REMEMBER
THIS TIME

REMEMBER THIS TIME

Gloria Kurian Broder
and
Bill Broder

Newmarket Press
New York

To the Kowal sisters of Luninyets:
Mary, Sarah, Ethel, Teibel, and Chaya.

First Edition

1 2 3 4 5 6 7 8 9 0 FC

Library of Congress Cataloging in Publication Data

Broder, Gloria Kurian.
Remember this time.

1. World War, 1914–1918—Fiction.   2. Soviet Union—
History—Revolution, 1917–1921—Fiction.   I. Broder,
Bill, 1931–   II. Title.
PS3552.R6194R4   1983   813'53   83–4249
ISBN 0–937858–23–4

Manufactured in the United States of America

Designed by Ruth Kolbert

ACKNOWLEDGMENTS

The lines of poetry quoted on page 115, beginning "Hail to you . . ." selected from the poem "Zydye" by Janka Kupala, printed in *Opposition to Sovietization in Belorussian Literature*, 1917–1957 by Anthony Adamovich. Munich, Institute for Study of the U.S.S.R. for Scarecrow Press, New York, 1958.

Spiridonova's speech on page 211 was adapted from *Memoirs of a British Agent* by R. H. Bruce Lockhart, copyright 1932 by R. H. Bruce Lockhart, with permission of the publisher, Macmillan, London and Basingstoke.

The lines of poetry quoted on page 203, beginning "But what can we . . ." selected from "The Twilight of Freedom" in *Osip Mandelstam: Selected Poems*, translated by Clarence Brown and W. S. Merwin, copyright 1973 Clarence Brown and W. S. Merwin, reprinted with the permission of Atheneum Publishers.

The events and background contained in this novel are based upon a variety of sources: individual interviews, tapes, books, and articles. For the details of the evacuation of 1915, we are particularly indebted to *The Way of the Cross*, by V. Doroshevitz, New York, 1916, and for the description of the Fifth Soviet Congress to *Memoirs of a British Agent*, by R. H. Bruce Lockhart, New York, 1932. We are grateful to the libraries at the University of California, Berkeley and the YIVO Institute for Jewish Research in New York.

We wish to express our special gratitude to Esther Margolis, who suggested that we write this novel, and who has given us constant help and encouragement during its creation.

[v]

OF

Polotsk

Vitebsk

Poryetchie

Viasma

Smolensk

Orsha

Yukhnof

Gorki

Mossaisk

Yelnia

Mstislavl

Mohilef

Roslavl

Shisdra

MOSCOW

GREAT RUSSIA

StaroBykhof

Cherikof

Bobruisk

Dovsk

Briansk

Karatchef

Rogatchef

Maglin

Surash

Starodub

Dmitrovsk

Rietchitsa

Gomel

Novosybkof

Mosyr

Gorodnia

Dmitryef

R. Pripet

T

HE

S

Glukhof

Igof

Rylsk

Ovrutch

Chernigof

MENT

Konotop

Oster

Sumy

Nieshin

KIEV

Shitomir

Radomysyl

rdichef

Vassilkof

Pereyaslavl

Kanef

0   20   40   60   80   100

Miles

────────── Kala's route during the Lyesk evacuation.

+++++++++++ Naftali's trip to Moscow.

**From 1815 – 1914 Russia ruled Congress Poland
and the Pale of Jewish Settlement
and Austria ruled Galicia**

**From 1915 – 1918 the German Army maintained
a front east of Baranovits and Luninyets**

PART ONE

CHAPTER ONE

T HE QUESTION SOMETIMES AROSE BETWEEN CITIZENS OF
Lyesk and citizens of Baranovits, Bialystok, and Pinsk
in the western provinces of Russia: was Lyesk a large village,
a small town or—as some suggested who had been born and
brought up there—was it, after all, an important and wonderful city? Located over five hundred miles to the west of Moscow and two hundred miles east of Warsaw, the town consisted of run-down barns, run-down houses, streets knee-high
in either mud or dust, an ugly hotel, poorly developed indus-
try, poor stunting soils, and an uncertain climate. As such,
Lyesk suffered from a certain lack of status in greater Russia.
Indeed, in the larger world no one noticed it was there. Still,
many of its inhabitants loved and defended their town, pointing with pride to the cobbled main square, the half dozen
two-storied houses, the gentle beauty of the river, the dense
birch wood, the spacious skies and—most important of all—to
the fact that Lyesk was an actual rail repair facility a short

way off the direct line from Warsaw to Moscow. By some great misfortune, however, aside from the equipment routed to the repair facility, trains came through less than once a day, after which there remained in the air only the cold sound of the wind sweeping over the bluffs or the croak of frogs from the river bottom.

Then unexpectedly, in the spring of 1914, a sudden prosperity descended on Lyesk. Two crews of dapper-looking workmen appeared from Mogilev Province and began to rebuild the railroad bridge and to repair a twenty-mile section of the metaled high road on the bluff to the south. Osip Blag, the White Russian owner of the hotel, bought new beds for all twenty-five of his rooms, and the furrier on Merchant Lane purchased a dozen new furs for his shop. For the first time in history, trains arrived every day of the week, then sometimes twice a day, almost every train carrying important-looking civilians, military officers, troops of young men, horses, and big guns on flat cars. Officials from St. Petersburg and Moscow, decked out in elaborate uniforms, stepped forth from special trains equipped with dining and sleeping cars and were met by local administrators who abandoned their former lofty stance and bowed and scraped, muttering about alternative transportation routes and emergency schedules. Friends and relatives of the townspeople who lived in nearby towns paid frequent visits to keep in touch with what was going on; and the town baker—Malkeh Chodorov, a woman with clear gray eyes, majestic breasts, and a long firm compelling chin—sent her daughters daily to sell bread and kvass at the station.

Everywhere in Lyesk—at the railroad where the festive priority trains rushed through, whistles blowing, flags flying, shades down; on the streets; in the shops; at the hotel; and in the town square—people mentioned the names "Germany," "Austro-Hungary," "Paris," "Serbia," "Magyars," "England," and "France," and as they spoke their chests filled and puffed, their eyebrows went up and down, and their eyes blinked and winked with solemn meaning. More than once the word "war" was spoken, but on the whole no one treated the idea seriously, many of the citizens declaring that even if there were to be a war it would last a week, several weeks at the most—anything longer would be to no one's advantage.

To the Chodorov girls—Ruth, eighteen; Kala, sixteen; Sophie, fifteen; and Ekaterina, fourteen—the world seemed suddenly to have expanded. They did not at first question the change very deeply. More to the point was the fact that—as anyone could plainly see—their town had ceased to be boring. Sitting down together, they composed a letter to their older brother Iosif, who had emigrated to America. He had left six months earlier—in late 1913—and by now his sisters had forgotten that they had never really cared for him. Rather, when they saw how much their father grieved for his only son and observed their mother briefly nodding at the mention of Iosif's name, they too began to think there had been something admirable about him. In the letter to Iosif they said that the town had changed and grown exciting, that their father had been awarded a contract for providing the army's horses with feed, that Stepan's hunchbacked cow had given birth to twin calves, that a bar with brass fittings had been installed in the reception room of the hotel and that, for his own sake, he ought to hurry up and come back home.

"But why do you advise him to come back?" their mother, Malkeh, rebuked them. "If he comes back, the Russian army will simply draft him. There's a war ahead." And she went on to bemoan the fact that at such a moment her daughters were just now reaching the age for marriage.

"Do you mean because there'll be fewer men?" Sophie asked.

"Because there'll be less choice of men," their mother half lamented.

At this the girls laughed and Kala said, with a sweep of her hands, "The world is full of men . . . Mama, look around you, there are men everywhere," her statement expressing her belief in the bountifulness of the world and at the same time her uncertain attitude toward the worth of men. "With so many trains coming in and out of Lyesk . . . these days men keep arriving from all directions."

And, indeed, the very next day a man in his mid-twenties, carrying himself and his suitcase with an air of virility and competence, descended from the train. Broad-shouldered and tall, with dark, somewhat heavy-lidded eyes and a pleasantly rosy complexion, he glanced up at the newly repainted sign over the station, then at the vendors in his path, and after passing up Nachman Liebes selling used clothes, Shmuel, the Holy One, selling crosses, beads, and pictures of Jesus, and the midwife Matryona selling honey and candy, he put his suitcase down in front of Kala Chodorov and bought a slice of apple strudel from her basket. "Delicious strudel," he pronounced, purchasing another slice. "You must have made it with your own two hands."

Kala grimaced and studied the ground. She had a broad face with high Slavic cheekbones, gold-flecked brown eyes that slanted upward, fiercely rosy cheeks, brown short-cropped hair, a small blunt nose, and a large expressive mouth, which was just now bunched up comically to the left.

"I said that it was delicious strudel. Why do you look so cross?"

"Because," she swung her left foot, stirring the dust, "everyone assumes that I made it. Even when they know I'm the only one of my sisters who doesn't bake, they keep asking: did I make the strudel, did I make the honeycake, did I make the prune tarts? If you really want to know who made the strudel," she said, "one of my sisters did." And she pointed here and there down the platform to where Ruth, Sophie, and Ekaterina had taken up their stations.

"All of them?" he inquired. "Those are all your sisters?" He raised his eyebrows so that, like weightless boats, they appeared to float pleasurably in his forehead. "Ahhh," he said, taking a deep breath, "if I were four men instead of only one . . ."

She nodded appreciatively, approving his response. "The

[6]

fact is, I do everything else. No one takes into account that I . . ." All at once she identified the stranger as Jewish. Pausing, she regarded him more closely.

"What's everything else?"

"I repair . . ." She stopped, her face beginning to blush. "I repair things."

"Never mind," he said, "a pretty girl doesn't need to bake strudel."

"But I'm too short," she said. "And my sisters are even prettier."

"You're pretty enough." Then he turned his head and went on to look at her sisters. "That one, you said. And the one in the wheelchair," he pointed with his chin. "And the blonde—dear God, what a beauty she is. Still, it's clear that she knows it. And all three, each one with a different color hair . . ." He lowered his voice. "She's in a wheelchair, your sister?"

"That's Sophie, my closest sister. She can do whatever anyone else can do and even more. Much, much more. She can accomplish anything she wants to. Do you see the boy behind her?" Kala pointed to a pale fourteen-year-old in a cap and short jacket who hovered around the wheelchair. "His name is Hershel. He's her slave. He's the miller's son. He does all our errands just to be close to her. She doesn't need him. There's nothing she can't do. It's probably she who baked your strudel."

"Oh, I don't doubt she can accomplish everything. It shows in her . . . in her . . . it shows somewhere. And what's that?" He indicated five bottles nesting in Kala's basket beside her baked goods.

"My mother's kvass."

The young man bought a bottle, drank it down in one gulp, shook himself, and then looked keenly at Kala. "That's no ordinary drink. That's no everyday run-of-the-mill kvass. Just let me guess." He took a few steps back. He began to speak in Yiddish. "Your family's name is Chodorov and your mother is Malkeh Chodorov. Am I right?" His eyes popped

[7]

open with astonished delight in himself, after which he waited for her to be impressed.

Shifting easily from Russian to Yiddish, she simply said, "Everyone knows my mother."

"You've missed the point. The unusual circumstance is . . . my name is Ephraim Savich. My father's name is Myron Savich and both my parents grew up with your mother in the *shtetl* Kletsk. They used to mention that should ever I pass through Lyesk, I must stop by and give your mother their best regards. Now that I'm here I'll do that. I'll just deposit this piece of luggage at the station and when you're ready— you're almost out of strudel—I'll walk back with you."

"You have to wait for my sisters," Kala said when he returned from the station. "I meet them by that rock and we walk back together. When we're together, that's when we're at our best. You'll see. And anyway, here comes Ruth," she announced as she caught a glimpse of her eldest sister threading her way toward them through the fair-like atmosphere of the merchants, gossiping and selling. "Here comes Ruth," she repeated happily, craning her neck to make certain that Ruth, as always, was a picture of dignity and restraint with her neatly combed red-gold hair, her delicate complexion, and brown intelligent eyes. In a proud whisper she confided to Ephraim it was Ruth who kept all the family accounts, having exhibited early in her life an aptitude for sums and a handwriting akin to newsprint; it was Ruth who baked all the honeycakes and all the jam-filled cookies; and it was no doubt because of these accomplishments that her sister moved with so serene and enviable a grace—her back straight, her neck arched, her head held high.

A short distance behind Ruth, Sophie followed, maneuvering her high old wheelchair with vitality and ease. "And here's Sophie."

"Sophie was born with . . . ?"

Kala stopped him by abruptly looking away. "An accident." Holding her head at a stubborn angle, she asserted again, "Sophie can do anything anyone else can do. She can

[8]

make her wheelchair turn cartwheels. She can run almost as fast as I can, using just her crutches. And for really long distances or awful weather Mama's given her her own small cart and a gray pony that Sophie named Mishka, because she really looks like a mouse. Sophie and I . . . though there's ten months' difference . . . we're almost twins."

Ten months younger than Kala, Sophie possessed similar features—high cheekbones, small blunt nose, expressive mouth, and rosy cheeks. But her face was cast in a slightly finer mold than Kala's and she wore her long black hair down to her waist. Kala hoped that this young man would notice that her sister's eyes were a blue that was almost black and that they possessed so unusual a luminosity that the merchants and the townspeople honored Sophie's radiance as she passed. "Sophie and I," Kala remarked, "we're chums . . . we're special friends."

Finally Kala aimed her finger at Ekaterina, who trailed yards behind, her head descended in a book. Ekaterina was the baby of the family, and with her white-gold hair, her emerald eyes and full, lithe figure, obviously the Chodorovs' one true beauty. "Ekaterina's often cranky," Kala warned— just in case Ephraim might find her too attractive. "She won't speak anything but Russian—even in the house." Then, grudgingly, she allowed, "It isn't all her fault. Ever since she was a little girl everyone stroked and patted her all over or else they pinched her. Everyone: every government official, every distant relative—even total strangers to town. So naturally she turned cranky. Now, of course, she always wears a frown. Except when she reads books. She loves books."

"Is that so?" Ephraim said as Kala's sisters drew near.

Kala pulled him toward them. "This is Ephraim Savich," she said, looping her arm through his as if to claim him. "Ephraim's mother and father knew Mama when she was very little. He's walking back with us to give her their regards."

At this, Ruth, Sophie, and Ekaterina, having glanced away from Ephraim, raised their eyes and peered at him closely—

almost as if they expected to discern in his person some lost image of their mother as a young woman.

"Do you still live in the *shtetl* Kletsk?" Ruth inquired politely in Yiddish as the group shuffled about and started up the hill toward the square.

"Oh no, I was born and grew up in Karlin, as did my brothers and sisters." After responding in Yiddish, Ephraim switched to Russian. "My father established and owns a lumber company there." From his vest he took a card, which he handed over to Kala. Then he got behind Sophie's wicker-backed, high-wheeled chair and started to push as though without thinking. With a brief laugh, Sophie broke away from him, propelling herself across the road where she spun playfully about in a show of independence before returning to her sisters. Ephraim held his hands against his sides and went on with his story. "I represent my father's concern. I travel around . . . occasionally I set up new branches. I've never been in Lyesk before, but with all the new construction going on here . . . ."

"Have you ever been to Moscow?" Ekaterina inquired coldly, speaking through the blonde locks that covered half her face.

"No."

"To St. Petersburg?" Sophie asked.

"No. Not there either."

As if she'd already given up all hope, Ekaterina tossed her head airily. "To Paris, London, Rome?"

Ephraim regarded her with a smile. "I've been to Warsaw, to Bialystok, to Minsk, Bobruisk, and Gomel; I've been from Kovno all the way to Rovno; I've even been to Kiev."

"Pooh," said Ekaterina. "You've hardly been out of Bye-lorussia." And she hung her nearly empty basket on the back of Sophie's wheelchair and left them at the turning before the square without saying goodby.

"Please don't mind Ekaterina," said Ruth, who had been walking with her. She glanced back at Ephraim, who walked slightly behind. "And please don't think she's running away . . . she's on her way to her tutor's house, because Mama knows the extent . . . the sincerity of her interest in books—it's a very real, deep interest—and though Ekaterina's already fourteen Mama still allows her to take lessons with the children of the Russian officials and landowners."

"She keeps on reading and reading and ruining her eyes, day and night, and she keeps on going to class. It's because," Kala giggled, "she loves Sophocles and Aristotle."

Giggling, Sophie echoed, "She loves Aristotle and Sophocles. She loves them madly—whoever they are." Then, as if reacting to some signal between them, the two girls burst out laughing. Once started they found it difficult to stop. They doubled over, they held their stomachs, they went on laughing—the sound at once joyous and jarring.

Ruth glanced anxiously at Ephraim. "They're not always silly like this. It just depends on the time of day."

"Oh, it's good to laugh, it's very healthy," Ephraim reassured her. "And it's very appealing, how much alike they sound. All the same, I think I'll walk next to you." And he stepped forward, joining Ruth. "I imagine," he began, "you and your sisters have admirers . . . fiancés?"

"No . . . no fiancés," Ruth answered quietly.

"She's already had three suitors," Sophie said.

"She rejected them," Kala finished.

"Shhh . . . Kala, Sophie," Ruth said.

They had cut across the cobbled square, mounting the wooden sidewalk in front of a homely little church. "No fiancés? What luck!" Ephraim Savich sighed luxuriously. He looked about at the two-storied buildings that constituted the center of town—several substantial residences, a dry goods store, the offices of the town police and administration, and the freshly painted facade of the hotel, all red and gold with a welcome flag over the door. "So this is Lyesk," he said.

The girls nodded with pride and then directed him down Merchant Lane—their street—an unpaved lane with open sewage ditches spanned by board planks. "I can't say I've heard too many wonderful things about your town,"

Ephraim continued, looking at the low wooden houses fronting directly on the roadway. Almost every building sported a sign advertising one sort of merchandise or another; customers loitered about gossiping as they waited their turn. Horses and cows browsed in vacant lots, now and then leaning over unpainted wooden fences to gaze incuriously at the people who passed. The lane ended at the countryside: orchards, fields, and a winding river at the base of a long hillside. "What do you find to do here?"

"What do you find to do here?" Sophie mimicked. "You sound like our brother Iosif. Before he went to America he always complained, 'I know every single pig, I even know the chickens.' "

"He went on and on," groaned Kala. " 'I know every single pig, I even know the chickens. I know the mudholes . . .' " she stopped short as, in front of them, a large pig and six chickens started their procession across the road. "As a matter of fact, that's a very nice pig, that one. Her name is Marie."

"And the names of the chickens?" Ephraim raised his eyebrows.

"Those are Nachman Liebes's chickens."

"I see," acknowledged Ephraim. "I understand. And how do you like living in a town where you know the name of every animal?" He addressed not only the three girls but made a point of also including Hershel, the miller's son, who trailed behind them.

"We love it," Ruth instantly declared.

"We love it," Kala and Sophie echoed.

And even Hershel came forward, removed his hat to reveal bright red hair smoothed down with a wide part, and stated that on most days he liked the town a lot.

"And where are the trees?"

"On Orchard Lane. On the way to the high road there are fruit trees of every kind."

"And lilacs," added Sophie. "Lilacs are my favorite flower."

"No other place is like Lyesk," Kala expanded. "It's a town where Jews no longer need a permit in order to live. Our mother was the one who went to Minsk and got the status of the town changed, just before Ruth was born. It's your own place. You feel free here, it really belongs to you. Yet it's not like a *shtetl* where you know only Jews. Here you're acquainted and you deal with Gentiles; they're even close to you, like good friends. Pan Josef Potocki, the Polish landowner, before he invests in flax, he comes to the bakery to consult my mother. And Stepan Ilyich Rozumov won't do anything concerning his horses before asking Malkeh's advice. And on top of all that we grew up sitting on the knee of Ivan Sergeyevich Dovrynin, the Stationmaster and Superintendent of the Rail Facility, while he told us stories. He used to say that his left knee belonged exclusively to the Chodorov daughters."

Ephraim shrugged, "That's fine so far as it goes. Gentiles are all well and good. But what is there for entertainment?"

"There's a whorehouse."

"Sophie!" warned Ruth.

"There's a whorehouse," said Kala, "there's the train station, the town square on Saturday night, the bakery and the bakery porch. Aside from the hotel, it's the only porch in town. People sit there summer evenings. Look!" Kala cried out as two droshkies—one driven by a soldier, the other by a peasant—wheeled around near the end of the lane and stopped in front of a building with a porch in front. From one droshky descended a short, vigorous official in a long coat and gleaming buttons; from the other, a languid gentleman in an English white summer suit with stripings. "It's Ivan Sergeyevich and Stepan Ilyich . . . both."

"Oh my goodness," exclaimed Ruth. "It's Wednesday. Ivan Sergeyevich shouldn't be here at all."

"Both on Wednesday, Stepan Ilyich's day," said Sophie. "Poor Mama will be swamped." And she excused herself, hurrying up the street with Ruth and Hershel.

Left behind with Ephraim, Kala grew still more expansive. She explained to Ephraim—hoping to sound important and adult—that he had just witnessed two of the town's most prominent citizens: Ivan Sergeyevich Dovrynin, Station-master, and Stepan Ilyich Rozumov, owner of Arabian horses and an immense estate, emerging from their droshkies to visit her mother. Neither man got along with the other—Stepan Ilyich having once corrected Ivan Sergeyevich's wife's pro-nunciation and grammar—and as a result they usually came to the bakery on different days: the Stationmaster on Tues-days and Thursdays and the landowner on Wednesdays. Hav-ing conveyed all this information, Kala threw Ephraim a shrewd sidelong glance. "Ivan Sergeyevich must need my mother's counsel badly to come on Stepan Ilyich's day."

Then all at once she grew aware of Ephraim's manly shoulders and she wished her sisters had stayed with her—without them around her she felt less attractive, a good deal less appealing. And yet, she reminded herself, it was she, not her sisters, Ephraim had singled out. She put her hand to the back of her neck and pulled at her hair, regretting she had trimmed the ends so short just to shock her family. An urge welled up in her to display her charms. Hoping to determine what they were, she considered jumping, leaping, telling jokes, performing cartwheels. She even imagined putting on her best summer frock, then remembered that when Dunya, the dressmaker, had measured her, Dunya had advised, "You're grown up now, Kala, and you've got to try to tailor your smile so it doesn't reach clear across your face. You have to show a bit of self-control. Arrange your smile so that it's just so wide"—with her thumb and forefinger Dunya had measured a certain space—"and not a single inch wider. That's what all the boys like."

"That's what all the boys like." The phrase ran through her mind. But did she like boys? In the past she had at times suspected she might turn into a boy herself. She smiled uncomfortably at Ephraim. Then, fearing that for no good reason her smile might spread too wide—that it might stretch in a foolish arc across her face—she brought her hand up and pressed it against her mouth.

At that moment she and Ephraim came up to the bakery

and Hershel rushed out the door, carrying two glasses of tea and two bagels for the drivers of the droshkies who chatted, perched on the porch railing. Close by, at one of the outside tables, three men sat smoking and drinking tea: Avrom Lavin, the tailor; Lazar Dovitsky, the stableman; and Mendel Feldshpan, until recently a modest tanner, and now the proud owner of a leather factory purchased for him by his father-in-law. Feldshpan, the employer of four hardworking young men, wore a dreamy faraway grin. He also wore a new suit fashioned for him by Avrom Lavin, the very tailor with whom he sat. From time to time Lavin glanced at the too-large brown gabardine suit, appraising it with critical admiration. The rest of the time the tailor busied himself waving his fist in front of Lazar Dovitsky's nose. Nor did Lavin slow his argument with the stableman when Kala and her visitor stepped upon the porch. Instead, with his free hand, he removed a gold watch from his vest pocket, brandishing it in the air toward Kala, who at once looked away, explaining to Ephraim, "He loves his watch but it rarely works more than a week after I've fixed it." She bit her lip. "I repair watches."

"Kala," the tailor called. He held his watch to his ear. He coughed. "Kala."

But Kala adamantly kept her back to Lavin and directed Ephraim Savich's attention to the fine craftsmanship of the bakery's generous Dutch door, the top of which remained open, hooked to the wall. "My father built it," she said. "It's the only Dutch door in town."

"One of the only porches and the only Dutch door? Your father's a carpenter?"

"Yes, he's a carpenter—that's his hobby. He also leases land —an apple orchard." She wanted to say a good deal more—to attribute to her father a multitude of impressive accomplishments. She wondered if she ought to mention he made delicious pickles. "He's a contractor too—for the army," she said; then felt ashamed she had neglected to add he had only been given one contract.

Inside the shop they paused before the crowd of hungry people trying to catch Malkeh's or Ruth's attention. "My father built the bakery," continued Kala, "as a wedding present for Mama." She threw her arms out to indicate the bright whitewashed walls, the beamed ceilings, the side-paneled front windows framed by flowered linen curtains, the rustic tables and chairs gleaming with shellac, and—along the entire west wall—a wide counter with glassed-in shelves filled with strudel and poppy-seed cakes and macaroons and apple turnovers and prune tarts. "And do you see that wonderful high throne behind the cash register? It swivels on casters. He made it for Mother but she never sits down. Instead we girls take turns sitting there."

Now it was Sophie in the swivel chair who wrapped baked goods in white paper, fastening the paper with thick twine wound on a bobbin hanging from the ceiling. With her fast, sure motions, she never bruised a cake, never chipped a warm fresh cookie. She might have wrapped the baked goods more quickly had it not been for two handsome matrons in their thirties who stood directly in front of her, gossiping and interrupting her efforts with questions about each cookie and every cake. All other customers were forced to reach around them or between them. Yet no one bothered to object, for Leah Kantorovits Feldshpan and Naomi Pearl Benjamin had always been in the way. Since their early teens, they had served the town as a two-woman newspaper. Through their large, mobile mouths passed every event that had touched the lives of the inhabitants of Lyesk. Both ladies were well connected: Naomi, the daughter of the Hebrew teacher, Reb Chaim Pearl, and wife of the government rabbi; Leah, daughter of the rude, powerful manager of the Potocki estate, and wife of the rising Mendel Feldshpan, now sitting on the front porch, whose leather factory, profiting from military business, contributed substantially to the town's new prosperity.

"It was a tumor as big as a melon," said Naomi, her glowing face fringed with a halo of thick tan frizzy hair, her blue eyes gleaming like fierce joyous stars, as she detailed the medical woes of the town bath attendant.

"And she had been so sure that she was pregnant," sang Leah, bursting with voluptuousness herself, but always nodding, always solemn.

Just then Naomi noticed the stranger at Kala's side. "And who is he?" she inquired of Kala.

Kala introduced Ephraim Savich to the two women, adding out of generosity, "His parents grew up with Mama in the *shtetl* Kletsk."

"Oooooh?" crooned Naomi. "The *shtetl* Kletsk."

"And what's happening there?" Leah asked.

"We live in Karlin now," said Ephraim.

"Ooooh," said Naomi. "Karlin. Very elegant these days, I hear."

"Very elegant," Leah addressed Naomi. "Two trolley lines now and a full-time, year-round Yiddish theater."

And the two women went on chattering, beaming, and inviting Ephraim into their talk about his hometown. Ephraim smiled absently; and Kala located her mother, who was on her way from the front table occupied by Stepan Ilyich, the landowner, and his chessboard, to the back table where Ivan Sergeyevich, his uniform buttons gleaming, nervously drank glass after glass of tea. Impatiently the Stationmaster awaited his hostess and then started in with his harangue. Kala observed her mother listen attentively, gazing at the wall. Then Malkeh asked a short question, hearkened to another bout of explanation and complaint, phrased another question and listened once again till, bit by bit, Kala saw the frustration and hopelessness subside from Ivan Sergeyevich's shoulders and face and his hand rest quietly on a glass now empty of tea.

To observe such progress filled Kala with wonder. Yet at the same time she suspected that Malkeh's wisdom was overvalued, that her reputation throughout the district was vastly undeserved, and that it was nothing more than the manner in

[17]

which she delivered her recommendations rather than anything she said or advised that drew Ivan Sergeyevich to the bakery on his enemy's day. Out of admiration as well as out of deep resentment she tried to pinpoint the exact locale of Malkeh's power. Precisely where did it reside?—in her full, long, heavy breasts, her girdled stomach, the implicit intelligence of her posture and straight back, her skeptical yet understanding eyes, her compassionate smile, or her long firm chin, which, by virtue of its peninsular shape, seemed in itself an instrument of justice?

It was her chin, Kala finally decided; it was most of all her chin. And it was this same chin Malkeh lowered as, catching sight of Kala, she advanced quickly toward her, took her aside, and in a low voice reprimanded, "Why are you here? Don't you have work to do? Why aren't you in the repair shop?"

Kala nodded at Ephraim Savich. "Mama," she said, "guess who this is. His parents grew up with you in Kletsk. His father is Myron Savich and his mother's name was Dessie Shlomovits."

Ephraim put out his hand. "I'm here on business," he offered warmly. "And when I mentioned to my parents I was stopping in Lyesk they told me to look you up. I'm here on business," he repeated. "I'm the main buyer for my father's lumber company—he calls me his partner but I know better. Do you happen to know Colonel Nikolai Sukharov in Pinsk, the regiment commander? We've just provided him with all the lumber for his new officers' mess."

At this Malkeh gave a short laugh and folded her arms across her chest. "Your Colonel Sukharov has been responsible for my friend Dovrynin's troubles today. The Colonel has just drafted Ivan Sergeyevich's best repairmen for work on the main line at Baranovits. Well, you're welcome here. Please feel free to stay at our house while you're visiting Lyesk. You have your father's coloring . . . your mother's eyes . . . now it comes back to me more clearly. And I see you've already met my daughter Kala."

"I've met all four of your daughters," he told her, "and had I known such beautiful young women existed in Lyesk I would have rushed here . . . I would have rushed . . ." He stopped. Kala could see he was hesitating because of the detached ironic assessment in Malkeh's eye. For some moments he met Malkeh's gaze. He matched it. Then, rather too ostentatiously displaying a ringless left hand, he asked, "Which of your daughters is the youngest?"

His question seemed to take Malkeh by surprise. "Why, Ekaterina."

"And the oldest, may I ask?"

"If you've met the four girls you certainly must have guessed that Ruth is the oldest. Ruth is older than Kala by two years at the least."

Ephraim's eyes turned toward Ruth, who, wearing a starched apron, carried more tea and another slice of sponge cake to Ivan Ilyich's table, her smooth red-gold hair setting off her serene and thoughtful profile. For some moments Ephraim watched her and he remained silent. When he spoke again the bantering sound was absent from his voice. His face looked very dark and somewhat drawn. In a tone of utter seriousness that dismayed and yet attracted Kala, he said, "I'm glad that Ruth is the oldest."

CHAPTER TWO

JUNE AND JULY OF 1914 PROVED UNEASY MONTHS IN LYESK. The new faces in town and all the extra activity disturbed some sense of propriety in the townspeople. Laughter turned quickly to anger; tempers grew short and incidents of violence occurred without apparent provocation. Three prostitutes attacked an itinerant gypsy fortune teller, crippling her with fence staves. They claimed she had given them the evil eye. On market day in the town square a driver became angry at his horse and beat it to death, and no one tried to stop him. When asked why he'd done it, he said, "Just look at the newspapers." And indeed people looked at the newspapers; they took to assembling at the station morning and evening to read the latest news: the leaders of all Europe were squabbling over the boundaries of small Balkan countries; a strike, begun in Baku, had spread north to St. Petersburg, where discontented workers erected barricades in the streets and exchanged shots with the police; peasants in

Chernigov Province had burned four estates; the price of food had increased thirty percent; and in a listing of national problems, alcoholism would soon surpass chicken pox and mumps.

The report of so much disorder and discontent unsettled Kala. She had always assumed that by virtue of some excellent natural law the larger unknown world would choose to operate in a relatively benign and rational fashion. The indications that it did not touched her with scattered restlessness. Unable to concentrate on the watches her clients brought to the repair shop, she escaped every half hour or so to run in the fields or to sneak behind the house, where she spoke her mind to Emmanuelle, the cow; Sir Leslie, the horse; and Mishka, Sophie's pony.

Three years earlier, upon the death of her grandfather, she had, against her will, taken over his watch repair shop. Thirteen years old at the time, she had objected she already had too much work. She had put her hands behind her back, but her mother had forced her right hand open, had pressed into it the small brass key to the shop and had folded Kala's fingers over the key.

"You were his helper," Malkeh reminded her daughter. "You know the tools. Besides, Iosif won't stay in Lyesk. Ruth keeps the store, Sophie is my master baker, and Ekaterina's much too young. At least your chores leave you somewhat free in the middle of the day."

"Not free enough," asserted Kala. "I need a lot of time for this and that. Not to mention you've given me much more work than anyone else." And spurred on by her sense of unfairness, she began to enumerate her early morning duties, her outrage mounting as she watched her mother step back from her and fold her arms as though only from this distance could she remain attentive.

But even with folded arms, Malkeh soon grew impatient. "It's true. You aren't imagining it. I do give you more work than I give your sisters. And the reason is . . . you have so much work inside you."

[21]

"So much work?" Kala cried out, trying to guess at her mother's meaning. "I have so much work inside me? In that case I'll just let it out."

"But it'll still be inside you," Malkeh said. "Because you have the need to work and an enormous capacity for work. The fact is, no matter how you look at it, my own daughter, you are capable of laboring longer and harder than anyone else in the family."

A lump of pride and horror—pride that her mother had singled her out, no matter the fashion, and horror that it involved nothing but work—formed in Kala's throat. She objected, "And that's what makes me different from other people—just work? Not ability—not talent like grandfather? And what if I'm a genius?" she asked, anticipating her mother's answer but resenting it—and hoping to confuse her.

"Work is every bit as good," Malkeh said. "In some instances it's even better. Of course, you'll break a number of watches at first and the customers with money will take their trade to Baranovits or Pinsk. But your skill will improve."

"Not quickly enough," Kala interrupted, then stopped, already regretting the amount of time she had spent with her grandfather in the repair shop. Yet the truth was, she had passionately loved the shop, imagining it—though hundreds of miles from any sea—to be the cabin of a ship. Long and narrow, with cupboards, drawers, and shelves to the very ceiling —with dozens of timepieces hanging everywhere—it was located in the north corner of the Chodorov house. As often as she could she had gone into it from the main house, enthralled that it possessed its own separate entrance and joyous that her grandfather always welcomed her company—that whenever she asked he told her stories about her mother's childhood in the village Kletsk. But with her grandfather no longer at her side, she foresaw that the shop would lose all its magic. She suspected that, bent over flywheels, escapements, and mainsprings, she would first turn lonely and then grow anxious as all around her, according to her skill, the broken clocks and watches either ticked or failed to make the smallest sound. She feared that days would pass with no one bringing her a single watch, or else she feared that the entire town would come rushing at her with all their watches, all their clocks. She saw herself shut up in the dark narrow room, listening while her clients related in detail the exact circumstances under which their timepieces had ceased to work. And she concluded that of all her duties, repairing clocks and watches appealed to her the least.

"Thank God for Sophie," Kala said—for as the years proceeded, with five free minutes from the bakery Sophie would thud along the lane on her crutches and, like a brilliant black and white bird, hop into the repair shop to bring Kala a cookie, a piece of gossip or a shiny kopek just for luck. With ten or twenty free minutes Sophie would squeeze herself and a bit of embroidery or mending into the small corner just beyond Kala's stool. Quickly, so as not to waste any time, the two girls would start to joke or laugh—for laughter was the greatest bond, the sacred sport between them. Sometimes Sophie would begin by imitating Osip Blag, the hotel owner, slurping his tea and munching his pastry, while Kala might mimic the tailor Avrom Lavin. On days when Kala appeared unusually frustrated, Sophie initiated her sister's favorite game, and from the walls and the drawers around them the girls removed all the timepieces. They divided these into two arbitrary piles, designating one heap as watches to be fixed and the other as watches to be thrown into the river. Then they would moan and writhe about like snakes and tear their hair, enacting the anguish of the watches' owners as their timepieces sank out of sight.

But with Sophie out of the shop and the watches in front of Kala, after a certain length of time the tediousness of the painstaking labor opened her mind to what she called "bad thoughts"; and she fretted that the hovel in which the midwife Matryona lived would not last another winter; she worried about the slow starvation of Luka Fomich's cousins, forced by recent famines to quit their land and seek a living in Siberia; she chewed her lip over the one-eyed beggar

Patch's arthritis. Most often her "bad thoughts" came back to the accident, ten years earlier, when Sophie had fallen in front of an artillery unit galloping through town. Why should life be so unfair? she asked herself. Why should she be able to walk when Sophie could not? Why had everything been arranged so badly?

To this list of injuries and injustices Kala added, on this early summer afternoon, the fact that Ephraim Savich had stepped off the train and had chosen Ruth instead of her. Had he done this, she asked herself, simply because she was younger? From Ephraim Savich her mind turned to the case of the driver who had beaten his horse to death on market day in the town square. She shuddered, tightly shut her eyes, and imagined that instead of beating the horse the driver had tenderly stroked its muzzle. Slowly the driver grew taller, more handsome, better in all ways than Ephraim Savich. Leaping on his grateful horse, he followed her through the town to the repair shop, where he turned into a Russian prince, whisked her from her stool behind the green felt counter, and took her off on horseback to Kiev.

Suddenly the door of the repair shop burst open and there stood Schlaymie Zuckerman, son of the *shoychet*, home on a visit from Baranovits. With his short legs, thick neck, and frizzy hair he looked, Kala thought, exactly like his parents. Fortunately, unlike his parents she had never heard him brag about the Zuckermans' elegant relatives with a large estate near Vilna. Rather he preferred to display nothing but contempt at the mention of such relatives, hinting that all privileged people would soon find cause to regret their wealth. Kala greeted her visitor quite eagerly, for in the past she and Sophie had admired his rebellious nature. As a child he had painted odd names on walls, applied glue to his teacher Reb Pearl's chair, and pinned up anonymous cartoons satirizing the mournful town police captain, Semyon Varsonevsky.

Home on vacation from the *yeshivah*, Schlaymie brought his alarm clock to be repaired. When he expressed surprise—precisely as he had the year before—that it was Kala who now presided over her grandfather's shop, she replied coolly, "Why not? I do everything else."

"What do you mean?"

"Except for the baking, I do everything else." She held up ten fingers and started counting. "I feed the animals. I milk the cows. I chop the wood. I grease the wagon. I stoke the bakery ovens. And whenever extra supplies are needed, I drive the wagon to villages two or three days away and I buy from the peasants."

"You do all of that? How wonderful!" Schlaymie breathed.

"That's all right for you to say but you're not the one who does it. All you do is study and pray. Try cleaning manure out of a stable on a hot summer day."

"You should be proud of such work," Schlaymie broke in, as though trying to stop her.

". . . or pounding frozen hay and chopping ice in troughs in the winter."

"Enough! I've known you all your life. You're practically a peasant. You could be Luka Fomich's daughter. You are made of different material from your sisters."

"I am made of the same material!"

"Whether it's the same material or not, you are a worker." Schlaymie grasped hold of her hand.

"Worker?" Kala tried to withdraw her hand. It alarmed her to hear him use her mother's words. "There's something wrong with you after all," she said. "I'm a girl, I'm not a worker."

Holding onto her hand now with both of his, Schlaymie leaned over the counter toward her, his brows beetling down over his hard little black eyes. "Kala Chodorov, with these callouses," he lifted Kala's hand, turning the palm toward her, "you have won a role in the future." He laughed. Then he peered over his shoulder to make sure no one had entered the shop, and from his inner pocket handed her three cheaply printed pamphlets.

Kala pushed the pamphlets back at him. "I'm not much of a reader."

"These are worth reading."

"Give them to Ekaterina."

"But these aren't for your little sister. These pages explain why Luka's cousins lost their land, who exploits the workers, how the Tsar finances pogroms, and how the governments of the world will profit while people die in the coming war."

"These pages explain everything?"

"Everything."

"Schlaymie, I'm not that dumb."

"These pages," he winked, "were written with heroines like you in mind." And Schlaymie turned about and quit the shop, somehow forgetting to leave his alarm clock.

When he had gone, Kala studied the covers of the leaflets, troubled that he had bestowed them on her. Why did he trust her? Why had he chosen her? Was there an aura some people possessed that showed they were sympathetic to—or even capable of performing—radical acts? Dismayed, she thrust the leaflets in a drawer, closed the shop, and rushed home to examine herself in Ruth's bedroom mirror.

Several days later there appeared upon the walls of the town square several provocative slogans in red paint:

A PAIR OF BOOTS IS BETTER THAN ALL CULTURE

ALL VALUE COMES FROM WORK

EXPLOIT THE WORKER, REAP THE WHIRLWIND

OUR BOMBS ARE LOADED WITH THE TEARS OF THE PEOPLE

That Schlaymie Zuckerman had carried his childhood pranks this far irked Kala. The outrageousness of the display, she thought, simply cheapened the young man's opinions—the words, in the boldness of their color, their size, and the thickness of the scarlet paint resembling nothing more than a circus announcement. Yet as she stood in the square, gaping, the slogans began to seem part of the threatening events of the last few months—born out of the ominous news filling the newspapers and the violent acts sprouting in the neighborhood. And when the police sergeant gave the beggar Patch a brush and a bucket and Patch began to paint the phrases out, Kala felt the words slide into her consciousness, joining her other "bad thoughts."

"A bucket of paint is better than all culture," joked Patch.

"And some paint is better than other," said the police sergeant. "These new revolutionaries are hopeless—you can't make head or tail out of what they're saying. Did you hear," he addressed Patch and Kala, "all the Fomich boys have been drafted?"

"All the Fomich boys?" said Kala with alarm. "How will Luka manage without them? They can't draft Gregori—he's got too many children."

"How many?" asked the sergeant.

"Six, including the twins."

"It shows he's a man," said the sergeant with an approving nod.

"Dmitri's the best planter. And Pyotr, he's too young to be drafted," Kala went on, thinking that she and Pyotr, Luka Fomich's nephew, must be almost the same age. They had been good friends since early childhood. Just this past spring they'd hugged and kissed in the fields. "How will Luka work the farm by himself? Think how unhappy the twins will be without their father, Gregori!"

She was interrupted by Avrom Lavin, who stepped up to her, ignoring the others. "Kala," the tailor wheezed, his black and white beard masking his gray face, "a person who repairs watches stays in one place and makes repairs. But no—five minutes you're there, five minutes you're gone. I can't understand why your grandfather trusted you to run a business."

Kala brushed by him, setting off across the square. "I can't think about watches now," she told him over her shoulder. "There's something else I have to do." And she headed up Orchard Lane toward Little Lyesk to offer Luka her help, calculating, as she walked, which part of the day she might fit the Fomich farm into her schedule.

The village of Little Lyesk lay between the town and the high road. It had belonged half to the Potocki and half to the

Rozumov estates, supplying serfs to both. After the Emancipation, all its peasants were given a bit of land, but the terms had been so harsh and the soil so poor that much of it soon passed back to the estates, and the peasants became landless wage earners. Yet, though Little Lyesk's poor huts remained barely more than holes in the ground covered with high thatched roofs, the village displayed a surprising pride in itself. Every roof was carefully constructed, the yards swept and planted with flowers. Well-pruned fruit trees grew up here and there along the lane, and a sizable orchard took up the rising land between the village and the estates.

The beauty and the order of Little Lyesk was the work of two men: Father Boris, priest for both town and village, and Luka Fomich, one of the few who had managed to keep his land and add a little to it. Luka's house and those of his sons—located in a large compound at the center of the village —were expertly crafted of wood. Within the fine picket fence surrounding the compound, Kala had spent hours of her childhood playing with the calves and foals and piglets belonging to the family. She had been treated like one of the Fomich children—invited to hayrides in the summer, sleigh rides in the winter, weddings, births, name days—invited on all festive occasions.

As Luka came toward Kala with his rolling gait, she looked at him, remembering that Schlaymie Zuckerman had commented she could have been one of his daughters. She hoped that the resemblance Schlaymie had observed was not physical. Luka's remarkable body came in two sections—his torso, that of a giant, with very long arms, wide shoulders, an immense chest and an even grander belly, all of this balanced upon the short thick bowed legs of a midget elephant. His small round head was capped with thick, faded, yellowish hair that stood up like stubble in the fields, while fine lines criss-crossed his bloated face. Embracing Luka, Kala said, "My mother sends her love," and was filled with well-being and pride that Luka, the village elder, called on her mother every Friday and that, sitting side by side in the Chodorov parlor, they arrived at many understandings that had far-reaching consequences for Lyesk. Disputes between the peasants and the Jews, between the Jews and the officials, between the peasants and the police, between the police and the landlords, and especially disputes concerning any inhabitant of Lyesk and the rest of the province, were mediated by a complex understanding between Malkeh and Luka. Peering in at them, Kala often believed that they looked so right together—each of them thick-armed and top-heavy, each able to communicate with the other while barely speaking, each one encircled by his or her own power—that she could not help but wonder what everything might have been like if they—like the shrewd king and the wise queen of some fabled land—had chosen each other and married.

"My mother sends her love," Kala repeated. She paused. "And I came because I heard your sons and Pyotr have been drafted, and I want to help."

"Not everyone's been drafted," Luka said. "Pyotr and Nikita will still be here."

"Just Pyotr and Nikita? That's not enough. Well, we'll all have to help each other. Terrible things are going to happen. Horrible things." She began to speak faster and faster, unable to stop herself. "There's going to be a war. There might even be a revolution. We'll have to do something."

At the sound of Kala's voice, Luka's favorite grandchildren, the twins Stepan and Natasha, scampered out of the barn. Hugging Kala, they demanded rides about the yard.

Luka stood by stolidly, balanced on his short bowed legs. "We Russians will win in ten, twelve days," he said, regarding Kala with his small deep-set eyes, a piercing river-green in color. "The war will end before it's even begun."

"Really?" she asked, eager to believe him.

"Truly. There's no need for you to worry. Let's see if you remember how to smile."

"Really?" A smile stretched across Kala's face. She laughed. Relieved, she flung the twins this way and that, swinging one around by the arms and the other by the feet. Their squeals brought Luka's other grandchildren running. Each child was small and very fair. They embraced Kala and took to shouting, "A snack for Kala! Kala wants her potato and milk."

Out of the cottage came Luka's wife Anya. Work and suffering had sculpted her face and bent her body. Yet her slim figure and enormous gray eyes revealed the remnants of former beauty. Smiling, but without uttering a single word, Anya placed Kala with all the grandchildren around a small wooden table in front of the cottage. Here, with the twins settled on either side of Kala, it soon slipped from the young woman's mind that she had come to offer Luka her help. She sighed while the shadow of the afternoon lengthened, feeling herself a giant dark child among tiny tow-haired dwarfs as she chewed the soft potatoes and lapped up the milk still warm from the cow.

CHAPTER THREE

I N THE EARLY SUMMER OF 1914 EPHRAIM SAVICH KEPT RE-
turning to Lyesk, where he pursued his business affairs
and at the same time courted Ruth—staying with the
Chodorovs as their overnight guest. He regularly brought the
four girls presents—on one trip giving Ruth a handsomely
bound blue ledger book, Kala and Sophie brightly colored
paper blossoms that opened up in water, and Ekaterina a
volume of Pushkin's poems. He invited Kala, Sophie, and
Ekaterina to join him and Ruth on picnics by the river, and
once or twice he put his arm about Kala's shoulder with affection and also, she thought, with regret, murmuring, "Ahh,
sweet Kala, if I were only two men instead of one." Malkeh
he regaled with his grand and rather too fanciful plans for
enlarging his family's lumber business. Expansively he
talked on, and while he rambled, he and Malkeh carefully
regarded each other, the humor in Ephraim's eye responding
to Malkeh's steady ironic gaze.

Yet it was Naftali with whom Ephraim scored his greatest success. He accomplished this simply by accompanying the girls' father to the synagogue and then joining him in a stroll over the high road bridge to the orchard on the other side of the river. When Naftali returned from the walk, Kala observed an expression of abashed pleasure and slightly disbelieving surprise on her father's face—as though his life might now hold in store more than he'd recently come to expect. For Kala knew that Naftali sorely missed his son. She understood that, uneasy with all women other than his wife, he had set out, upon marrying, to surround himself with an ample number of substantial, protecting sons. Unluckily, out of the four males he and Malkeh had produced, Iosif alone had survived infancy and childhood. Recognizing Naftali's need, Malkeh had then given over the major care of Iosif to her husband. From the moment Iosif learned to walk, Naftali kept him by his side where he purred at him from early morning till late at night. During the apple harvest they often slept in the cottage at the orchard. From time to time, early in the morning, Kala had come in the cottage to see Naftali perched on a chair next to Iosif's cot. In between Iosif's crashing, buzzing snores, she had heard her father murmur, "That's the way, that's the way, my son"—as if by keeping watch he participated in and encouraged Iosif's growth. Yet even so, to Naftali's bewilderment, when the boy, grown strong and stocky as a squat garden wall, sprang to his full height of five feet six, he began to criticize Lyesk. Bitterly the young man railed: he not only knew all the horses, cows, pigs, and chickens in the region but, even worse, every shop on Merchant Lane—the shoemaker's, the smith's, the furrier's, and the butcher's—suffered from a paltriness of merchandise that, combined with the hillocks of mud and the unchanging route of the livestock, morning and evening, imprinted upon the countryside an inescapable dreariness and monotony.

"How can you keep on living here?" he had questioned his sisters until at last, in the spring of 1913—the innocence in his light blue eyes alternating with keen suspicion—he had embraced his mother with genuine emotion, pecked each sister with a quick, dry kiss, struggled, flailed, and fought his way out of the arms of his father, and set off for America— where he settled in Detroit.

To no one's surprise, Iosif's departure shocked Naftali. It even altered his loyalty toward Lyesk. Lapsing into long sighs, at odd moments he took to bursting out, "To Detroit! Let's go to Detroit! Here we are . . . going off to Detroit!" Nor did such maundering cease until the evening of June 29, 1914, when Ephraim Savich announced his intention of moving to Lyesk. The town had just received news that Archduke Francis Ferdinand, heir to the throne of Austria-Hungary, had been assassinated by Serbians.

"So it's war for certain," Ephraim said. "Now I see no way to avoid it. And if there's war this family might well use the help of an extra man."

"But why should we be concerned with Serbia?" Sophie inquired.

"Because the great powers," Ephraim said, "have been looking for an excuse to battle one another."

"Germany and Austria, Russia, France. Even England," Malkeh named, looking into the distance.

"And it will be the poor who mainly suffer, the helpless," Kala warned, narrowing her eyes and glancing around for corroboration. She had been reading Schlaymie Zuckerman's pamphlets—pondering and questioning their accusations.

"They have no right," said Ruth. "Men will be killed."

"Thank God, Iosif is in Detroit," Naftali said.

"And when, God willing, I marry Ruth, I'll set up a lumber office in Lyesk. My father will agree, I'm sure. With all the new construction and the trains, this location is perfect."

Malkeh lifted her brows and inquired, "And the draft, Ephraim Savich?"

"My work exempts me."

"Men lose their exemptions."

"You mustn't worry—none of you must worry." Ephraim

waved a husky arm through the air. "The army will need its lumber even more in days to come. And if it comes to that, there are always replacements to be bought. I know how to proceed. They won't take me."

"They won't take him," Naftali echoed. "He'll open a lumber outlet."

And with these assurances in mind, the Chodorovs gathered in the parlor to hear Ruth play her three pieces on the piano. Through the open window came the sweet smell of baked earth. Frogs croaked on the river bottom, Emmanuelle the cow groaned, Mishka neighed, Sir Leslie whinnied, and a chorus of crickets in the fields answered a lone cricket lost in the chimney; and as Ruth played on she struck fewer and fewer wrong notes until at last she played so acceptably that Kala felt glad that Ruth would marry Ephraim.

The month of July bore out Ephraim Savich's prediction of war. By imperial decree, the Tsar ordered martial law for the western provinces. Civil courts were suspended and the western railways, including the station at Lyesk, came under the jurisdiction of the War Department. At the same time that the nation moved toward war, the discontent of the Russian workers and the peasants erupted. In the month of July, Minsk suffered three strikes against factory conditions and wages; and only sixty miles from Lyesk, peasants rioted, killing an estate manager and his family and burning a country house and three barns.

Day by day, as the mood of Lyesk darkened, Kala reread passages of her revolutionary pamphlets, struck by the truth of their prophecies. It impressed her that their authors had written about what was actually taking place. She declared to Sophie that if Russia went to war it would do so only because the Tsar could not feed and clothe his people. She predicted that the people would at once rise up in protest. On August 1, 1914, war was declared. A few days later, at the Lyesk railroad station, Kala learned that when the Tsar had appeared on the balcony of his Winter Palace to announce his decision, everyone in the immense St. Petersburg square—man, woman, child—dropped to his knees. This show of reverence astonished Kala. It confused her, for though Lyesk was momentarily prospering, she had been told that all through Russia the royal family and the government had fallen into disfavor because of economic disaster and police repression. Yet now a wave of patriotism was sweeping across the empire. Kala read that even the angriest critics of the regime—men and women whose names had appeared in Schlaymie Zuckerman's pamphlets—now reversed themselves and rose to grand eloquence in defense of the motherland; and in the first week of August, in Lyesk itself, crowds gathered at the station to cheer as the trains from the east came—every two hours, car after car of singing, optimistic young men and their officers, whose eyes faced toward the enemy they would soon defeat, for it was well known the Russian forces vastly outnumbered the Germans.

The first report—two great victories in East Prussia—had barely reached Lyesk before it was followed by news of a terrible disaster at Tannenberg. The Germans, moving swiftly on improved rail lines, turned heavy artillery upon the Russian soldiers, who floundered in the mud. The enemy then cut through two Russian armies and began a drive toward Warsaw, in the direction of Lyesk. Almost immediately the trains began to wend their way back from the north and west, filled no longer with prosperous officials and singing warriors, but packed with the Russian wounded in retreat—pale men with stricken eyes and missing limbs who sometimes cried out piteously like children.

Malkeh directed Kala to cart baked goods to the station. On the first morning Kala contacted the officers in charge of each train as she had been instructed. After setting a price, she helped pass out the bread and cakes. As she moved along the corridors of the trains, it seemed to her that the wounded had been loaded like freight directly from the battlefield.

[35]

Wherever she looked she saw raw wounds caked with dirt and oozing blood. Once or twice she all but fainted from the stench of the jammed carriages and the terrifying moans issuing out of every corner. Despite her desire to run through the train casting her breads and cakes from side to side with closed eyes, she exchanged a few words with whichever soldiers would look at her. The wounds she saw throbbed and pained as if they were her own—for since early in her childhood she had felt a peculiar susceptibility to other people's hurts. Horrified, she reflected that here were ordinary young men who, until a few weeks ago, had never harmed a soul. By what law had they been punished? Exactly what had been done to them, she wondered, and what had they themselves done, to brand them with such a look of apology and shame? How dare the government destroy the spirit of its Russian people!

One by one she approached her sisters, demanding to know their attitude toward the fighting. Ekaterina evaded the question, wanting nothing to do with it. Ruth tried to reassure her that life was God's mystery and that there must be some purpose to it all. Sophie, misreading Kala's mood, blew an imaginary trumpet and pronounced, "If the war comes to Lyesk, then we shall fight."

Kala withdrew and brooded. She asked herself why her sisters were so evasive. She wondered if they could keep on pretending that the trains bearing the wounded simply did not exist? Then one day toward noon she glimpsed Ekaterina pausing on the hill that overlooked the station—evidently having detoured several blocks on her way to her tutor's. Unseen, Kala watched her beautiful fair-haired sister peer down at the train. She witnessed Ekaterina's lips pursed in absent concentration and with troubled dislike—almost as if, thought Kala, Ekaterina gazed into a foul murky-bottomed river and the water sent back a bitter taste, which her sister's lips refused to acknowledge but which she could not manage to spit out. Uneasily Kala wondered how the war might touch her youngest sister if Ekaterina remained so distant and grand.

She never saw Ekaterina staring at the soldiers again, but a few days later—at the opposite end of the platform, just before the Stationmaster called out his warning—Kala caught sight of Sophie. She carried nothing in her arms, not so much as a small basket of rolls, but her long black hair reached down her back and her cheeks glowed as she strained up from the wheelchair and called and waved to the soldiers. Kala started toward Sophie, then paused, puzzled, for it struck her that there was something too excited and intense, too tenacious, about the gaiety with which Sophie waved and tossed her head and signaled to the men. Then all at once Kala understood that Sophie was telling the soldiers that she was one of them—that she, in her wheelchair, was also wounded; that she was trying to tell them through the breadth of her shoulders and the tilt of her head that if they looked at her they could see it made no great difference, crippled or whole.

Kala backed away from the privacy of this encounter. She hid behind a pillar. Her temples throbbed as she reflected that here was her closest sister revealing to strangers a more complicated, less matter-of-fact attitude toward her handicap than she'd ever allowed Kala to suspect. Here was her sister using her own body to present a message of hope to the soldiers, when, in Kala's presence—even in their longest talks—Sophie had always maintained that she believed in nothing.

Excluded and embarrassed, she spent the rest of the day avoiding Sophie. When it came time to prepare for bed on the sleeping porch which they shared, Kala slipped away to the repair shop and took up her tools, returning an hour or so later to stop in at Ruth's and Ekaterina's bedroom. Ekaterina was already asleep but Ruth was sitting up in bed, her hands clasped. "Are you praying?" Kala asked cautiously.

"I'm just awake."

Kala nodded. Then she began, affecting a conversational tone, "You never go to the train station, Ruth. I've seen

Ekaterina there, I've seen Sophie. I saw Sophie by the trains today . . ." She stopped, not knowing how much further she might continue without betraying Sophie.

"It's too hard to see all those injured men," said Ruth. "To see them suffer, and for no reason. So I've been praying a lot—more than usual. I've asked God to end the war."

"And do you think he will?"

Ruth inclined her head. "He may very well."

Kala groaned. "You're out of your mind. Not a single soldier will be saved by your prayers. God has nothing to do with the war. This war," she paused, ". . . I've begun to think the Tsar sent us to war just to save himself and his nobility." She peered at her sister, curious about the effect of her new ideas.

"Shh, Kala, where did you hear that? You're right but only to a certain degree. Shhh, you'll wake Ekaterina."

But Ekaterina had already lifted her head from the pillow and was looking at Ruth and Kala, her daytime vexed expression still absent from her face.

"Shh, you'll wake Ekaterina," Ruth repeated. "What's depressing is, today in the bakery I heard that the Russian government is blaming its defeats on the Jews."

"There's something wrong with the government, I already told you. It's been going on forever—the tsars can't rule their country and so they incite the peasants against us. We know what used to happen in Mama's village—twice a year at least."

"Poor Mama," said Ekaterina drowsily, "just think, living in a one-room hut that became a tavern on market days."

"I'm not talking about that, ninny," said Kala. "I'm talking about pogroms. She told us. Those same peasants who drank and ate at her house—they patted her head and praised her baking—once or twice a year the government got them drunk and turned them loose on the Jews. There she was, a little girl, hidden up in the rafters watching men she knew trampling on her family's few precious objects. Next door they did terrible things to the neighbor lady. The same thing has been going on everywhere else and would have happened here if it hadn't been for Mama—the way she handles the authorities. The Tsar is evil."

"Kala," said Ruth. "What is the Tsar, after all, but a man? Still, it's terrible, it's depressing. And today the government claims that in certain *shtetls* in the war zones Jews are hiding whole regiments of Germans. Jews are now considered German sympathizers and spies."

"I don't think I'm really Jewish," Ekaterina broke in. "If I ran away to London or Paris, even to Moscow, no one would ever guess."

"Ekaterina!" Ruth said.

"German spies?" Kala frowned. Then all at once the loneliness she'd experienced when she'd left Sophie waving to the wounded at the station—the estrangement and the sense that everyone lived alone—seized her, and to combat it she said, "Let's all go see Sophie together."

Without objecting or asking questions, Ruth and Ekaterina got out of bed and headed up the hall, following Kala to the porch at the back of the house.

Kala bent over her sleeping sister. "Sophie," Kala called, "Sophie." She tapped her on the shoulder. "Sophie, what with the war going on and the soldiers wounded and the Jews being considered traitors and spies, you have to wake up and talk to us. Otherwise we'll be lonely. Our town might become like anywhere else."

CHAPTER FOUR

"K ALA," MALKEH SAID, A SMALL SMILE OF SATISFACTION touching the edge of her lips, "run across to the orchard and tell your father we've just had word that Ephraim's borrowed a droshky and he'll be here by seven tonight."

Kala understood the meaning of her mother's smile: this evening Ephraim and Ruth would doubtlessly set the date for their wedding. Already it was the last week of September; the family had been waiting all month for this moment, hoping to have Ruth's future settled before the Germans took Warsaw—a possibility that seemed more and more likely.

Kala hitched a wagon ride across the river and located her father standing in the middle of the orchard. He looked, she thought, as if he had been planted and was growing there, like one of his younger apple trees. Except for his high work boots, he was dressed as if for a celebration in a white shirt and gabardine suit, his derby hat perched squarely on the top

of his head. Off to one side of the orchard rose the small
cottage in which, during the harvest, Naftali sometimes spent
two or three consecutive nights in the company of the peasants
and the temporary help who worked for him. Yet even when
he awakened in the cottage, Kala was certain that, exactly as
at home, Naftali washed and shaved carefully and with the
greatest attention, put on his fine snow-white underwear, his
garters, first one sock, then the next, his shirt, his cravat, his
suit, his hat—donning each item with a childlike deliberate-
ness born not only of vanity but also out of an attachment to
the motions involved in dressing and out of a strong belief
that from his efforts he would emerge a fully defined, a fully
completed, satisfactory Jewish male adult.

As Kala reached her father she said, "Hello, Papa." Naftali
nodded slightly. She was struck, as always, by the faintness of
his interest, which she knew also extended to her sisters. She
had observed that now and then, like a sweet tooth, he favored Ekaterina. But on the whole—though he entertained
fervent hopes for his daughters' future, though he was generous toward them with money and wanted to protect them
from every harm—they were finally his daughters and not his
son. Often it seemed to Kala he showed little interest in telling his girls apart. Yet here she was, she thought with a measure of bitterness and regret, more of a boy than her sisters,
described through the town as a "Cossack," an incorrigible
tomboy—and still she disappointed her father by failing to
make it all the way. Standing on tiptoe, she leaned to kiss
him. "Papa," she offered by way of compensation, "Ephraim
is arriving tonight. He's borrowed a droshky and he's expected by seven o'clock. So come home early. You're the first
person he always wants to see."

"Ephraim's coming?" Naftali's childlike, crafty, clean-cut
face crinkled with instant pleasure. "Ephraim's coming and
we didn't expect him for two more weeks!" Then his eyes
turned bright as he allowed himself his favorite question,
"Any news of Iosif?"

"No. No news."

[41]

Naftali turned and walked toward the cottage, which was set in a hollow, shielded from the river and the high road. "Ah well . . . we can't expect a letter every other day, certainly not if it comes all the way across the ocean."

Kala trailed her father, pleased to be breathing in the faint, bittersweet smell of the soil baking under the warm sun. The leaves of the trees had turned such a deep green that they appeared almost gray in the shadows. Now and then she reached up to touch a branch companionably, thinking that soon they would be bare. From the small rise above the cottage she noticed a pile of new lumber to one side and the beginnings of an addition to the back of the small building. Surprised, she questioned her father.

"The cottage was too small," he said, picking his way down to the bench next to the door of the cottage.

"For what?"

Carefully he laid out his kerchief and sat down, plucking each trouser slightly to preserve its crease. "Just too small," he murmured and then continued without a pause, "I suppose you've been down to the train?" Since the Russian retreat, when the trains began to bear cargo of bandaged, suffering soldiers he had given up visiting the railroad. Before that, in the prosperous weeks preceding the war, he had gone to the station fairly often—to shake hands and gossip with acquaintances, to gaze at the strange bearing of newcomers, and to be in touch with the latest news. Dressed in his fine suit and carrying his ivory-handled cane, he had hovered near the most imposing of the officials—not attempting, Kala knew, to insinuate himself into their presence but simply edging near in an effort to overhear the ins and outs of important business. One day in the spring he had backed onto the foot of an official who had then turned, included him in the conversation, and within the next five minutes awarded him a contract for providing the army's horses with feed. Now even the chance for another army contract failed to lure him to the station. "It's a different world. The trains keep whistling all day long. They never stop coming. Well, it's the fault of the government and what can we do about it? Did you take the soldiers any of Malkeh's kvass? Malkeh's kvass will give them courage. Did you bring them a taste of my pickles?"

"Papa?" Kala wandered about the yard. "They say that the Germans are advancing on Warsaw itself, and they may soon cross the Bug River."

"They're coming closer." Naftali made a sound, halfway between a cough and a groan. He recrossed his legs, adjusting his trousers once again. "We'll have the war on our doorstep, just wait and see. The Germans are smarter soldiers than the Russians. You can stop them once, or twice. You can stop them three times, but Papa Velvel's soldiers always find a way." He turned and gazed shrewdly at the unfinished addition. "There's a lot to do."

"Papa Velvel?" Kala laughed. "What a silly name for the Kaiser."

Her father hummed to himself and then looked up at the deep blue sky where small white clouds stood motionless. "Well at least Ephraim's on his way here, and early at that. We'll sit down together, he and I, and together we'll come to some conclusion. We'll decide on a date for the marriage. Go home, Kala," he dismissed her with a grand wave, "go home and make sure someone has washed and ironed my dress shirt. And I want you to press my striped trousers."

When she did not obey, he waved again, as if he were directing a parade. She stood motionless. "I can't press your trousers," she said.

"Of course you can."

"I have to get back to the repair shop." Kala spoke sharply, annoyed that he should act as if the entire family had nothing to do but care for his clothes. She wondered why her mother had married a man who had never learned to read in any language—a smart man, a shrewd man, who could not even sign his name. Had it been only for his chiseled face and his property—the house, its garden, the bakery, and this modest parcel of trees which he leased? It humiliated her that his favorite pastime with his daughters was to gather them around him and enumerate the riches in their dowry. With his head inclined, his voice low with wonder, he liked nothing better than to name the kinds of silver, the number of feather pillows, the amount of linen in the hand-carved chests belonging to each daughter. When he had finished with Ruth and Kala, he said proudly, "To Sophie I've given the largest dowry of all. Still, to be reasonable, she can't expect a handsome man or a tall man or an educated man. She can't even expect a young man . . ."

That he repeated such statements drove Kala mad. But most of all it rankled her that she was more like him—despite his fair skin and pale eyes—than like her mother. She too was excitable, impulsive, irritable and tended to make unreasonable demands on her family. Now they stared at one another —her father the first to avert his eyes, fussing over an imaginary spot upon his sleeve. Without a word Kala turned and ran up the hillside in the direction of the river. Before she reached the summit she turned, waved, and called out, "I'll see you later, Papa."

At the crest of the hill, Kala paused. Below, the orchard continued to the river, beyond which ran the railroad tracks and the back lots of the town. On a rise across the river, the buildings of the town looked more substantial than they were. Downriver, around the bend, the steeple of the station rose above the branches of the willows that grew along the banks. As she ran down a lane of trees, she lost control of her motion and felt as if her body would far outstrip her legs, sending her head over heels into the river. Still she did not slacken her pace. Even more quickly she thrust herself down the slope, veering at the last moment onto a sandy path which led along the river. Sliding to a halt, she chuckled at her acrobatics. Then, instead of returning downriver to the high-road bridge south of town, she made her way north to the railroad bridge, an ancient, frail-looking wooden trestle affair that had recently been strengthened by massive beams and supports. Without pausing she crossed, jumping from tie to tie outside the trestle. At midstream she stopped and sat down to peer at the swift water emerging out of the shadow of the bridge below. Momentarily the sun passed behind a cloud and she felt the chill of the coming winter. The water, just a moment before a translucent blue and green, turned gray and looked hard as stone. Along with the coming rains and the mud which would encompass the town and all of their lives, the war was edging closer, and she wished she had embraced her father before leaving him.

Somberly she proceeded across the bridge and up through the field of tall yellow grass. As she walked, the sun reappeared, warming her once more. The sound of flies and bees and small birds filled the bright air and the still grass cracked and popped from the heat. Soon, she thought, all this comforting noise would cease and be replaced by the sound of hard, driving rain and wind. And then would come the snows.

Entering the repair shop, Kala arranged her tools, adjusted her eyepiece in her eye, and picked up Avrom Lavin's gold watch.

Presently a knock sounded on the door. When she rose and answered, a young man inquired, "Are you Kala Chodorov?"

"Yes I am," she said.

The stranger moved gracefully into the shop, his head held at a shy yet reassuring angle. He had auburn hair and a reddish mustache and his clothes hung softly on him—so colorful and casual a mixture of multithreaded scarf and jacket and cap that Kala gaped at him, thinking he was like some wonderful decoration she might have glimpsed through someone else's forbidden window, or like a blue, rose, and gold ornament in Father Boris's church. Quickly she dropped her eyes. Her fingers flew up to her eyepiece to make certain it was still there, and she took her place behind the counter. "Do you have a watch?" she inquired.

Instead of answering her question he replied, "You're exactly as I expected," the sound of his Russian cultivated and gentle. "Yes, you're just as I imagined when my cousin first told me your grandfather taught you his trade and put you in charge of the clocks and watches of Lyesk." He leaned forward lightly and waited for her response.

He kept on waiting until she felt pushed to respond, "Oh if someone has a very expensive or a particularly valuable watch, they go somewhere else. There's a watch repair man in Baranovits named Augushevits." She blushed.

But her modesty failed to concern him. He shook it off. "I was told you even fixed the great clock in the railroad tower and that you know how to do everything from raising prize roses to shoeing a horse, to helping cows deliver their calves."

She had never heard herself described in so reverent a tone and it made her think there must be something very wrong with this elegant stranger. She noticed how young his voice sounded, younger even than his face. "Do you have a broken watch . . . ?"

He shifted a knapsack from his shoulder to the counter and rested his hands upon it. "As it happens, my watch isn't broken." Turning his head about, he gazed into all the corners of the shop. "I have a different sort of problem," he continued, and now he fixed his eyes on her. "I've got a more complicated sort of problem." He stopped short. "First let me introduce myself. I was born in Vilna. I've been studying in St. Petersburg for the past few years and I've come to Lyesk to spend a bit of time with my cousins."

Kala forced herself to listen to his words, although, to her chagrin, all she wanted was to consult his beautiful blue eyes —as clear as the sea she'd read about in storybooks. "Who are your cousins, what's your family name?" And she waited for him to mention one of the aristocratic Russian families who lived on the square.

"Zuckerman," he told her. "Rachel and her son Schlaymie. They're second and third cousins on my mother's side."

"Zuckerman!" she exclaimed. "You're Schlaymie Zuckerman's cousin?" At this she remembered that the *shoychet* and his wife had often bragged about their wealthy relatives in Vilna and she burst out in laughter.

Stepping back, the young man smiled and shook his head. "What a wonderful laugh. But are you laughing at the Zuckermans or at me?" Without waiting for an answer, he repeated, "What an absolutely wonderful laugh!"

Something akin to envy sounded in his voice. She felt uncomfortable again, just as she had when he'd praised her talents. But he was examining her once more with his dreamy, intense, and earnest eyes and she could not force herself to turn away. She felt as if her whole body were blushing now. She glanced down to make sure she was decently clothed.

"Listen," he began, leaning toward her. He struggled for words. "Schlaymie said you're sympathetic to our cause. When he left he told me that if I needed help, I could call on you."

"Schlaymie's a fool."

"He gives that impression. But it's just an act."

"I don't know why he's bothering me. He forgot to leave me his alarm clock but he left me some pamphlets—I haven't an inkling what's in his mind."

"He said you believe what we do. And that you would help."

"Help in what?"

His shoulders sagged. He shook his head. "I'm sorry I troubled you." He started for the door.

"I don't mean to be rude."

He returned to the counter. Without fully opening his knapsack he reached inside and fumbled around. His hand emerged holding a curious clock mounted horizontally in a small rough wooden stand. From one side of the stand protruded a large winding key; from the other side, four wires. The uncovered face of the clock showed only an hour hand. Turning the key several times, he held the clock first to his ear and then out to Kala. "You see, nothing happens. Nothing at all. I tried to fix it myself, God knows—I tried for three

[47]

days but my mechanical ability . . ." He gave a short laugh, revealing a set of small, perfect teeth. "Maybe you can just help me figure it out—without a lot of bother."

Kala took the apparatus and examined it. It was an alarm clock which someone had altered. The mainspring appeared in good shape. She turned the winding key. Just as he said, nothing happened. "I'm not sure I can do anything," she said. "It's no longer an ordinary clock. It's a timing mechanism."

He fixed her with a gaze so intense Kala felt a wave of suspicion pass over her. She gave herself a shake and held the clock to the light, peering into its works. "It's for a bomb, isn't it?" She tried to appear unperturbed.

The young man sighed, the return of his eagerness and his intensity draining away. "It's for a bomb. To be truthful about it—it's a time bomb." And having rid himself of these words, he threw out the other contents from his knapsack: a cookie tin, a metal cannister, two batteries hooked up to four wires, some soft twine on a spool, an instruction sheet, and other odds and ends. "I'm supposed to add the explosives and the caps when the timer is fixed."

In dismay Kala gazed down upon the array of materials on her counter. She picked up the cannister meant to hold the explosives. The cold metal sent a shiver up through her arm. She began to rotate the cannister so that it would fit with the clock and the batteries in the snug tin box and as she did, she became aware of the young man's head leaning over, his fine hair barely touching her forehead. As he raised his eyes, seeking hers, she had the sense he was trying to enlist her aid through his beauty. She wanted to thrust the cannister away if only to protect herself. At the same time she was filled with an immense curiosity about the bomb itself—about the potential of its explosive power. She grasped the metal cannister in the palm of her hand and felt oddly pleased when it seemed to swell and grow larger—when it seemed to bulge and press against her fingers. All the same, she said, "I don't believe in bombs. They just hurt people."

[48]

"I'm of two minds. My friends and I have talked about that a lot. You have to fight against evil."

"Not with bombs."

"But then with what?" She said nothing. "I don't want to trouble you. The truth is, I have to leave this somewhere. You don't have to fix it if you don't want to. I'd be back for it in a few days."

She hung her head. She wondered if he wanted to see her again, and if she wanted to see him. "I guess you can."

Very softly he said, "Thank you." He replaced all the parts of the mechanism in the knapsack, put it on the counter, and asked that she not mention his visit to anyone.

"How can I mention your visit," she asked, "when I don't even know your name?"

"Oh I beg your pardon. I forgot to introduce myself. My name is Mikhail Kossoff." He gave a bow, and at the door he said, "If you fix the timer, it's for the good of the people." He closed the door firmly after him.

"The last thing I mean to do is fix it," she muttered to herself, and hurriedly locked the knapsack in a cupboard. What with Schlaymie Zuckerman's pamphlets and Schlaymie's cousin's bomb, she thought, her repair shop was rapidly being transformed into a revolutionary center. She closed up for the day and slowly walked the short distance to the bakery. Inside she saw Sophie alone by the cash register and the store empty except for two customers at a back table: she had chanced upon a perfect time to communicate with her sister. They would have such a laugh. If she were to share her tale about Mikhail Kossoff and the clock-timer with Sophie, she knew her sister would keep the secret. But instead of mounting the porch steps and walking through the Dutch door, she found herself backing away. She and her sister, she reflected, had the right to lead their separate lives. She remembered Sophie waving to the wounded soldiers, and she thought that she too had come into possession of something she wanted to keep entirely for herself.

CHAPTER FIVE

B Y SIX O'CLOCK THAT EVENING THE ENTIRE FAMILY HAD
returned to the Chodorov house and were busily preparing for Ephraim's arrival. In the kitchen Malkeh and
Sophie cleaned and seasoned the fish; Ekaterina and Anya
Fomich's cousin Radish buffed and polished the silver and
brasswork. On an ironing board set up in the dining room
Ruth pressed a satin damask tablecloth. On another board
nearby Kala ironed her father's trousers. Naftali circled about
her, carefully instructing, "Here! There!" and directing her
to the wrinkles she'd missed. The household was buoyant
with excitement, for almost everyone in the family had grown
fond of Ephraim Savich. Naftali declared that not since his
son Iosif had he seen so splendid a Jew. He went so far as to
claim that Ephraim's eyes, which were brown and heavy-
lidded, resembled Iosif's, which were thin-lidded and blue.
Even Ekaterina—to whom Ephraim had presented a volume
of Pushkin, and then a volume of Herzen, and on a third

visit a volume of Turgenev—had gradually exempted Ephraim from her habitual scorn.

Malkeh alone retained certain reservations. The fact was, she approved of Ephraim's family, she commended his age— he was six years older than Ruth—she endorsed his prospects, and she admired the kind of gifts he brought Ruth from his travels. "Who else," she said to her daughters, "would give his fiancée office supplies from Minsk?" Not cumbersome necklaces, gaudy silk scarves, flowers, or unwholesome candy. No, Ephraim showered Ruth with paper clips. He surrounded her with the finest lead pencils. He overwhelmed her with the best grade of copy paper. But then he squandered all his credit with Malkeh by bringing Kala and Sophie toys manufactured in the Orient: acrobatic wooden figures on sticks; charming brightly colored fans of undulating crepe paper; magic tricks within boxes, which he and the two girls would work until the three of them laughed uproariously right beneath Malkeh's eyes. Shooing away her daughters and the toys, Malkeh advised her future son-in-law, "Kala and Sophie have stayed childish enough. They don't need anyone to encourage them."

Her admonition accomplished very little. Instead, Kala noticed that Ephraim soon took it upon himself to close in on her mother and try to elicit from her some playful response. At breakfast—no matter her objections, no matter if they engaged in a lengthy tug-of-war—tenaciously he held Malkeh's chair for her while she sat down. Then he insisted on pouring out her coffee and spreading her roll with butter and jam. If she wanted a second roll, he spread that too with butter and jam. His manner suggested nothing short of chivalry and good cheer. Yet Malkeh made it apparent she perceived his gallantry as an overbearing and irresponsible challenge, as an attempt to undermine her, a contest between them of wills.

Even for Kala there were times, when Ephraim joked, that she found him too foolish or extreme—such as when upon entering a room he manipulated his eyebrows and said, "Never fear, Ephraim Savich is here." Nevertheless, on one

[51]

such occasion, unexpectedly Malkeh laughed. Her mouth flew open. A sound burst from it like a clap of thunder and her face softened like that of a carefree girl's. Momentarily she appeared liberated from all the years of hard wisdom and judicious fairness. Naftali, Kala, Sophie, and Ekaterina turned to her with startled pleasure, then glanced with gratitude at Ephraim.

As for Ruth, she never once removed her eyes from her betrothed. Out of pride that it was she who, in all the world, he had chosen—and in her wish decorously to conceal that pride—her dignified features took on a look that was secretive, ecstatic, and smug.

It was an expression neither Kala nor Sophie could bear. During the warm summer nights—long after everyone else had gone to sleep—they pulled their beds close to one another, analyzed Ruth's facial expression, leaned out the window, and under the stars complained that Ruth was too orderly, too neat, too proper, too contemplative, too kind, and that she might one day turn into treacle. They lamented that soon she would leave their sphere of influence and her faults would multiply and flower—she who had been their second and less exacting mother, a gentle parent who had quietly herded them here and there. While they talked they contemplated the barnyard, the pastures, and the hills across the river where the family orchard was located. The glittering stars in the still skies seemed to press down upon them. The fresh smell of dew on the fields mingled with the odor of the barnyard and made them yearn to keep on living forever.

"And she never questions the existence of God," Sophie murmured.

"Not only God. She never questions Mama."

"Ah, well."

"And what a total lack of interest in Karl Marx."

"But Kala, why should she be interested in Karl Marx?"

"And then, of course, we seldom know what she's really thinking. Do you suppose she hates us?"

For some moments there was silence. "If she hates us,"

Sophie slowly reflected, "she'd never say so. We'll never know."

"Sophie, ask her."

But as there seemed no way to pose that question, in its place they resolved to advise Ruth that if she kept the same absent, prissy look for any length of time Ephraim would abandon her and marry one of them.

"If she keeps it up," said Sophie, "he'll marry me."

"No, I'm older," Kala reminded, "he'd have to marry me."

"Then he might as well marry Ruth."

At exactly half-past seven Ephraim stood at the door with his familiar worn suitcase and a new carryall slung over his shoulder. Though he appeared tired, his smile somewhat forced, he greeted and embraced each member of the family with a kiss, a special handclasp, a whispered joke. As he stepped into the house, he turned and beckoned to someone who remained in the street some paces back. For an instant Kala thought it might be Mikhail. But after much coaxing, a man Ephraim's age stepped into the house. Ruth, Kala, Sophie, and Ekaterina stared for an instant, then quickly looked away for, as handsome as Ephraim Savich was, the stranger was just as ugly. Shorter than Ephraim by as much as a foot, he had a pockmarked complexion, a mouth shaped sadly like a button, and vast peach-colored ears that stood out from his head like butterfly wings.

"This is my good friend Mordecai Berg," Ephraim said. "We have known each other . . . we have known each other," Ephraim knitted his brow in a comical half effort to remember, "forever—at least since *cheder*."

"Any friend of Ephraim's," beamed Naftali. "Ah, Ephraim, you look so happy and healthy. It's time to eat. Malkeh has prepared a special meal and after dinner I'll show you the latest letter from Iosif." Tucking his arm under Ephraim's he led him into the dining room.

[53]

Very swiftly Ruth set an extra place for Mordecai Berg, putting him—at a signaled request from Malkeh, who had noted his shyness—next to Ephraim. From here Mordecai faced Ekaterina, a look of awe settling on his face, so that Ephraim murmured, "She's beautiful, isn't she?" then warned, "Easy, my friend, she's not for you." After that, while Naftali recited the blessings for the wine and for the bread and Malkeh served the soup, Ephraim seemed to grow abstracted and a bit morose until at last when the platter of *flanken* was brought in, he stared at the meat and announced the time had come to make his confession.

"What is it?"

"I've been drafted into the Russian army."

Ruth turned pale. "So that's what's wrong," she said as Naftali moaned, "Bad news, bad news!" and Ekaterina exclaimed, "You'll be an officer, of course."

"Ekaterina!" Malkeh reproved her. "There are no Jewish officers in the Russian army."

"She's been reading all those novels," Sophie said. "He'd have to join the Austrian army to become an officer."

To the family's surprise, suddenly Ruth interrupted their talk, her voice shrill. "Never mind all that. Never mind the chatter." She bent across the table toward Ephraim and whispered hoarsely, "When do you leave?"

"Aie, aie!" Naftali kept groaning. "We should have expected it. With the war coming closer . . ."

"And what kind of war is it? What kind of war is it?" Kala shouted, responding to the hysteria in her sister Ruth's voice. "There's nothing for us to gain. It's the Tsar's war."

"Oh, Kala," said Ruth, her hands to her cheeks as if she had a toothache.

From her armchair at the head of the table—a position which, side by side, she shared with Naftali—Malkeh accused Ephraim with a single sentence: "I thought you paid someone to take your place."

Ephraim looked down at his plate. "No. I thought about it. I turned it about in my mind. But I could not see paying someone to lose an arm or a leg or even a finger when it ought to be my arm or leg or finger." He laughed. "And now, of course, when I've changed my mind, it's much too late. They need every man they can lay their hands on . . . not to mention that the examiner in Pinsk has got something or other he holds against me. He used to be our customer, but there was a misunderstanding. Besides, who could I find? Who would be willing to die in my place? Who could I ask?" Pointedly he directed these questions to Kala, Sophie, and Ekaterina, at the same time avoiding Ruth. His tone momentarily softened. "For example, would I ask a friend?" He turned his head and looked at Mordecai Berg.

And so did everyone else. Without so much as a word, they fixed their gaze on Mordecai in earnest concentration. Before this evening they had never glimpsed him. Yet now they seemed to be asking, as though they'd known him all their lives, "Mordecai, go to war for Ephraim."

Mordecai shifted uncomfortably in his seat.

"Anyway," Ephraim clapped his friend resoundingly on the shoulder, then leaned way back and surveyed him with an air of proprietary approval, "anyway, the army has rejected Mordecai." He heaved a sigh of envy and resignation. "The army has rejected Mordecai, God only knows why. And since I, too, like all of you . . . have no sympathy for the foolishness of this war, I've decided to follow Iosif's example and run off to America. Right this moment the authorities are no doubt following my trail. In the morning I set off for Brest and Warsaw and then it's border-crossing time."

Now he put down his knife and fork and for the first time looked directly at Ruth. His eyes moistened and the sound of self-sacrifice quavered in his voice. "And so in my place I have brought you Mordecai Berg. I consider him almost my brother. That is," to lighten the statement he grinned, "if I had a brother."

Ruth's hands began to tremble. At this Ephraim shifted his attention to Malkeh. Then as if addressing Malkeh's superior reasonableness he went on, "I have told Mordecai what a good wife Ruth will make—what a marvelous girl she is, how kind and capable in every way, what a splendid cook, whose handwriting . . ."

"What are you saying?" Kala's voice rang out.

"Maybe this is all a mistake," Mordecai murmured.

Ignoring him, Ephraim continued, "I have told Mordecai about Ruth's handwriting—how it is the most beautiful and legible in all the province; that she has a special way with keeping the monthly accounts, an intuition about numbers."

As he spoke, he seemed to grow more and more depressed. Scowling at his plate, he pushed it away, at which Ruth got up, her back and shoulders peculiarly bunched together. She quickly left the table.

"You stupid man!" said Ekaterina. "You could have bought a substitute. You don't have the brains to know where your self-interest lies." She rose and followed Ruth to the bedroom at the back of the house.

"This really isn't right," Mordecai said.

Addressing Ephraim, Kala persisted. "Do you mean that once you're safe and settled in the New World, you'll send for Ruth to join you?"

"That's not what he means," Sophie drily remarked.

"Perhaps I do. And if I don't . . . it's a question of fairness. I have no papers. I have to cross all of Europe—two battle lines. The odds against my ever getting to the ocean are great, and then there's the passage. And even if I accomplish all that, how can I know how long it will take me to find my way in the New World—to learn the language, to be hired at a job . . ."

"Ruth will wait," said Sophie. "Ruth is someone who would even want to wait."

Silence greeted Sophie's statement. There seemed no proper way to digest it. Even the sound of Mordecai cutting up his food ceased abruptly, mainly because—unlike anyone else—Mordecai had eaten everything on his plate. It was finally Malkeh who broke the spell. "So you're from Karlin too?" she questioned Mordecai, at the same time filling his plate with a second helping of *flanken, kugel,* cauliflower, and potatoes.

"I am."

"And your parents?"

"From Karlin too. They own a small dry goods store."

"So you're from Karlin?" Naftali joined in weakly. "I have a second cousin there. Name of Levy."

All at once Sophie shouted at the two young men, "Go away. Both of you. Leave! We want nothing more to do with you." She hobbled swiftly on her crutches to the other side of the table and snatched away Mordecai's plate. He was left holding a fork in his left hand, a knife in the other—both of which utensils Kala then captured in a single motion. She swept away Ephraim's plate, cringing when she remembered how he'd said, "Ahh, Kala, if I were only two men instead of one."

As Kala and Sophie made their way to the back of the house they heard their mother explain, "The girls are over-wrought, as you can well understand. However we have plenty of room and I can see no reason to make you go out again so late in the evening. You must spend the night."

"Ephraim, I don't belong here," Mordecai said.

"Nonsense, you're doing a good deed."

"So you're a good friend of Ephraim's?" Naftali uttered sadly. "Tell me," he inquired, "exactly what does your father sell? Does your father sell English suiting?"

In the bedroom that Ruth shared with Ekaterina, Kala and Sophie found Ekaterina stretched out on Ruth's bed, reading a book. Ruth sat on the foot of the bed, looking straight ahead—as dignified and composed as if she were in *shul* listening to the rabbi. At the sight of so much restraint Kala burst out sobbing, keeping in mind the qualities Ephraim had enumerated—what a marvelous girl Ruth was, how kind and capable, what a splendid way with numbers, what exceptional handwriting. Unable to contain herself any longer, she threw herself into Ruth's lap. At this Sophie, too, began to sob. The two girls cried louder and louder. Presently

Ekaterina, disturbed by so much noise, glanced up from her book. Suspiciously she eyed Kala and Sophie. After a few moments—bit by bit, as if she were being drawn in against her better judgment—Ekaterina let loose a single tear from the right eye, another one from the left eye, and then all at once, two more tears simultaneously.

Ruth's eyes alone remained dry. And at the knock on her door it was she who rose and quieted her sisters. At the door she found Ephraim Savich, his head extended oddly from his neck as if in supplication.

"Please don't cry, Ruth," he pleaded. "Please don't cry. Why are you crying?"

Coldly Ruth surveyed Ephraim. "You've made a mistake," she informed him, presenting a face as smooth and dry as stone. "You've made a mistake. No one here is crying."

In the morning when Kala came in from chopping wood, Ruth's former betrothed was gone but Mordecai Berg sat at the kitchen table drinking coffee. Apologetically he raised his eyes to Kala, as if reminding her Malkeh had invited him to stay while at the same time asking her forgiveness that he wasn't Ephraim Savich.

CHAPTER SIX

MORDECAI BERG REMAINED THE WEEK. WHEREVER THE girls turned he got in the way, awkwardly stumbling to let them by with the same odd smile of apology on his face. He was in the kitchen when anyone was in the kitchen. When no one was there he went into the yard and got in the way of the cows and the chickens. In the day he hovered by the dividing curtains in the bakery as Malkeh and Ruth attempted to pass through carrying trays. Early evening found him in near collision with whichever daughter was trying to set the table. Yet Malkeh and Naftali gave no sign they minded. After dinner they invited him into the parlor and on the third night they asked Ruth to play the piano for him.

Ruth's musical recital brought Kala straight to her mother. Appalled that her parents permitted, let alone encouraged, such goings-on, she thrust her face in front of Malkeh and railed at her for pushing so unacceptable a suitor at her sister

—and at a time when Ruth had just been jilted by her true love.

"The country is hard at war," Malkeh replied, regarding Kala with her clear gray eyes. "There will be very few men around—for any girl."

That her mother delivered so undignified a statement in a flat matter-of-fact tone shocked Kala even further. She withdrew to recover and then confronted Ruth as her sister left the parlor. "Ruth," she whispered urgently, "you mustn't play the piano for Mordecai again. It's wrong. He isn't worth it."

Ruth looked away, then said with her quiet smile, "My piano playing isn't worth very much. That isn't a problem."

"It isn't that bad. It's too good for Mordecai. What I want you to know is . . ."

"I know." Ruth stopped her. "I understand. You don't find Mordecai enormously appealing. Mordecai's . . . different from Ephraim. But if you think about it, Ephraim was really never meant for me. I remember I had misgivings in the beginning. If I had paid attention to them . . ."

"But Ephraim's the person you wanted to be with . . . to marry."

Ruth winced. "I shouldn't have allowed myself to believe that."

"But how can you act so calm?" Kala raised her fists and shook them furiously. "Why aren't you tearing your hair? Why don't you act like a normal person? Listen, don't let Mama and Papa talk you into Mordecai. You have to get rid of him. Throw him out the window. Throw him in the river. You can do it. You're stronger than he is. I'll help you."

"And if it's God's will?"

"God's will? Is it His will that you marry someone you don't care about? What sort of God do you believe in? Does your God know enough to be just?"

"Ah, justice." Ruth nodded, her features framed by smooth red-gold hair. "Justice is . . . God's mystery."

[60]

Kala ground her teeth. "What does that mean? It doesn't mean anything. You iron everything out so that it loses all meaning. Justice is man's goal. Justice comes from the work of man. It has nothing to do with God."

"Except, Kala, that you know as I do, that everything proceeds according to God's will."

Unable to tolerate one more moment of such an exchange, Kala charged for the back door and headed toward Emmanuelle and Sir Leslie. On her way out she glimpsed Naftali and Mordecai at the thick oak dining-room table. The two men had just spent the day together in the orchard and they now sat next to each other, their chests and shoulders obscured by the smoke from their pipes. Naftali, bent toward Mordecai's large, peach, transparent butterfly ears, was ecstatically counting out the number of feather pillows, the kinds of silver, the amount of linen in his eldest daughter's dowry.

"So many feather pillows," Mordecai interrupted Naftali. "But you must please give Ruth time to decide for herself."

Kala fled into the yard. She paused before the animals, stamped her foot in disgust, and went on into the repair shop. Here she sent a glance at the locked cupboard containing the broken clock-timer; but Mikhail Kossoff's bomb seemed no more than a frivolity when compared with the prospect of her sister marrying Mordecai Berg. And yet, she told herself, she ought to be fair to Ruth's new suitor. Recalling Mordecai's concern for her sister, she felt a twinge of fear she might be judging him too harshly. She resolved to be more kind. But when she went back into the house and caught sight of Mordecai, she wished he would simply go away.

At the end of the week Mordecai left for Karlin. He promised to return very soon. On the same day, toward the end of the afternoon, Ekaterina burst into the house from her tutor's, shouting, "Mama, Mama, a train just passed through the station filled with Jews from the war zone."

Malkeh called her daughters together in the kitchen. Although she appeared upset, they stopped some distance away from her, knowing she preferred to touch them with her wide clear eyes and the firmness of her voice. "The evacuation has begun," she said. "The Jews are being sent away from their villages. The Russian government is afraid that Jews in the war zone will help the Germans in their advance. So they've put I don't know how many people, how many whole Jewish villages on the trains."

"Where are they sending them?"

"Further into Russia—somewhere or other. No one knows. The Russian government doesn't know. So now when we hear of any such trains stopping in the Lyesk station we'll carry down as many breads and cakes as we can. If the trains are delayed for any length of time or if the cars are shunted into the yard for repairs, we'll invite as many as we can to stay with us overnight. We'll accept no pay—that goes without saying."

"And what if they offer us money?" Ekaterina asked.

"We'll accept no payment."

"Just because they are Jews?" Ekaterina pursued.

Quickly Kala looked to her mother.

"Yes, because they are Jews," Malkeh said, raising her long and regal chin. "First because they are Jews," she repeated, smiling the compassionate yet utterly implacable smile that had helped establish her reputation for wisdom. "And then because they are people. We take payment from the Russian army only because the government pays handsomely for food and drink supplied to its soldiers. But we accept no money when we give to the poor or the hospital or the old folks' home. There's nothing in life so important as sharing with the needy and the homeless. That's the tradition of our people. That's what we believe."

Such grand words as these brought a flush of pride to Ruth's, Kala's, and Sophie's cheeks. But Ekaterina bit her lip peevishly. "How dreary," she sighed. "To keep on being pointed out—to keep on being eternally reminded that we're Jews. We're even expected to give Jews special treatment."

"Not only because they are Jews," Kala insisted, modifying her mother's statement. "First and foremost it's because they

[62]

are people, unjustly treated." She glanced around, ready to argue, but neither her mother or her sisters objected.

Two days later a refugee train stopped briefly in Lyesk, and Malkeh sent her daughters to the station to offer their baked goods personally to the Jews. Hershel appeared at the last moment and began pushing Sophie's wheelchair. The procession started up Merchant Lane where the shopkeepers added small offerings to the girls' baskets as they passed: a scarf, an old blanket, a jar of jam, a packet of hard candy, candles, matches. From Merchant Lane the sisters and Hershel cut into a field of tall grasses, a narrow path providing a short cut to the station. Here Sophie wheeled herself about in circles while Kala and Hershel chased her. Descending the hill, they examined the merchants' gifts. They giggled at the dry left-over *kugel* Faygeh Shneir had thrust upon them. They chortled over the moth-eaten scarf Nachman Liebes had so ceremoniously handed over. They sniffed at Sarah Finkel's packet of candy, then put it to their ears and shook it. "One hundred years old," Sophie estimated.

"Two hundred years old," exclaimed Hershel. At the bottom of the field, Kala, Sophie, and Hershel paused on the hillside to survey the railroad. About them the day closed in, growing warmer and grayer. As Ruth and Ekaterina came up from behind, Kala recalled that often when they stood on this spot Ruth, with her mild voice, invited her sisters' admiration of the railroad's gabled wooden tower, commenting that so picturesque a structure lent a special character to Lyesk. But today the tower and the red and gold sign bearing the name of the town lay shrouded in a still mist, and, after glancing around at her sisters, Ruth simply peered down and was silent. From the square, Ivan Sergeyevich's droshky broke into view, hurrying through the gloom to the station. Below, the train was already in, white steam rising from its engine to join the mist. As Hershel's and the girls' eyes grew more accustomed to the thickened air, they made out a long line of refugees who waited their turn before the three spigots at the station cistern of water, under which a fire burned all day. In their hands the people held containers of every size and shape with which to bring hot water to the train for their tea.

"They keep looking over their shoulders at the train," Sophie remarked.

"It's because they're afraid the train will leave without them and they'll lose their families," Ruth instructed.

Kala hurried toward the line of refugees and began distributing her bread and cakes. Moving ahead, she soon found herself very near the train, staring up at one of the open cattle cars crowded with heaps of household articles and lumps of people huddled together in family groups. At the rail of an open car she noticed a boy and a girl standing alone. Both were very small and wizened—neither older than nine or ten. They gripped each other's hand as if stuck or frozen together out of fear, and they stared out at the station with identical large brown eyes which Kala thought almost looked blind. Everything about them appeared to her as gray as the fog—even their dank hair and the rags that covered them. Rummaging in her basket, she discovered two thick slices of honeycake, which she thrust up at the children. "Take them," she urged.

In their free hands—without releasing their clasped hands —the children took hold of the cake, their blank gazes shifting to Kala's face.

"Go ahead," Kala said. "It's cake. It's delicious. Eat it."

Taking small bites, the children obediently consumed the pastry. Timid smiles gradually lifted the corners of their mouths. "It's very good," the girl said. "Did you make it?"

"My sisters did," Kala said, recalling that of the two cakes she had ever baked, one had burned and the other had failed to rise. Then all at once she wished that, like her sisters, she too sifted flour, measured sugar and salt, kneaded dough, and whipped together eggs. "I usually don't do the baking," she explained.

At this, the children seemed to lose interest in Kala; and in a moment they were gone. Kala, feeling oddly spurned by their quick departure, backed away from the train. She col-

[64]

lided with the immense girth of the short peasant midwife, Matryona, and nuzzled against her for comfort, speculating why Matryona—one of the poorest among all the peasants—should also be one of the fattest. After Matryona had hugged and released her, Kala observed that the midwife, who was handing out her pots of honey, managed both to refuse and to ignore any money offered her by abruptly dropping her chin to her chest.

"But Matryona," Kala grabbed hold of the older woman's wrists, "there's something wrong with you. These are not your people. You're not a Jew."

"These are people," Matryona crooned in her deep baritone voice, "and they need my honey to sweeten the taste of our sour stationmaster today." She pointed to Ivan Sergeyevich, who was shouting, "On the train, on the train!"—an unusually shrill pitch to his command.

Kala glanced about to identify the source of the Stationmaster's annoyance. She caught sight of a bent old man in a long coat who moved carefully away from the cistern, a broken pot of hot water cradled cautiously in his sleeves. "On the train!" repeated Ivan Sergeyevich, shoving the old man and jostling the pot so that the hot water spilled out upon the platform.

"Ivan Sergeyevich," Kala demanded, leaping away from Matryona and confronting the Stationmaster—her indignation against him all the more extreme because she'd often dangled from his left knee in her childhood—"Ivan Sergeyevich, why do you act so badly? How dare you treat an old man so brutally?"

Ivan Sergeyevich's eyes widened. "Me, dear girl? What did I do?"

She stuck her face up in front of his. "You pushed him—as if he were nothing—just an ugly dog."

The Stationmaster's surprise shifted to consternation. "You're mistaken, dear girl. Of course I didn't push him. Whom did I push? It doesn't interest me to push anyone. I just don't want them to miss their train."

[65]

"You pushed him," Kala said. "You just want to get rid of him and the rest of these people." Then while she accused Ivan Sergeyevich, she saw that the expression on his face was peculiar and distraught. She felt bad, realizing he no longer found his duties as Stationmaster simple. She reached out and touched his arm, then quickly finished distributing the contents of her basket. Without waiting for her sisters, she headed back toward town, thinking that the war was changing everything and everyone.

That night as she slept she dreamed that she encountered once again the large-eyed dank children, but this time the fluffy loaves of bread she gave them were loaves formed by her own hands and she was able to comfort and reassure them when she said, "Here is some bread. I baked it especially for you. As I sprinkled it with poppy seed and brushed it with the white of eggs, both of you were in my mind."

In the morning she woke up, finished her chores as quickly as possible and returned to the house to scrub her arms and hands. Her mother, Ruth, and Sophie had already left for the bakery but Ekaterina—assigned to help Radish wash the windows—was sitting on the piano bench, her back to the piano, her blonde head in a book. "Ekaterina," Kala scolded, "why aren't you helping Radish?"

"I'm supervising," replied Ekaterina, without looking up.

Exasperated, Kala quit the house and went to the bakery. It was still early and the store was empty. The floor had been freshly scrubbed and the wood tables washed down. Naftali's pickles rested in a deep barrel by the door, while Malkeh's kvass stood in tall-necked bottles in a row behind the cash register. Trying out a chair, Kala surveyed the bakery with envy and pride: its whitewashed walls and ceiling, the side-paneled front windows, the generous Dutch door. This, she thought, was the domain of her mother and her sisters: the place from which she'd been banished. She began to hear the murmur of her mother's and sisters' voices as they baked, and she got up and crept toward the curtains that divided the back from the front shop. As she drew closer she identified the aroma of her mother's inner circle: apples, cinnamon, and yeast. She even believed she could detect the rather sour smell of the cough drops Malkeh kept in her mouth all fall and winter. What did they talk about? she wondered. Why had they excluded her for so long? Was her mother leaving her out on purpose so that she might speak about womanly things to Kala's sisters? She thrust the curtains aside. "I'd like to bake," she requested. "I'd like to try my hand at whipping up some cakes."

"Come in and bake then," invited Malkeh, barely pausing in her conversation and continuing to chop apples in her wooden bowl. "The reason that the Russians think we're spies," she said, "is the same reason the Germans think of us as brothers. It has to do with the similarity between the Yiddish and the German languages. When Germans speak we can understand what they say . . ."

A bit shyly, Kala tied on an apron, nudged Sophie to make room at the table, and dumped eight cups of flour into a large container.

"But it can't be anything other than a joke," protested Ruth, "it must be a joke that the Russian government believes those impoverished Jewish villagers own secret telephones on which they give information to the enemy?"

"Each villager with his own telephone," Sophie took up, gaily bending from her waist, rolling out thin sheets of strudel dough with her powerful arms and shoulders. "Just imagine the *shoychet* of one of those little villages tiptoeing to the outhouse where he dials the German high command. "Hello, General?" he says in Yiddish. "The General answers, "Hello, Itzchele"—Sophie raised up her rolling pin—"where are the forty-third Hussars tonight?"

No one laughed. Kala made a slight attempt. Ruth, who was filling empty trays with macaroons and oatmeal cookies, poked her finger into a puffy macaroon, musing dejectedly. "So there they are on the train . . . with no houses to go to, no work, no prospects."

"It's the fault of the Tsar," Kala summed up, gladdened

by the communal exchange and more than happy to join in. "After all, it's the Tsar who started the war when he couldn't feed or clothe his subjects. And it's the Tsar who—now that the army is losing—has made scapegoats out of the Jews. Now if we could only replace the Tsar . . ."

"You're wasting flour," Sophie remarked.

"If we got rid of the Tsar and everyone worked together . . ."

"You're still wasting flour," Sophie warned. "And more than that, you're wasting baking soda."

"You . . . you're crowding me out." Kala jabbed her sister with an elbow.

"Kala, why are you here today?" her mother asked. "Wasn't Shmuel, the Holy One, supposed to bring you his wristwatch this morning? Hurry, girls." She rushed out to the front. "The shelves are still empty . . . if you like, I'll come help you. Sophie, Hershel is here for deliveries."

Left to herself, Kala happily measured sugar, beat eggs, kneaded with enjoyment, pounded with force, and patted her dough into pans. How much better this was, she thought, than tinkering with the hard, unyielding surfaces of clocks and watches. She slid the pans into the oven, stood still for a moment, and then paced back and forth in front of the oven to encourage her cakes to take proper shape. While she waited, she scrubbed the pastry boards, the mixing spoons, and Malkeh's wooden bowl. At last she took a deep breath and carefully removed the pans from the oven. Full and golden, her cakes kept rising even while she held them in her hands. But when she set them down, their centers fell, their sides collapsed, and they shriveled, each one to the size of an egg.

Sophie swung in at that moment, pausing on her crutches before Kala. She drew her fine black brows together. "Kala," she began, ignoring the row of fallen cakes, "if the Tsar is to blame—if that's what you honestly think—what can you do about it?"

"What do you mean?"

"What can you do about it? Can you join a group that wishes to overthrow the Tsar?"

Kala faced her sister, surprised. "That's very well for you to say, Sophie. You're not bothered by the Tsar. You can ask such questions because you're not involved. But for me," she twisted her mouth to one corner, "I'd have to believe in revolution from every single angle. From every single angle." She felt the impulse to tell her sister about Mikhail Kossoff and his bomb, an impulse that she kept in check. "And how will I ever know what I truly believe?"

"It'll come to you," Sophie assured her, swinging out of the room, almost crashing into Ekaterina, who arrived in a rush, mixed together a quantity of cookie dough, dropped the dough from a tablespoon onto a large baking sheet, and began to arrange nut meats in the center of each raw cookie. Silent at first, Ekaterina soon started to talk, addressing the spaces around her—empty or filled. "I'd like to be a philosopher," she said, "or an actress. I'd like to live someplace where I'm surrounded by people who think and write and compose music or paint important pictures. But not in St. Petersburg. There it matters if you're a Jew. Everyone would want to know how I got to be there, what right I had to be there, why I was given a permit, and so on. No, I'd rather live in Paris or London, where none of that counts. I'd go regularly to the Bibliothèque Nationale and the British Museum and the place where I lived would be filled with books and people of talent . . . true culture . . . people of learning." Suddenly she stopped, having noticed Kala's cakes. She gasped and sent her sister an accusing glance. "What are those, Kala?"

With a sigh Kala answered simply, "I made them."

CHAPTER SEVEN

T EN DAYS HAD GONE BY AND STILL MIKHAIL KOSSOFF FAILED
to return. Untouched, the broken timer remained
locked in the cupboard. Kala wished she had simply refused
to accept it. If instead of the handsome stranger, she accused
herself, Schlaymie Zuckerman, with his short neck and hard
little black eyes, had come to her shop offering a broken
bomb rather than merely his pamphlets, she knew she would
have chased him away.

Two, and then three more days went by. Perversely, her
desire for a glimpse of the young man increased. She began to
fear that some terrible disaster had befallen him. She imagined him surrounded by police, manacled, and taken off to
jail. By the end of the second week, she marched up the lane
to ask for news from Schlaymie's father, the *shoychet*.

The frizzy-haired *shoychet* disclaimed any "Kossoff from
Vilna."

"We never heard of a Kossoff from Vilna," echoed his wife.

"Mrs. Zuckerman," Kala pleaded, "remember how you used to tell us about your grand cousins in Vilna? Remember how you described the hundred poplar trees that led to their estate? Remember that you said their name was Kossoff?"

The *shoychet* and his wife glanced at each other, then marched Kala into the slaughtering shed. There, next to the bloodstained block, they begged her in harsh whispers to remain silent about the young man's visit. "We've had enough trouble with our own son, God rest his soul." Mrs. Zuckerman wailed, while Mr. Zuckerman poked a finger at Kala. "You've seen the trains coming through, young lady. The government thinks we're all spies and revolutionaries. Wait and see, they'll find an excuse to evacuate the Jews of Lyesk."

"But he's a relative . . ."

"We have no relatives," Mrs. Zuckerman declared.

"We don't even have a son. In our eyes Schlaymie no longer exists. Ever since he left the *yeshivah*, every single day we say the prayer of mourning for his soul."

Kala regarded the Zuckermans with horror. "But Schlaymie has done no evil," she tried to explain. "He thinks he's working to help mankind."

At this Mrs. Zuckerman raised her thin hand to Kala's lips. "Shhh, shhh, shah."

Mr. Zuckerman summed up, "Mankind doesn't need Schlaymie."

Kala walked back to the repair shop. Unhappy with the Zuckermans for abandoning their son, her mind produced a softened image of Schlaymie—his little black eyes kinder than before, his short neck slightly longer. But it was Schlaymie's cousin who occupied the greater part of her thought. She envisioned him alone, without friends, stumbling, cold, hungry, and denied by his own relatives. Wanting to make contact with him, she reached into the cupboard and gently removed his knapsack, recalling how it had hung carelessly from his shoulder. She was about to return the knapsack to the cupboard when her curiosity took over and, locking the door to the shop, she spilled its contents out onto the counter: the one-handed clock mounted in its small rough wooden stand, the batteries, the metal cannister, the cookie tin, and a hand-printed instruction sheet. She pored over the instructions and set about trying to repair the clock. Step by step she stripped the mechanism, removing the dial, letting down the main-spring slowly, taking off the top plate and dismantling the wheel assemblies. Soon she discovered the problem: the balance wheel of the escapement had been bent out of line, moving the lever so that the pallets had jammed the escape wheel. Carefully she realigned the balance wheel, adjusted and remounted the pallet lever and the escape wheel, and proceeded to reassemble the movement. When the clock sprang to life, she grinned, pleased with herself, for each time she managed, from the jumble of pieces strewn over her green felt counter, a correct arrangement of metal parts, each time she created the proper order, allowing a machine to measure the passage of time, the skills her grandfather had taught her seemed honorable and worthwhile.

With a new proprietary interest, she now lifted the cannis-ter and examined it, thinking that if the cylinder were filled with explosive powder and the proper detonator cap attached, it would become a powerful instrument. She gave a shudder of fascination. What had Mikhail Kossoff planned to do with the bomb? Visions of a great blast drifted idly through her mind: a racking explosion within the Lyesk police station, in the bell tower, on the steps of the Potocki mansion, in the stove of the House of Study. But was it possible for a bomb to advance good causes? Could a bomb help people fight for justice? She knew that Mikhail Kossoff and Schlaymie Zuck-erman were not alone—that they belonged to a party of men and women who believed they could overthrow the Tsar and end the injustice and suffering of the people around them. Wasn't that what she too wanted—to remove a government that paid thugs to injure Jews and helped landowners starve their peasants? Yet it seemed to Kala that the Tsar and his government were much too distant and grand to be over-thrown.

Ready to test her repair, Kala set the mechanism's alarm for fifteen minutes. She meant to work on Dunya the dress-maker's locket watch while she waited, but instead, as the timer ticked away, she found herself compelled by the move-ment of the mainspring, the balance wheel, and the pallet lever of the clock within the tin box. She reflected it was by such movements that time passed, war was declared, armies moved forward and back, and ordinary people were affected. This, she decided, was what Schlaymie Zuckerman and his pamphlets called "history": just a mainspring uncoiling. She went on to recall the dazed eyes of the wounded soldiers on the trains and the fear in the posture of the refugees lined up before the cisterns of water at the station, and she wondered how many people would be harmed before justice was achieved. Would a new government bring improvement? Did a social system make life unfair, she asked herself, or did life by itself make life unfair? She mused that even Ruth's God either could not or else did not choose to place His finger upon the machine of time to stop the suffering dealt to His creatures. Whirrr, click! Fifteen minutes had passed. The trigger mechanism tripped, making contact with the battery-operated electrical system. The clock-timer had been re-paired. But where, she wondered, was Schlaymie's auburn-haired cousin?

Two mornings later she discovered a note on the floor of her shop. In a large, childish scrawl, the author asked that Kala bring his knapsack to the birch forest after eleven o'clock that night. Kala, realizing she had decided in advance she would go, studied the short note, disappointed by the crudeness and innocence of the uphill script. To fortify her-self she opened one of Schlaymie Zuckerman's pamphlets. She shook her head at every second statement, reading again that the Tsar had created the war, that history was on the side of revolution, and that those who fought for the people would eventually live in peace and brotherhood with their fellow men.

The rest of the day passed slowly. An extreme loneliness

overtook her and she kept reliving the afternoon ten years earlier when Sophie had tripped and fallen in front of an artillery unit galloping through town. She and Sophie, small girls of five and six, had been playing outdoors, tossing a piece of smooth white stone in the dirt when the wagons had loomed up. She had screamed as Sophie fell, her cry willing the caisson wheels to turn in another direction. But the horses' hoofs had beat ahead and the wheel rolled on to crush her sister's legs. As the memory repeated itself, a low moan escaped from Kala, and she asked herself, as she had earlier: did a social system make life unfair or did life make life unfair by itself?

Just before bedtime she sought out Emmanuelle, Sir Leslie, and Mishka, Sophie's pony. They, she knew, were prepared for any sort of confidence from her, for with her family tiring of her dinner talk about the evils of the Tsar, she had taken her musings to the animals instead. This evening, however, the animals turned their heads away. Giving up, she entered the house through the kitchen, went into the sleeping porch, exchanged a few words with Sophie, lay down and then suddenly sat up, at a loss to figure out what had made her decide to bring Mikhail Kossoff his clock-timer. Woefully she stared at Sophie in the next bed, telling herself she and her sister ought to lead their separate lives. Otherwise, how much easier it would be, how much less lonely, if she could simply have said, "Sophie, I met a true revolutionary the other day. And guess what?—he's Schlaymie Zuckerman's cousin."

Kala heard the wind blow from the north and felt the house shudder. She listened to her sister begin to breathe evenly. Once the winter rains began, she reflected, she and Sophie would have to take their belongings from the airy sleeping porch and move inside to the smaller room behind the chimney. At this prospect—and at the notion that Mikhail Kossoff was even now hiding in the forest waiting for her— her loneliness grew more acute and with it came the unsettling touch of fear. She slipped out of bed and leaned over her sister, shivering—though not from the cold. "Sophie," she whispered. There was no response. "Sophie," she sang out, wanting to embrace her sister and, for a moment, imagining Sophie was dead. "Sophie!" But the wind shook the house and Sophie remained huddled, asleep beneath layers of blankets.

Kala put on her clothes. She went out the back door, stole around the house and into her shop, where she placed the clock-timer and case in a gunny sack, protecting it with straw and old rags. It comforted her that at least she was heading for the familiar birch wood. Setting forth, she mimicked the posture of her sister Ruth—her back straight, her neck arched, her head held high—as if, like Ruth, she were accepting her destiny, her fate. Stealthily she slipped through the railing of the back fence and left the shelter of the barn. The north wind caught at her skirt, billowing it out. Overhead, towering clouds moved swiftly through the sky, obscuring the dim moon, which displayed a vast ring of light about it. She could see that the rains would come this week, and she groaned at the thought of the mud that would overwhelm Lyesk.

Once she had descended the hillside, she stepped off the path into the high weeds and peered behind her to make sure no one had followed. The wind blew. It let up and blew again and the grasses made a strange rustling sound around her. As she approached the birch wood she began to hear the river and the deeper sound of the wind through the bare heights of the full-grown trees.

At the edge of the wood Kala paused. She called out his name once. "Mikhail!"

She waited. When she got no response she entered the wood and followed the path, which twisted as it approached the river bank. In the center of the forest she stepped off the trail, fearing she had called out too soon. Surely the noise of the wind had carried her voice away. "Mikhail!" she tried again, hesitantly, because the young man's note had directed that she call only once. Above her head the slender boughs of the treetops swayed turbulently.

Pulling her jacket about her, she sat down on a fallen tree. Resentfully she thought of Sophie, comfortable under her covers. Then from the direction of the river came the sound of someone clambering up the bank and moving clumsily through the woods—of some creature breaking boughs and colliding with trees. Kala slipped off her seat. She placed the sack in a hollow beneath the tree and crouched, waiting. Soon a figure loomed up on the path and went past. Silently Kala followed until she came to the edge of the wood, where a glimmer of moonlight revealed Mikhail Kossoff. She came up beside him and murmured his name.

With a cry of fear, Mikhail wheeled around as if to defend himself, then threw his arms about Kala and hugged her with relief. Stammering an apology, he released her. "Thank God it's you. How wonderful that you've come! What a time I've had this last week. I thought you were the police. Did you bring my package?"

Kala gazed up toward the town, where a few late lights still glimmered. Her heart pounded from his embrace. "It's best not to talk too loudly." She took his hand and drew him into the wood. By the fallen tree she knelt and lifted the sack from the hollow.

"Does it work? Are you certain it works? How clever you are!" Enthusiastically he pressed several notes into her hand.

"No, no," Kala waved the money away. "I want to contribute something . . . to you and to Schlaymie Zuckerman because . . ."

He appeared somewhat startled. "But you don't even know who we are."

"I know enough. What I want to know now is—what will you do with the bomb?"

"To tell the truth, I'm not certain," he replied without a pause. "The whole operation has gone wrong from the beginning. I've been wandering up and down the river, sleeping in caves and hollows. My comrades were picked up by the police, so now I'm on my own—without even a place to hide." At this, having summed up his situation, he slumped down, folding up against the fallen tree.

Kala looked down at him with dismay. It seemed extraordinary to her that someone with such fine manners and so cultivated an accent would admit his problems openly to a stranger—with hardly an introduction.

"I might have remained with the Zuckermans. But my poor cousins! They almost died of fright when they realized I was involved with their son. There was no way to stay with them once I realized the situation. Schlaymie hadn't bothered to let me know they'd been mourning for him."

"That's very sad for Schlaymie," she said, feeling worse for Mikhail.

"For Schlaymie? Oh, he doesn't care. He's got too many other things on his mind."

"I went to ask the Zuckermans about you. I was worried something might have happened."

"Thank you. I thank you for that."

She nodded. She was glad he had raised his head when he thanked her. Earlier today, when she'd imagined this meeting, she had never thought of him as slumped down against a tree. She had somehow conceived that his ideals and the easy grace with which he moved would carry him aloft. Perhaps they still would, she thought. "I know a safe place where we could go," she said, trying to make out the exact color of his eyes. "It isn't far from here." For a reason she could not fathom, she lowered her voice, hoping it would emerge sounding older, more experienced. "I could take you there."

He shook his head. "I ought not to involve you any more."

"It's a tree house my brother Iosif built. It's hidden away and private. You could rest comfortably and think out what your next move ought to be. Just come with me," she said.

He followed her and they crossed the railroad bridge. They had proceeded some hundred yards along the bank when he stopped, took her arm, and guided her several steps off the trail. Reaching into the hollow of a tree stump, he retrieved a package. "These are the powder and caps. I hid them here soon after I left the knapsack with you."

Kala, reminded of the young man's purpose, did her best to ignore his words. Uncomfortably, she continued toward the Chodorov orchard and climbed over the hill to the cottage. Here she gathered a lantern, a package of tea, some crackers, and a bundle of twigs. If only, she thought, she had met Mikhail under different circumstances, she would have enjoyed their acquaintance a good deal more. She could have introduced him to her family. Yet even now she pictured Naftali, Malkeh, her sisters, and also Iosif, standing in the orchard just behind the next tree, admiring Mikhail and exclaiming, "How exceptionally handsome he is! Look, it's Kala he's chosen, and not simply because she's the second eldest. What an excellent Russian he speaks and what a splendid bomb they're carrying!" Kala made a rueful face and her spirits sank.

Then, to assure herself the young man still paced by her side, she glanced at him and without a moment's hesitation he returned her glance, happily.

Quitting the orchard, they scrambled down one side and up the other of a steep ravine, after which they entered a thick woods full of underbrush. Within a few minutes Kala singled out the great old tree she sought. After locating a crude ladder, the sturdy rungs of which were bound with baling wire, she and Mikhail climbed the ladder through the boughs of the tree and pulled themselves through the trap-door of a tree house. They set about putting up the stovepipe and lighting a fire. Outside the wind blew. The tree swayed slightly and the walls shuddered. Up through the floorboards came a steady draft; but in a few minutes they felt quite warm, sitting cross-legged in front of the small, crudely fashioned stove.

Presently Mikhail unpacked the bomb, the detonator caps, and the explosives. He began to study a slip of hand-printed instructions by the light of the fire. Shrugging, he set the

[78]

clock for an hour. As it started to tick he grimaced and scratched his head. "To be honest, I'm rather confused. Apparently," he pointed to the mechanism ticking away between them, "I can do anything I want to do with it—so long as it helps our effort." He laughed, not too gaily. "Who would you blow up with it?"

The question puzzled her. After a minute she suggested, "The Tsar?"

"I suppose—the Tsar. He's as good as anyone else." He sighed and shook his head. "There were four of us—we got the order from Schlaymie. We were sent to attach our time bombs to a command train. The train's due to pass through Lyesk this morning. This very morning!" he said in an anguished tone. "But now that I'm by myself I'm not sure if the Party wants me to go ahead."

"The others were picked up?"

"Two were caught boarding the train in Minsk and the third disappeared. For all I know, the authorities are simply waiting for me. The others had experience. I wasn't even told the details." He began to get up as if to pace but, realizing the enclosure was too small, he sat back again and stared at the fire. "On top of that," his voice grew faint, "I'm not very brave."

"Yes you are," she contradicted. "Otherwise you wouldn't be here."

For a brief moment he looked hopeful. Then he shook his head again. "There were to be three bombs, and here I am with no help and a defective timer."

"A defective timer! There's nothing wrong with the timer —I fixed it. What's wrong is that you want to explode a bomb. There's something wrong with you! How can you be sure that innocent people won't be hurt—children? Good people?"

"But innocent people are being hurt every day."

"Not by us."

"If we just stand by watching, we're guilty too. And if we blow up the train and stop the war, we'll save who knows

[79]

how many lives. With a German victory, the Tsar will fall."

She eyed him dubiously. "Just by blowing up one train?"

"This is only one of many operations. There are hundreds of other undertakings to happen simultaneously." He forced a smile. "Personally, I'm about as ignorant of tactics as I am of mechanics. I leave all that to people smarter than I am. Not everyone is born with a brilliant mind, you know."

She looked at him quickly to try to figure out which one of them he meant: himself or her.

"Well, not everyone is," he insisted. "That's why we have to depend upon collective wisdom. And that's why I joined the Socialist Revolutionaries. I chose the best party, the party that wants to give back the land to the people who work it, the party closest to the peasants. Schlaymie had joined it earlier, and it was the right thing to do except . . ." he pointed to the bomb, ". . . except there's a problem. I haven't been able to bring myself to hurt anyone."

"I understand," said Kala.

"But it's no good. I'm a member of the Party. I have my responsibilities."

She looked at his unkempt and unshaven but nevertheless comely person. She had the sense she could follow him and his worthy goals to the ends of the earth. Sitting close to him, she could smell the sweat of his body. He had evidently not bathed for many days. A tenderness crept through her so that she wanted to kiss the pale flesh on the back of his neck and to console him by gathering him into her arms as if he were a child. But the fact was, she thought, he might not want her to.

As if in response, Mikhail shut his eyes and buried his head in Kala's hair. His lips touched her ear and then her neck. Excited by his touch and perplexed by her contradictory emotions, she drew back but not very far. "What we've got to think about is—do you have to explode the bomb? Can't you decide not to?"

He took her hand. "If individuals," he said, "made those decisions on their own, there would simply be no party."

"Still . . ."

"And to tell the truth, I want to act—it's on my conscience. I've got to do something to make things better." He began to assemble the bomb.

"Oh, if there were a way to make things better without hurting anyone, I too would like that. If there were a way . . ." She paused. "What if we blew up the train tracks?" she offered, feeling foolish to suggest anything. "No one would be harmed."

"No, that wouldn't work. The tracks could easily be repaired."

She gave him an ironic half smile. "What a peculiar problem—choosing what's best to blow up." Her smile held for a moment. Staring at the fire, she recalled that when they crossed the river before, the railroad bridge had swayed, its heavy timbers moaning. The thought passed through her mind that if they blew up only the bridge, Mikhail would not be hurt. She hesitated. "What if we blow up the railroad bridge—the one we crossed. Then the command train would not be able to get through. It would tie up the whole line. With the rain, the bridge might not be rebuilt until the very end of winter. We would hurt no one and we would at least harm the war effort."

The young man fixed his eyes on her with admiration. "What a good idea! What an excellent idea! How extraordinary you are." He looked away. "It's the most effective use I could make of a single bomb."

Kala reached for the cannister. "But we'll have to hurry," she warned, "or else I'll change my mind. Besides, it's almost time for Reb Keppel to knock on the shutters and wake the men for morning prayers." She helped Mikhail pour the explosive into the metal container. Her hands trembled. They doused the flames of the stove and descended to the ground.

They reached the bridge in that still moment just before dawn. A soft light from the eastern skies reflected off the surface of the moving water. Without hesitating, Kala slipped over the side of the bridge and crawled along the

[81]

supports until she found herself on the main timber underneath the rails. She called up to Mikhail, who set the timer
and handed the time bomb to her through the ties. She
bound the bomb in place. Below, the water swirled around
the base of the bridge and sent a hollow echoing sound into
the air. She felt frightened, as if she might never escape the
shadows of the bridge.

The young man was waiting when she crawled back up on
the ties. With joy and relief they embraced. Their lips met at
first gleefully, but then, tasting each other's flesh, with hunger. When they parted he moved to one bank of the river and
she to the other. They waved and fled in opposite directions.

CHAPTER EIGHT

THE EXPLOSION ROCKED ALL THE BUILDINGS. IT CAME AT dawn, entering the dreams of the people of Lyesk. There had been scarcely any flame and a dark, foggy dawn had obscured the smoke. When a railway watchman discovered the site of the explosion, townspeople gathered just beyond the birch woods to marvel. While they stood there, mouths agape, the first drops of winter rain fell upon their heads. No one moved. Then the cold rain increased in force and the citizens of Lyesk began to stamp their feet and to clap themselves to keep warm. Over the years they had heard news of estates burning to the east, of the massacre of Jews to the north and south, of executions, riots, and strikes. But until the coming of the war their small region had remained untouched by violence. Now, on October 14, 1914, they witnessed the fact that the railroad bridge just north of the depot had blown up in an eruption so forceful that not one of the supports of the bridge was left standing. On either side

[83]

of the river lay charred debris. The center of the bridge, none too steady even with the recent reinforcement, had totally disintegrated. Splintered lumber, wedged this way and that, left a track downstream along the banks. A pile of wood had come aground on the small island before the bend, clogging the river so that it sent up a spume of water.

Kala finished her morning chores. Wearing an old leather cap of her father's and a peasant jacket of sheepskin, she waded through the back fields to the birch wood, then out on the river bank. A few townspeople lingered near the site, watching while the police and the soldiers dug through the wreckage. She found it difficult to believe that the railroad bridge, such an important landmark in Lyesk, no longer stood on its site—that the tin box which she had attached to the support under the track had so totally removed it. She tried to tell herself that the destruction would help save the lives of many people, but looking at the empty space on the river, she regretted the act—unable even to reconstruct the steps by which she had become an accomplice.

"It's a German artillery shell," she heard a handful of citizens conjecture as they turned away from the site.

"It was an old bridge."

"It's a time of sorrow for Lyesk."

"Maybe not."

"Can the Germans be that close?"

"If they are, we're in for it. Someone ought to look for shell casings in the river bed."

Kala trailed the group, trying to convince herself that the old bridge would have fallen down anyway. She wondered how people would react if they knew of her part in the explosion. She considered jumping into their midst to confess she was the criminal. Even more strongly she felt the impulse simply to run far away and hide.

She did neither. Instead she went to the repair shop and was still debating what to do when Reb Keppel, the *shammes* of the synagogue, stole in so quietly that Kala feared he had found her out. Dangling his pocket watch on its gold chain,

Reb Keppel inclined his solemn narrow face, all the while regarding her with a look of the most grave concern. "I've noticed something wrong," he began.

"Something wrong? What could be wrong?" Her terror gave way to relief. She wanted to be freed of her secret! "Yes, yes, there's something wrong."

The *shammes* nodded at her knowingly. "The explosion," he murmured, "has affected my timepiece."

Startled—thrown off her path—Kala inquired with annoyance, "What's wrong with the watch?"

"It runs both fast and slow now—sometimes one, sometimes the other."

"That isn't possible."

"It runs both fast and slow and its accuracy is essential to my duties."

"Well give it to me, I'll see what I can do."

"But do it carefully. It has a very delicate mechanism." Reluctantly Reb Keppel lowered the watch to the worktable without releasing its chain. "No need to pry anything," he warned, waving his fingers against any brutal move. Then with his hand still clutching the gold chain, he leaned toward Kala far over the counter. "Our little explosion," his mournful voice intoned, "has been blamed on the Jews."

"On the Jews! Which Jews?" Kala's hand flipped up and slammed down while inserting a pair of slim-nosed pliers into the watchworks.

"On the Jews in general. Kala, what are you doing—no force, no force!" He pulled on the watch chain to halt the girl. "You can go on working, but work gently."

"But someone told me," Kala objected, "that the bridge was destroyed by a German shell."

Reb Keppel advanced her a look of great pity. "My poor child," he said. "Whoever heard of a shell that could fly two hundred miles? Unfortunately the Germans are too busy running away. At the very moment of our little explosion the Russian army was turning Hindenburg back from the gates of Warsaw. No, as bad luck will have it, we won't see German shells for some time now. No, if you ask me, it's not the Germans. It's . . . a mystery . . . a political mystery."

"So long as it isn't the Jews. Reb Keppel, I can't concentrate while you stand there. You'll have to trust me and go away and leave the watch and come back." She half escorted, half pushed him to the door, closed the door after him, and then leaned against it, afraid he would return, and thinking there was something wrong with Reb Keppel—that he moved about too quietly and stealthily. Even his wake-up knock on the shutters of the faithful, she reflected, was much too insidious, much too light. If, as he claimed, the Jews had been blamed for the explosion, how could she confess without its having repercussions on other Jews? She wished the *shammes* would not always insist on suggesting more than he knew.

The door opened and Sophie entered, the mud thick on her boots and crutches. Placing an oatmeal cookie on Kala's shoulder, she announced, "I'm taking fifteen minutes off." She settled herself in the desk chair in the corner and removed from the pocket of her starched apron a length of embroidery thread and a hoop of cloth. "No one is talking about anything else but the railroad bridge. Naomi and Leah are in heaven. Ivan Sergeyevich says the traffic is backed up for miles on both sides of the river and that passengers and freight have begun to be transported by wagon over the high-road bridge. It's very slow though and the mud makes it worse. Everyone's got his own idea of who did it. Naomi thinks it was a revolutionary."

For a few minutes nothing could be heard except for the tinkle of Kala's tools. Then Kala lifted her head. "Sophie?"

"Yes?"

"What would you say if I told you I know who blew up the bridge?"

"Don't tell me, let me guess."

"You'll never guess."

"Then who?"

"Me."

"Kala Chodorov . . . you? You blew up the bridge?"

Kala enjoyed a brief surge of satisfaction.

"You yourself? You blew it up?" Sophie's bright cheeks glowed. "You did it, I know, because you thought it was right, but Kala," her voice dropped very low, "why ever did you?"

"I don't know," Kala replied, ashamed that the destruction of the bridge had not proceeded purely out of her belief—ashamed that it had somehow just happened—that it had been bound up with her attraction to Schlaymie Zuckerman's handsome cousin. "Don't ask me any more."

"Well, fine then, if you don't want me to ask you . . ."

"No, no, I want you to. I want to tell you. It was . . ." She took a deep breath, freed her hands of the repair tools, and spread her fingers on the counter, "It was . . ." She hesitated again.

"You don't have to tell me," Sophie said. "And to be honest," she knitted her fine dark brows together, "it might not make sense to me. And perhaps it ought not. So let's put an end to talking about it, for both our sakes."

"For both our sakes," miserable, Kala acquiesced.

She vowed to put the explosion out of her mind. She was helped by the fact that Ruth's fate was being decided at this time, for ten days after the explosion Naftali had traveled to Karlin, Mordecai's home, by wagon. Here he stood in a synagogue with the father of Mordecai Berg, the two men grasping opposite ends of a very white handkerchief while a rabbi read to them the terms of the marriage contract between Mordecai and Ruth. When the contract had been read, the fathers exchanged gifts, toasted their children and themselves with schnapps, and shook hands. Naftali returned from Karlin and Ruth selected a Tuesday in early November for the marriage ceremony, requesting a Tuesday because, as she pointed out, the Bible said that when God created the world, on the third day He spoke the words, "It is well!" not once but twice.

Without so much as an instant's delay, Malkeh ordered the

invitations, reserved the synagogue, arranged for the feast, hired the band, and retained Dunya to sew gowns for Ruth, herself, and the girls—as if there were no war. Kala and Sophie pursued their mother desperately. "You mustn't let it happen," they demanded. "Tear up the invitations, cancel the synagogue, dismiss the band . . ."

"Stop!" Malkeh said. "Both of you stop!"

"But it can't be allowed to happen. Marriage is for the rest of Ruth's life." The two girls surrounded their mother, wringing their hands and pleading, "Mama, it's Ruth. Ruth deserves somebody wonderful."

"Go away," Malkeh told them. Then unexpectedly her lips turned up in a wry yet gracious smile. "Mordecai is almost wonderful."

"Almost? Then you agree. He isn't."

Coming into the room, Ekaterina regarded her sisters haughtily. "If Ruth wants to marry Mordecai, what business is it of yours?"

"She's our sister. She has so many talents. Such beautiful handwriting," Kala said.

"Such beautiful handwriting. Such an ability with sums," Sophie went on. Then Sophie inquired point blank, "Ekaterina, would you marry Mordecai?"

"Oh . . . me." Ekaterina pushed her blonde locks further into her face.

"Oh you, Ekaterina," Kala and Sophie jeered. "No—you would only marry the Kaiser's son or the Prince of Wales."

"What a foolish discussion," Malkeh said.

"But Mama, why are you in such a hurry? Why not put it off? They hardly know each other. We hardly know him ourselves."

The two girls had each latched onto one of their mother's arms. "Unfortunately, Ruth has already been engaged," Malkeh reminded them, disentangling their fingers, pushing them away. "And there's nothing wrong with Mordecai. He'll make a good husband. Just wait and see. The marriage should happen as soon as possible. Everything is so unsettled—there are still so many rumors about the bridge."

Reminded of her folly, Kala's anxieties mounted. And indeed, as it turned out, the rumors concerning the bridge did not take their final shape until the Wednesday just preceding Ruth's wedding. On that Wednesday afternoon Kala was painting the cart and wagon, preparing them to be used as extra vehicles for guests in the wedding procession, when she sensed something awry. Slipping into the back door of the bakery, she found the store full of customers, with Sophie and Radish in attendance. Everything appeared normal except that Malkeh occupied a chair at the last table, her arms folded into one another. Beside her, delivering an earnest harangue, perched Father Boris, the Russian Orthodox priest —a man loved by the peasants of Lyesk as much for his orchard as for his piety. The priest grew more than twenty varieties of pears alone, branches of which he would graft onto any tree in the neighborhood at the slightest show of interest. Although he was said to be over seventy, he had remained supple and strong. Quick brown eyes peered sympathetically out of a rugged, lined and wind-burned face framed by white hair. Today, as always, he talked in spurts, the expression on his face turning from solemnity to joy. As Kala approached from behind, he leaped up out of his chair in enthusiasm, shouting to Malkeh, "There you have it! You can deal with the Colonel! You're the one to do it!"

When Malkeh shook her head back and forth skeptically, the priest subsided, his mouth drooping, his eyes sad.

"He as much as told me he was willing to listen to an offer. There you have it!"

"Mama?" said Kala.

Malkeh's spine stiffened, her arms fell to her side. "Ah Kala, Father Boris has been kind enough to warn us that the Russian government has formally blamed the destruction of the bridge on German spies—namely Jews. We are the scapegoats . . . it's not unusual. Father Boris thinks we may very

[89]

well be evacuated and relocated. The district colonel arrives in town today."

Kala clutched the back of her mother's chair to keep her balance. The beamed ceilings bowed down and the curtained windows buckled as the full horror of her act sank in: along with the bridge, she had destroyed her family's future. Through her mind traveled an image of the Jewish refugees lined up before the cistern of water in the railroad station. She would have liked to set off that instant for the police station; unfortunately she realized a confession from her would implicate the Chodorovs and the other Lyesk Jews still further. The whitewashed walls were still shuddering when she opened her mouth. "It isn't the Germans . . . the Germans are retreating. If whoever did it . . ."

"It doesn't matter who, my dear," said Father Boris, patting her hand. "The government prefers its own explanations."

"To make things worse," continued Malkeh, "there's to be an inventory of all animals and rolling stock owned by Jews."

"That's not official," explained the priest. "It's evidently our own Police Captain Varsonevsky's idea. Colonel Sukharov doesn't like those documents, those silly forms any more than you do. He's afraid the whole district will be inundated with the Captain's paper. That's why you should see the Colonel, Malkeh. There you have it! For all I know, the whole evacuation idea may be the Captain's."

"Well, we'll go then," Malkeh said, getting up slowly, "you and I, Father Boris, we'll visit the Colonel at the hotel. After that I may have to make some calls in town. Kala, tell Sophie to close up when it's time. Tell Radish . . ."

As Malkeh gave her orders, the front door opened and a cold draft swept down the length of the warm, moist room. Three men entered: the dour captain of the town police, Semyon Varsonevsky; his police clerk, known only as "Wart," for the great wart which protruded from his chin; and the dimpled, red-faced Government Rabbi, Jacob Benjamin, the husband of Naomi, his blond curly locks falling over his

forehead from beneath his Russian-style fur hat. Wart carried
with him a large pad of legal paper, a pen and ink pot; the
rabbi had in hand his own small note pad and pencil, while
the long-faced captain swished a riding crop through the air.
When the three newcomers saw that Malkeh was leaving,
they immediately turned and followed after her. Kala too
went out the door. She headed for the barn to continue
painting the cart and wagon. In the middle of the yard she
stopped, hearing the Chodorov piano. Ruth, Kala remembered, was in the parlor with Dunya for the final fitting of
her wedding dress. Eight consecutive notes, struck one by
one, pealed mournfully out of the house. When Malkeh had
purchased the piano, she recalled, no one in the town had
been able to fathom why her mother, committed to all things
practical, had gone out of her way to buy so frivolous an
object. Visitors to the house had put on a show.

"Oh, you have a piano!" Mendel Feldshpan had exclaimed,
stepping up to it, poking once at the white keys, another time
at the black keys, and pushing at four keys with his fingers
pressed close together.

"Oh, you have a piano!" Avrom Lavin had wheezed. "Just
like the Russian colonel . . . better yet, just like Pan Potocki."

"Oh, you have a new cow!" Lazar Dovitsky, the stableman,
had joked, protecting his hands by clasping them behind his
back.

Of the sisters, all except Ruth had refused to take any
lessons. Ruth alone, in her kindness toward their mother,
had taken sixty piano lessons during which she learned three
pieces—one of which she now played with halting sorrow.
Very carefully Kala listened to the poorly executed, sad
music, hearing in it both Ruth's misery and the accusation
that she, Kala, had caused the exile of the Jews from Lyesk.

That night Malkeh attended a special meeting of the Jewish Council to discuss her interview with Colonel Sukharov
and Father Boris. Waiting for her return, her daughters sat
in the dining room, all the wedding dresses spread out on the
oak table ready for hems. Kala had always enjoyed sewing

with her sisters—just as she'd liked walking with them. Stitching serenely in their midst, the softness of some fabric in her hand, she had the sense they lent her a portion of their femininity and beauty while, in turn, she offered them the straightness and evenness of her hems. Tonight, however, the taffeta fabric of her wide-skirted pale green gown felt too heavy and burdensome for her hands, too dense for her needle. Anxiously, she drew her fingers along her cheeks and chin and kept on glancing at her sisters. At every sign of restlessness they displayed—each time Ruth or Sophie or Ekaterina paused or stared into a basket of thread and needles or got up and stood by the window, looking out at the darkness—Kala guessed they were confronting what it would be like to be sent away from their home in the night. That Mikhail Kossoff's bomb had produced such results continued to stun her. She judged the consequences out of all proportion to what she and the young man had done. Yet the truth was, she admitted, that they had committed a dishonorable act. She had no right to go on sewing, no right to her sisters.

"There isn't much to report just yet," said Malkeh when she returned. "After Tuesday we'll see what has to be done. Until then we'll look forward to Ruth's wedding."

On the Sabbath before the wedding, Mordecai and his family, who had arrived from Karlin the night before, attended synagogue with the Chodorovs—Naftali dragging Mordecai and his father forward and installing them in the best seats. A rumor had spread about town that there was a plan afoot to bribe the Colonel; yet the majority of Jews had already started to prepare for an evacuation. Some, hoping to evade the authorities, had dismantled their wagons to hide them in attics and bedrooms and had tethered their horses and cows out in the forest; others had drawn up plans to send the elderly and small children to relatives in nearby districts. Sitting with the women in the upper gallery of the synagogue, Kala gazed at the congregation and observed that for the first time in her memory its members remained in place during the entirety of the service. No one gossiped; no one stared at the Chodorovs' future in-laws; no one paraded in the hallway to show off a new coat or a new pair of shoes. Naomi Benjamin Pearl and Leah Kantorovits Feldshpan kept their eyes steadfastly on their children; and all the children, instead of wildly chasing one another around the building, stayed quietly by their parents' sides. At the end of the service the Chodorovs and the other members of the congregation nodded at each other to communicate that this might be their last Sabbath in Lyesk.

But on Tuesday the Chodorovs awoke, their mood transformed by the brilliant change in the countryside. A great frost had struck in the night and daybreak revealed delicate traceries of white spread out for miles. Never could Kala remember the sky so blue—a hard, clear, fathomless blue. Trees glinted as though they had been lit from inside, and the dazzling white disc of the rising sun seemed to cast no warmth; it could have been a full moon that rose in the middle of the sky.

Late in the morning Ruth went to the *mikveh* for her ritual bath. While her mother and her sisters watched, old Rivkah, the attendant, cut the nails of Ruth's fingers and toes, gathered the leavings into a pile, and burnt them with great care, mumbling prayers. She warned the giggling Sophie and Kala that if every nail were not burned, poor Ruth would have to wander about trying to find the remaining ones after her death. Three times the old lady pushed Ruth down into the pool, the water closing over the young woman's head. Every time she came up, Rivkah declared solemnly that Ruth was "a kosher daughter of Israel!" All the way home Sophie and Kala jested that now it would be all right to eat their sister's flesh. Their mother said she did not find them very funny.

In Lyesk there remained the hope that a reprieve from the evacuation would somehow come. With the exception of people buying last minute provisions for the road—should they have to go on the road—business on Merchant Lane

[93]

ground almost to a halt. No one wanted to prepare too much, or to lay in anything that could not be carried. As a result, most of the wagons and carriages frequenting the streets belonged to the wedding party as it traveled back and forth between the houses, with the hoofs of the horses and the wheels of the carriages making a fine crunching sound on the frozen mud. Gradually the whiteness disappeared from the fields and from the branches of the trees. The biting cold remained, as did the blue skies. Down by the river, the bare birch forest gleamed like a grove of icicles, motionless in the still air.

Toward the latter part of the afternoon, three carriages drew up to the Chodorov house and the groom's family disembarked—mother, father, two sisters, a brother, and assorted uncles, aunts, and cousins, all in their wedding finery. In their midst stood the diminutive Mordecai in his black and white formal attire, with a very high top hat perched uncertainly upon his head. Solemnly the Bergs paraded into the house, through the dining room, and into the parlor where Ruth, wearing her white satin bridal dress, sat in a chair piled high with cushions, surrounded by her sisters and by her mother and Naftali's two sisters, who had given up their solitary retirement and traveled all the way from Minsk. As Mordecai entered the parlor, he put his hands over his eyes so that he would not see the bride and bring their union bad luck. A veil of delicate lace was placed in his hand and he was guided by his mother, who made sure the veil dropped from his hand over the bride's head. Then Malkeh fixed the veil in place properly. Standing there, his hand still over his eyes, Mordecai mumbled the speech expected of him concerning the duties and responsibilities of the bride. He knew it all by heart, but somehow the injunctions embarrassed him as though he were ordering this superior woman to act in a way she already knew much better than he. When he had finished, he remained standing as if in search of something further to say. Then at last he spoke out clearly—having put together his thoughts: "And everything that the wife

[94]

must do for the husband, for the home and the children to come, the husband must do for the bride, the home, and children."

Kala and Sophie glanced at each other. With a certain unwillingness they shrugged, then nodded, to give Mordecai his due. Then the groom turned and the Bergs and the Chodorovs threw rice and grain over the heads of the wedding couple, murmuring wishes for many, many children. Mordecai and his family trooped back to their carriages and set off to the synagogue. Two large cabs pulled up in front of the Chodorovs' for the bride and her family. It was past five in the afternoon, and already darkness was falling. Ahead of them as they moved toward the synagogue, beyond the dark roofs of the town and the low dark fields, the western sky still burned orange and green and blue across the whole horizon. And to Kala it seemed she gazed into an icy fire that promised her nothing but loss and despair.

Ruth's wedding took place in the paved courtyard of the synagogue, which had been set with folding chairs and surrounded by oil lanterns on high tripods. A small stage had been erected in the very middle of the yard. On the stage stood the *chupah*, a gorgeous embroidered cloth mounted on four polished cedarwood poles. The first three rows all the way round were cordoned off by ribbons for the family and honored guests, who were ushered to their places by Hershel, wearing a new blue suit with a sprig of berry in his lapel, a red muffler around his neck, and the tip of his nose and his cheeks as rosy as his plastered-down red hair. He walked stiffly with one chilled hand ready to right the white silk holiday *yarmulkeh* that kept slipping from side to side on his head. As the Chodorovs' carriage drew up, Kala could see that almost all the guests had arrived and were standing at their seats, clapping their gloved hands together and stamping their feet against the cold. To avoid the chill breeze, the groom's immediate family stood clumped together on the stage, attempting to appear at their ease. Under the canopy the groom and Rabbi Hershfill, learned rabbi of the congregation, awaited the bride, while at the wrought-iron gateway to the courtyard, Reb Keppel paced back and forth, shoulders slightly hunched, his gold watch in his hand.

As Naftali briskly escorted Ruth toward the stage, Kala noticed a number of empty chairs in the reserved section. She realized that every one belonged to a gentile, and her heart sank. Ivan Sergeyevich, the Stationmaster, was missing—despite the fact that he had come to the bakery twice a week, Tuesdays and Thursdays, during the entirety of Ruth's life. Osip Blag, the hotel owner, had not shown up, nor had a few others among Malkeh's well-to-do Russian customers. Their conspicuous absence slightly dampened the festive mood in the courtyard, reminding the guests that the stigma cast by the explosion had reached as far as the Chodorov wedding. Kala, on the other hand, was happy to see Father Boris, the midwife Matryona, and Luka Fomich with all his numerous family, as well as Stepan Ilyich Rozumov, the bakery's Wednesday regular who, resplendent in his uniform of nobility, had brought his son and daughter.

As Rabbi Hershfill lifted the bridal veil to reveal to the groom the face of his bride, in case he should have any second thoughts, Kala remarked the look of sweet sadness that had settled over her sister's features. The joy that had burned in Ruth's eyes for Ephraim Savich had been replaced by resignation. Kala reflected that she too had entered a dark realm in which none of her dreams could ever be fulfilled. But where Ruth had done nothing to deserve her fate, she, Kala, had betrayed those she loved by destroying the railroad bridge. She would give up everything, she decided, she would accept any punishment. Still, she knew there was no way to make amends.

Now Rabbi Hershfill lowered the veil and announced the happy occasion which had brought them all together. He pronounced a short benediction and read the marriage contract aloud. When the contract had been signed by the bride and groom, Ruth's veil was raised and the rabbi began a speech to the couple which, because of the biting cold, he kept short. "Ruth and Mordecai, the 'house of faith' which you begin to build on this day does not reside in walls, possessions, or land. It will grow spiritually between you. Like this *chupah*, you will carry your 'house' with you wherever you go and you will find your true comfort and safety within this invisible trust."

"You see?" said a wedding guest aloud. "We'll have to carry our house with us."

The bride and groom exchanged rings, saying, "Behold thou art consecrated unto me by this ring, according to the law of Moses and Israel." Each sipped from a glass, pronouncing the blessing over the wine. Mordecai then took the glass, placed it within a linen napkin provided by the *shammes*, put it on the floor of the stage, lifted his foot high, and crushed the glass.

"*Mazeltov!*" came a great shout from the audience, and everyone rose to embrace, while the hired orchestra—two fiddles, a flute, a horn, a bass viol, and a drum—struck up a joyous melody and began to march off toward Merchant Lane. By now it was completely dark and the oil lanterns around the courtyard cast flickering shadows against the pavement and the synagogue walls. Reb Keppel cleared the aisles for the bridal parties, but once they had embarked in their carriages, a bedlam of confused shouts and cries, of music and singing, of carts clashing against one another, of harnesses rattling and horses neighing, filled the air. For a while it seemed as if no one would be able to escape the courtyard to make his way to the wedding feast at the Chodorovs'. Reb Keppel saved the day, however, taking out his watch and bringing order out of chaos, and soon all were gathered and the wedding feast began.

In the Chodorov house the furniture had been pushed to the walls and long tables had been set up. Because tables for the children had been placed in the bakery, the youngsters ran back and forth between the two buildings. Mordecai—expected to deliver a speech—simply offered a toast to the bride and her family, an act at first applauded by those spared the strain of such tedium but later commented upon with disapproval. Many more toasts and speeches followed, but no one minded or listened because the meal had begun.

After the first course Naftali stood and raised his glass toward the bride and groom. "A special toast from your brother Iosif in the New World. We have had a letter from Iosif. He too is now a father. He has a son named Caleb. A toast to Iosif, who misses us and misses all of Lyesk. Hooray for Iosif and for Caleb too—what a pity they aren't here!" Swallowing his full glass in one gulp, Naftali walked to the center of the room, signaled the band to begin the music, and invited the beggar Patch and Matryona and Rivkah, the bath attendant, to join him in the first dance. Within an instant the other guests followed suit, men rising to dance with men, women with women, and now and then men and women dancing together in modern style.

Just after the soup course, an authoritative knock was heard on the front door. A hush fell on the company. Kala ran to answer, hoping Ivan Sergeyevich had finally decided to join the celebration, for the Stationmaster's absence, she knew, had wounded her mother. When she threw the door open, there stood an unfamiliar lieutenant.

"Is this the home of Malkeh Chodorov?" he asked.

Kala nodded, speechless with foreboding.

"Colonel Sikharov requests permission to enter."

"Of course," said Malkeh who had followed her daughter to the door. "We would be honored."

Down from the carriage stepped a gentleman with a full gray beard, wearing a splendid dress uniform, with gold braid across his chest, many colored ribbons, gleaming medals and buttons, gold stripings down his trousers, and a fine sword. "My compliments, Madame Chodorov," said the Colonel.

Behind him, the Lieutenant took a large white box tied with an elaborate bow from the carriage and followed as the Colonel, with Malkeh on his arm, entered the house.

Silence greeted their appearance. The Colonel moved gracefully across to the table of honor where the newlyweds sat. Malkeh introduced the Colonel and he presented his gift. Malkeh then invited the Colonel and his aide to join them in supper. Graciously, the Colonel accepted. Malkeh placed him next to Ruth and the aide next to Mordecai. Before the Colonel sat down, he raised a glass to the couple.

"I wish you long life and happiness and I sincerely hope that you will always be able to remain here in Lyesk with your family and friends. I know that there has been a shadow over your celebration and I regret my part in the situation. Unfortunately, I am not responsible for certain policies, nor can I control the necessities of war. However, our hostess, Malkeh Chodorov, was kind enough to share her wisdom with me about this situation. She pointed out how essential this community has been to the support of this region and what a disaster your removal would be. I know there are times when it seems that Petrograd is far away, but you must never forget that the Tsar loves his subjects, all his subjects. I know that you will do everything in your power to aid in the war effort against the Germans, and for this reason I expect that you will still be here when victory is ours. Long life, happiness, and many children to the bride and groom."

The cheering lasted many minutes, and while the Colonel drank and ate, toasts were offered in his honor. At each table the guests speculated on how many roubles, how many bottles of brandy, how many sides of beef the Colonel's reprieve had cost the Jews of Lyesk, and on how the cost would be divided up between them when the reckoning came. The weakest cheer came from Kala—so dazed was her relief. Three times Rabbi Benjamin tried to approach the Colonel to make a speech by right of his office as government rabbi, but each time his wife Naomi pulled him away and sat him down far from the main table, scolding him for his absurd ambition.

CHAPTER NINE

DURING THE WINTER OF 1914–15 THE RUSSIAN ARMIES, sustaining terrible losses, advanced, retreated, and advanced against the Germans and the Austrians. Even Lyesk suffered. Luka Fomich's three oldest sons fell in the north, Osip Blag's brother-in-law died in the south, along with Ivan Sergeyevich Dovrynin's son-in-law and Stepan Ilyich Rozumov's two younger brothers. In the spring, when the Germans began to drive once more toward Warsaw and the Austrian and German offensive gathered force in the south alongside the Carpathian mountains, the Russian government instituted a scorched earth policy, ordering its armies to burn towns, villages, and fields, and evacuating the populace to deny the enemy all local supplies and manpower.

Soon after the Lyesk River thawed, a military work crew arrived to construct a makeshift railroad bridge. Trainloads of wounded continued to return from the distant front, and from time to time fresh army units on their way to battle settled down in the region for a period of several weeks or so to train and provision themselves. Troops were quartered in local houses. In the Chodorov house four or five soldiers at a time occupied the parlor. Because most of these men were peasants, the Chodorovs felt comfortable in their presence as well as appreciative of the soldiers' good humor, the meagerness of their demands, and the extra rations the army provided. Ungrudging and generous toward the men, Malkeh requested as her sole restriction that the soldiers not bang on the piano or sleep on its top. At the same time she made it very clear that she and Naftali would allow nothing in the way of forwardness between the soldiers and her daughters.

No sooner had the boarders unpacked their gear than Kala felt a great kinship with them. It pleased her to know that they woke in the morning, washed, dressed, shaved, left for their maneuvers and parades, and returned to her family every night as if they belonged to the Chodorov household. Often she imagined that these were Luka's missing sons who, miraculously restored, had come back to live in her house. The surge of new yet familiar voices, the increase in the number of footsteps, the gain in a sense of a camaraderie and life buoyed her up, saving her from her low spirits through the winter—from her anguish over the half-dozen deaths in the town and from missing or thinking about the vanished Mikhail Kossoff.

As the summer of 1915 approached, the battles to the north intensified. Train traffic increased, the turnover of local troops accelerated, and on the high road the trek of homeless refugees steadily thickened. One Thursday in June, Kala received a list of spare parts for clocks from a supplier in Minsk. Surprised, since normally she did not order from this company, she tore the envelope open and studied the list. She was about to slip the sheet into her spare parts folder when she noticed upon the back a poem scribbled in a tumbling, awkward, immature hand which she recognized as belonging to Mikhail Kossoff. She read the poem through, tugging with disapproval at her left eyebrow, for it began:

"Soil of Lyesk arise!/In the warmth of your sand/Grow wheat, barley, prunes, and justice." Why was he writing her? Who had ever heard of a prune growing? Was he joking, a terrible poet, or simply a fool? She read the poem once more. In the last stanza the author implied he would soon visit again the acid soil of Lyesk with its oats, wheat, and—in the place of prunes—this time he substituted "its beautiful brown-haired girl."

All day Kala's mood alternated between joy and depression. She took the poem to bed with her that night. As she lay under the sheet, she heard the soldiers quartered in the house—Nikita, Alyosha, and Ivan—come down the lane from the tavern, singing drunkenly. She listened sympathetically, knowing they were about to leave for the front.

"Sophie," Kala said, sorry she had kept Mikhail a secret from her sister, "are you sleeping?"

The singing grew louder as the soldiers entered the house. In the parlor one of them took to mooing like a cow.

"I'd like to be," Sophie sighed. "Tomorrow's *shabbas.*"

Kala crossed over to her sister's bed and sat down, lighting the lamp. "Sophie," she thrust Mikhail's poem into her sister's hand, "here's something I want you to read. Ignore the handwriting."

After a few moments Sophie asked, a bit suspiciously, "Who wrote this?" She finished the poem, turned the order sheet over, scanned the list of spare parts, and then read the poem again.

"A friend."

"A friend? What friend? It doesn't rhyme."

"Rhyme isn't the whole world. Listen Sophie, what do you and I know about poetry? Whenever we heard a poem in class we fell asleep."

Sophie handed back the poem, "I just hope he's nice." She reached out and turned down the lamp until it went out. "Now don't talk to me. I'm going to sleep."

"But don't you want to know any more?" pleaded Kala, still perched on her sister's bed.

"Not if you never told me about him before he wrote the poem."

"But I'm telling you now. Why do you suppose he used the word 'prunes'? Is it a joke?"

"It was probably the only word he could think of," Sophie growled, and then she spoke no more.

Kala stayed for some time on the edge of Sophie's bed. Then she tore the parts sheet in half, in quarters and eighths, and made her way back to her own bed. Down below she could still hear the voices of the soldiers, not quite as boisterous, dropping into ordinary conversation. Wakeful, she thought of Mikhail's dreamy intense blue eyes and regretted she had destroyed his poem. "Soil of Lyesk arise! . . ." the lines flew through her head, but this time, her mind alighted not upon the word 'prunes' but upon 'justice.' At least, she thought, Mikhail was attempting to do something to stop the war—at least he wanted to change the government intent upon destroying Russian land and innocent lives. In the warm summer night she found herself remembering the brief moments when she and Mikhail Kossoff had touched. Angrily she admitted she wanted to be with him again.

In the morning, as they dressed, Kala and Sophie made no mention of the poem. Sophie went off to the bakery and Kala to the barn for her morning chores. Inside the barn stood Ivan, one of their boarders, looking the worse for the past night's rowdiness and waiting to help Kala for the last time. Kala reflected she would miss all three of the soldiers quartered with her family, but Ivan more than the others. From the moment he had set foot in the house, whenever possible, he had followed Kala and Sophie about, joking with them in a hoarse voice that honked wistfully and helping Kala with the yard work. A private from the Ukraine, he had a crooked nose, a blond forelock that imitated the nose's crooked curve, and a pair of frightened, watchful, yet eager eyes. Often in spurts of animation, he had compared the Chodorov animals —sometimes favorably, sometimes unfavorably—to his own cows and horses far away.

This morning, when she caught sight of him, Kala declared, "Look how much Sir Leslie likes you!"

"How can you tell?" Ivan responded, his face thrust forward with anticipation.

"Because he winks in a certain way I've never seen before, twice like this," Kala blinked her eyes twice, rapidly, "and snorts, just barely, as if calling your name."

Ivan nodded wisely and with a resounding noise kissed Sir Leslie's nostrils.

After breakfast the family said goodby to their boarders, wishing them luck and loading them with cakes and breads and jams and cheeses so that they could hardly walk upright down the lane. The soldiers kept on turning and waving and shouting back their thanks. Then, a few hours later, they were gone from Lyesk.

In the afternoon the new casualty lists were posted at the station and Ekaterina brought home the news that Luka Fomich, the village elder, had lost his two remaining sons who had fought in the south for the Carpathian Mountains.

"It isn't believable," Kala said. "It can't happen like that . . . all five sons lost in less than a year. And no word of his nephew, Pyotr, in months." Heartsick, she gave herself over to her tedious work. As the heat of the sultry day continued, her sorrow increased. She wondered whether Luka Fomich would pay Malkeh his weekly visit before sundown. Then just before five o'clock a stream of housewives started past her open door, each woman carrying a kettle of *cholent*. Because Sabbath laws prohibited fires, the Jewish women brought their Saturday night suppers to simmer in the bakery oven, which retained its heat all through the holy day. The appearance of the housewives was Kala's signal to head for home to help her mother prepare for Friday night dinner.

Malkeh had left the bakery early, taking Radish with her— as if it were an ordinary Friday, rather than a day when she had learned of the death of Luka's last two sons. While she chopped and seasoned the fish, prepared the *matzoh* balls, roasted the chicken, and laid the noodle dough to dry, Radish went about the house washing the woodwork and the windows and waxing the floors. At the kitchen door Kala met Sophie and Ekaterina. She could see that they had been crying, but now, as if to keep Luka's loss from overwhelming them, they shouted and clapped, alerting Radish that they had come to help.

"I always do everything myself," Radish complained.

"Little darling," Kala said, at odds this afternoon even with such an expected statement from Radish, "why do you always grumble?"

"Radish," said Sophie, "you always carry on—you always grumble like a hive of bees."

"Radish," Ekaterina advised, ignoring the fact that she herself liked nothing better than to grumble, "I see no point in your always raising a fuss."

Then the sisters joined in to help polish the furniture and buff the brassware—taking particular care with the parlor since it was here the soldiers had been living and here Luka would sit with Malkeh, speaking about his sons.

Now Reb Keppel came through the streets, ringing his hand bell and intoning in his nasal voice the call to the baths—reminding the men they must be clean to usher in the Sabbath Bride. At once Mordecai arrived home from his job with the tailor Avrom Lavin and promptly set off with his towel and clean underclothes. Ten minutes later, Naftali rushed into the house and rushed out again, shouting back his list of instructions to his daughters and berating Kala, Sophie, and Ekaterina for the minimal interest they showed in his clothes. Soon—in the company of Mordecai—he returned from the baths, his voice echoing through the rooms as he called first to one daughter and then to another to fetch his shoes, his shirt, his trousers, and the rest of his Sabbath outfit. As he dressed, he compared his daughters' abysmal care of his clothes with the excellent attention Ruth gave her husband's. Fifteen minutes later he and Mordecai left again.

Kala and Sophie drifted to the front window. They watched while Mordecai and Naftali, carrying their prayer books and elaborately embroidered *tallis* bags, fell in with the other Jewish men who paced solemnly toward the synagogue. Kala fancied that the men appeared transformed from ordinary citizens to dignitaries who bore important messages to God—their black silhouettes embossed upon the apricot light of late afternoon. Here and there a light breeze kicked up the dust from the lane, filming over the green leaves of the trees and the black silk and gabardine of the men's coats and hats. At this moment, down the street in the opposite direction, came the Russian soldiers still quartered in the other houses on Merchant Lane. The soldiers' uniforms drooped from a hot day's work and they appeared much larger than the Jewish men, and younger—many of them almost schoolboys. Kala, wincing to see how carefully the two groups made way for one another, stepped back from the window.

She and Sophie then joined their sisters and mother at the bathhouse. They returned quickly to dress so they would be ready for Luka Fomich. Normally the village elder brought along his favorite grandchildren, Stepan and Natasha, the twins—identical not only to each other but also to their grandfather, from their tow heads to their sturdy bowed legs. But this evening Luka came alone. Kala embraced the village elder. Then she watched him follow Malkeh through the dining room where he paused, as always, to take in the fine settings of the *shabbas* table—to gaze appreciatively at the cut-glass crystal, the gleaming silver, and the starched linen that hung in graceful folds. Entering the parlor, he and Malkeh descended into chairs that faced the piano. Ordinarily, side by side—at once majestic and familiar—they would murmur, discuss, raise objections, and arrive at certain conclusions crucial to the citizens of the region of Lyesk. Today, from the parlor door, Kala heard Luka formally announce to his friend the death of his sons. Malkeh shut her eyes and nodded.

In the kitchen Kala ladled up a fresh bowl of Friday night *matzoh* ball soup. Placing the bowl on a tray with a spoon and a cloth napkin, she carried it into the parlor, where she found her mother and their visitor sitting silently. Luka's small deep-set green eyes, which in the past had seemed to pierce every object around him, were fixed dully upon the floor. Kala set the tray upon Luka's knees. After a bit he raised his head and scrutinized the soup. He handed the tray back to Kala and stood up. As he started for the door with Malkeh, an unnatural stiffness in his wide shoulders and short thick bowed legs, he appeared sorrowful, stoic—almost an old man for the first time.

Kala returned the tray to the kitchen.

"What have Mama and Luka been saying?" Sophie asked.

"Nothing."

"Mama should be comforting him. They should be talking and crying."

"They should be crying together," Kala agreed.

"But all they know is how to make decisions together."

All they know is how to make decisions together. "Oh well," said Kala in a low voice. "What good are tears anyway?"

CHAPTER TEN

T HE CHODOROV SISTERS GATHERED IN THE DINING ROOM TO
watch their mother light the Sabbath candles. Leaning over the twin candelabra which ascended from the center
of the table like stately branching trees, Malkeh covered her
eyes with her hands and prayed for each member of the
household—for health, for success, for husbands to wed her
daughters, and for the gift of many children. She glanced
appreciatively at the pregnant Ruth. The setting sun passed
through the dusty atmosphere, the room glowed with a rosy
light, and the last gleam of the day gilded Malkeh's strong
and handsome face. "Blessed art Thou, O Lord our God,
King of the Universe," she repeated in a hushed and urgent
whisper, "Who hast hallowed us by His commandments and
commanded us to kindle the Sabbath lights. Gather Luka's
sons to Thy bosom and guard over the Fomich family."

In the middle of her prayers, without warning, a sudden
shower burst upon the town, rattling off the roofs, washing

the leaves and buildings free of dust. The sound of dogs bark-
ing and children gleefully shouting floated in through the
window, mixed with the drumming of rain. While the girls
were still closing the windows the rain stopped as suddenly as
it had begun and the procession of Jewish men started back,
moving much more swiftly on its return.

In the house the Chodorov girls began to chatter, despite
their sorrow over Luka Fomich's sons. Hunger loosened their
tongues. "Good *shabbas*, good *shabbas*," Kala and Sophie announced to one another. And turning, they rushed to tell
Ekaterina that in the distance they had glimpsed their father
who brought from the synagogue another fat merchant, like
the one from Gomel who, two weeks before, had touched
his fingers to Ekaterina's breast and asked for her hand in
marriage.

"Good *shabbas*, good *shabbas*." Naftali entered the house.
"Everyone come meet our special *shabbas* guests. Here we
have our good friend, Patch, and our own Hershel—see how
tall Hershel's grown—and for once we also have a real angel
of the Lord to test our hospitality." He looked around.
"Where has he gone to?" Naftali stuck his head out the door.
"Oh, there you are." He returned with his arm about the
shoulders of a handsome bareheaded young man. "Here he
is."

Kala gasped and sidled out of the entrance hall. She hid in
the kitchen, busying herself by dishing up the *gefülte* fish
onto saucers.

"Mordecai!" Naftali pointed out the visitor's summer suit
to his son-in-law. "How long has it been since you've seen
fabric like this linen?" Appreciatively he took hold of the
young man's lapel, rubbing it between his thumb and forefinger. He shook his head in wonder. "Nowadays you never
get a chance to see cloth like this. And to think . . . he's a
cousin of the *shoychet* Zuckerman's, though actually he
comes from Vilna." Then Naftali introduced Malkeh, Ruth,
Sophie, Ekaterina, and at the end inquired, "Where's Kala?"

"Kala!" Ruth called, waddling into the kitchen, accompanied by Ekaterina, who whispered, "Kala, guess what? Papa's brought home a decent-looking guest. Come see. Things are improving at the synagogue or else Papa's taste is getting better."

Against her will, Kala let her sisters lead her back to the hallway where she arrived in the midst of Naftali explaining, "I have a son Iosif, but he lives in America . . . in Detroit, Michigan. When he was eighteen years old he had enough of Russia. Have you ever heard of Detroit, Michigan? That's where the motor cars come from. And here," he said, favoring Kala with a glance, "is my second oldest daughter." His eyes narrowed shrewdly. "She's the strongest of the lot."

At this presentation Mikhail stepped forward, took Kala's hands in both of his, and stood gazing down at her for so long a time that the Chodorovs, after appearing somewhat nonplussed in the beginning, began to look uneasy and to shift about uncomfortably on their feet. A deep, dark reddish flush suffused Sophie's neck and face, and Mordecai for some reason stamped his foot, as if in anger. When the young man still did not release Kala's hands Ruth murmured, "How very strange." Finally it took Malkeh to sum the matter up. "It appears you know each other."

"Not very well," demurred Kala in a small cracked voice, glancing at Sophie, whose color by now had toned down and who was carefully examining the new visitor.

"Well enough," Mikhail contradicted. "Under the circumstances. Eight months ago . . . perhaps it was nine . . . I was visiting my relatives and at their suggestion I brought your daughter a clock of great importance to me . . . no one else could have fixed it."

"No one else?" Naftali ruminated over this statement, raising his eyebrows. "You could have taken it to Baranovits or Pinsk. Certainly if it was valuable. No matter, it's fixed now. Come," he took Mikhail's arm, "come sit with us at our *shabbas* table." And he and the younger man proceeded side by side until the dining-room entrance, where Mikhail paused to let all five of the Chodorov women, as well as the beggar Patch, enter before him. Growing impatient at this display of manners, Naftali let go of Mikhail's arm, took hold of Mordecai's arm, and gave Mordecai a slight shove into the dining room, all the while muttering into his son-in-law's butterfly-shaped ears, "In Vilna we'd still be at the door."

At the table Naftali spoke his lines by heart: "Let us give thanks to the Lord our God for all the kindnesses He has shown unto us and hope that we are deserving to welcome in the Sabbath. Please remove, O Lord our God, from all of us and our nation, sickness and suffering and poverty and the threat of war. Please, O King of Glory, Lord of Peace, may the Sabbath angels," he turned his head to regard the three guests as if they, significantly, were the angels in question, "usher us into happiness and peace for now and evermore."

Then as everyone prepared to be seated, Ekaterina carried a bowl of water about the table so that the diners could sprinkle water over their hands three times.

Seated across from Mikhail, Kala hardly knew in which direction to look. She would have preferred to rest her gaze on Mikhail Kossoff if only to remind herself what he looked like, but instead she looked at the table and asked herself, was he different from the man she remembered? And why was he in Lyesk—had he come just so he might see her? At first this notion annoyed her. Then surreptitiously she glanced around to determine if her family had properly assessed his cultivated Russian and the beauty of his eyes. To her dismay something in the demeanor of the *shabbas* diners suggested they found Mikhail Kossoff rather odd—in particular the fact that when the men removed their hats and put on *yarmulkehs*, their heads turned toward Mikhail as though to determine whether he were enough of a Jew to produce his own *yarmulkeh*.

Out of his pocket came a simple silk cap—a cap like everyone else's. But when he placed it on his head it appeared somehow more stylish than pious. Unfolding his napkin, he whipped it onto his lap in a single too casual gesture and lifted his wine glass too gracefully between his thumb and forefinger and sang out the words of the blessing so that they sounded like an exotic serenade.

Hershel alone appeared impressed. "I had a birthday last week," he announced. "I'm fifteen." He looked eagerly between Sophie and Mikhail and added proudly, "Any day now I can expect to be drafted."

"Hershel, stop that!" Sophie rebuked. "You only frighten and upset us."

"Already fifteen?" queried Naftali. "You still look fourteen—even thirteen, like a *Bar Mitzvah* boy. You've got time, Hershel, before you go running away from the army—though not too much time. Papa Velvel is on his way."

"The Kaiser's children will take Warsaw and keep on coming," said Patch, finishing Naftali's refrain while in the midst of chomping on his third helping of chopped liver. Patch, because of his poverty and his piety, was a frequent recipient of Chodorov hospitality. At the table he seemed totally at home except that he allowed himself nothing but small portions of food, taking innumerable helpings as the meal progressed—just to make up. "The Kaiser's children will take Warsaw and keep on coming," he repeated, his mouth bulging.

"But don't you see, Sophie," said Hershel earnestly, "I don't intend to fight in this war. My friends and I are training to be pioneers. Before I'm taken into the army I will be on my way to Palestine to make a homeland for the Jews— with these hands." He held up his hands for Sophie to see. Then, realizing that everyone else was studying his hands, embarrassedly he lowered them to his lap.

"And what about you, Mikhail?" Malkeh inquired, gently retrieving the chopped liver dish from Patch and offering it to the new guest. "Have you served on active duty yet?"

"Or are you medically unfit?" asked Mordecai, hopefully.

"I've been a student for the past four years, and of course exempted for that reason."

"A student where?" Malkeh asked.

"St. Petersburg."

"St. Petersburg!" Ekaterina raptly clapped her hands. "So you know painters, sculptors, philosophers."

"It's not St. Petersburg any longer," ventured Mordecai. He cleared his throat. "They call it Petrograd now . . . because that's more Russian."

Ekaterina laughed excitedly, her emerald-colored eyes fixed upon Mikhail. "St. Petersburg! We have someone in our midst who has actually lived in St. Petersburg! At last! Tell us what it's like!"

"St. Petersburg?" repeated Mikhail, as though Ekaterina's fervor had flustered him. "Petrograd," he glanced at Mordecai to show he had heard his correction. "Well, it's very large."

"Yes?"

"Filled with bureaucrats and officials."

"Well, of course. That's to be expected. But I want to know about the libraries, the cafes, the palaces, the writers and the painters." Ekaterina beamed upon the visitor, dazzling her sisters who had never seen her display such warmth.

"Actually," Mikhail went on, "Moscow is the city for the arts. Oh there are artists in St. Petersburg too, of course, cafes and palaces. But I was enrolled in the Institute of Agriculture."

"Don't joke," pleaded Ekaterina. "You don't know how much this means to me. What are they reading at the University? Are they reading Lermontov and the Imagists? Are they reading Pushkin and Saltykov-Shchedrin or are those writers considered old-fashioned?"

"I can't really say," Mikhail laughed placatingly. "At one time I meant to read all of those authors myself. I even opened Saltykov-Shchedrin." At the memory a pained look came across his face. "But to be honest—there were so many technical manuals I was expected to get through. You can't imagine how many manuals they give prospective agronomists. Anyway," he shrugged, "I got my degree."

"But in agriculture? And you never read Lermontov?" Ekaterina wrinkled up her nose.

"Not a page," Mikhail declared firmly. "In Petrograd I learned about land—what to do about soil, how to distribute the land more equitably."

Ekaterina's nose wrinkled up still further.

"And now that I've graduated," Mikhail continued, "I'm serving temporarily as liaison between the War Department and various volunteer charities. I'm out at the old Post House with the Sisters of Mercy. Our agency's setting up relief stations through the countryside, giving aid to the poor who've been evacuated before the advancing Germans. Our armies are burning everything behind them."

"Burning? Why?" asked Ruth.

"To deny the Germans all resources," Mikhail said.

"And that only makes sense." Patch vehemently nodded, reaching out for his fourth helping of chopped liver. "If I were Grand Duke Nicholas, I wouldn't want to feed the German army."

"Unfortunately, it's the poor and only the poor who've been set loose on their own." Mikhail's voice rose. "There's not one official, not one landlord, not a single family of wealth on the road. Only the laboring poor and the peasants. And at the front where four million have died: only the laboring poor and the peasants."

Kala experienced a drumming in her ears, as though Mikhail's presence had placed her under water.

"Four million!" Ruth protested. "Not four million already!"

"And who knows," Mikhail pursued, "I wouldn't be at all surprised if the industrialists were at the bottom of this whole evacuation—hoping for cheap labor in the heartland."

"That's strange talk," commented Malkeh, "from someone working for the War Department."

"The relief stations are really the work of volunteer charities—Northern Help and Mutual Aid and the Sisters of Mercy. The government gives us little or no support—our liaison is merely a gesture to keep order."

"Still I'd be more discreet," Sophie advised.

"We're all friends here," Mikhail said.

"That's right," said Hershel, eagerly waving his fork, "all Jews and we should be turning toward Palestine right now. Palestine is where our future lies. In Palestine no one will accuse us of being parasites . . . we will work for ourselves."

"We're all friends," agreed Patch. "All Jews. We aren't peasants." He dug into a towering *matzoh* ball, momentarily submerging it, after which it rose to the surface of his soup like the tip of a rounded iceberg. "Oh if I had a zloty for every time this white beard had been pulled by a peasant I'd be Rothschild."

Mikhail laid his utensils on the table. He shook his head. "No, no. Polish peasants perhaps, Roman Catholics. But your White Russian peasant, your Byelorussian, he's an entirely different sort of fellow. He's a kind and modest fellow—he would never pull your beard out of malice. No, the White Russian peasant has been a subject race for almost as long as the Jews. There's a poem that says both share their captivity in common, both wait for the Messiah to restore their land. It goes . . . the lines go . . ." He stood up, and while the *shabbas* diners stared at him, he delivered in the Byelorussian dialect:

"Hail to you, all-Byelorussian Jews
  I have faith in you, although Tsar and Slav
  The old and young everywhere, spit black dirt on you."

He paused to peer significantly from one end of the table to the other. Then as if for emphasis he repeated, "The old and young everywhere, spit black dirt on you."

A stunned silence greeted Mikhail's recitation. Quickly this changed into an almost unanimous indignation. "What kind of poem is that?" Naftali demanded. He pounded angrily on the table.

"A lot of nerve!" exclaimed Patch. " 'They spit black dirt on you!' "

Carried along by the others' displeasure, Kala failed at first to identify her own grievances. When they swept into her mind, she thrust her chin forward, frowning at Mikhail fiercely. "The Jews of Lyesk were almost evacuated last fall."

[115]

She all but spit out the words. "We were almost evacuated though we were nowhere near the front. Someone blew up our bridge. The authorities blamed it on the Jews."

"On the Jews?" Mikhail echoed disbelievingly.

"Yes. On all of us. And they would have sent us to Kazan or Novgorod if it hadn't been for Mama. She went to the Colonel and pleaded our cause."

"Actually we bribed the authorities," Naftali explained. "We did it very well. We gave them boots, flour, silver, roubles, brandy, beef."

Kala glared at the visitor. "We bribed them. And a bribe is nothing to be proud of."

"They blamed the Jews!" Mikhail said.

"Papa Velvel is on his way," Naftali said.

"The Kaiser's children will take Warsaw and keep on coming," Patch agreed, taking his first, then very quickly his second and third helpings of the noodle pudding. "And it won't be such a tragedy for the Jews."

CHAPTER ELEVEN

THOUGH NO ONE HAD INVITED HIM, MIKHAIL ARRIVED THE next evening in time for Saturday supper and was met at the door by Sophie. "So you're Kala's poet!" she greeted him, an inquisitive expression on her face. Birdlike, she turned her head this way and that to examine him from all sides. "Well," she said in a friendly tone of voice after hopping around him on her crutches, "I just hope you're nice."

This evening Mikhail appeared a good deal different from Friday night. Mild and quiet, he sat through dinner listening to the others. Every so often he caught Kala's eye and smiled at her, but when she turned away he made no further attempt to capture her attention. After his display of the night before, she felt grateful that at least he now remained unobtrusively in the background. Indeed, the Chodorovs had just grown used to Mikhail's presence—having almost forgotten it—when Kala rose to clear the plates and Mikhail leaped to his feet to help her.

"What are you doing?" Naftali called out in alarm.

"I'm helping Kala clear the table."

"Sit down, young man," Naftali directed, pushing his hands toward the ground. "The women will do all that."

"Oh, it's quite all right." Mikhail gathered up Sophie's plates and reached for Ruth's—at which Ruth stood up and tried to take the plates away from him. "You mustn't bother, you mustn't trouble yourself," she half urged, half pleaded.

"Sit down, young man!" Naftali commanded, then added fussily, glancing over toward Malkeh, "I don't know how you were brought up over there in Vilna . . . but if you won't look to your elders, then look at Mordecai. Mordecai does everything he can think of doing for his wife. Sometimes he does too much and goes too far. Yet Mordecai would never consider going about picking up dirty dishes."

Very softly—almost too softly to be heard—Mordecai whispered, "Sit down, young man, sit down."

But Mikhail had already carried his stack of dishes into the kitchen.

When supper had been cleared away, Naftali took out his watch and announced it was time for the family's weekly Saturday night stroll. From outdoors crickets could be heard chirping shrilly and frogs croaking hollowly in the river bottom. Presently, out of the house stepped Malkeh and Naftali —Malkeh in a gray silk dress, its full sleeves gathered at the wrists. Carefully she matched her steps to Naftali's as he strode along by her side, tapping now and again with his ivory-tipped malacca cane, a bowler topping his head. Behind them Ruth and Mordecai waddled and wobbled—Mordecai imitating Ruth's gait in empathy with her condition. Sophie, in her wheelchair, and Ekaterina followed behind them— both girls wearing tightly bodiced, gaily printed summer dresses—their bare arms gleaming in the moonlight. And still further behind—separated from the others by a definite space, by a gap which Sophie and Ekaterina appeared to encourage —Kala and Mikhail tagged onto the end of the party. An expression of calm contentment rested on Mikhail's face, a stricken look of embarrassment lay on Kala's.

"I wanted to say . . ." Mikhail began.

"This is hardly the place to talk," interrupted Kala, shaking her head.

"But I've come back to be with you . . . to explain."

"This is a very small town," Ekaterina said, twisting her head around, for the Chodorovs, who had already circled the town square once, were now circling its cobbled stones again. "It's very small, particularly for anyone who has lived in St. Petersburg. And not only small, it's very boring."

"Oh Ekaterina!" Sophie rebuked.

"You'll see tonight," Ekaterina told Mikhail. "You'll get an idea of how boring it is," she went on as, at every turning, someone the family knew emerged from behind a building, around a gas lamp, out of a doorway, or from the midst of a field. Nachman Liebes leaned upon the hitching rack in front of Dovitsky's stable. Sarah Finkel and Shmuel, the Holy One, lounged in front of the hotel porch. The Russian landowner Stepan Ilyich Rozumov and his daughter Natasha ambled around the town square, trailed at a respectful distance by the Police Captain Semyon Varsonevsky, Varsonevsky's sister, and her two daughters. Still further behind, the Stationmaster, Ivan Sergeyevich Dovrynin, and his wife dragged their heels to avoid running into their enemy, Stepan Rozumov.

"It's never boring to see the people you know." Kala glanced pointedly at Mikhail. "It's just boring to see those you don't know."

"In a way we know each other very well," Mikhail insisted.

"Not well at all." Kala let the distance between herself and her family increase as they continued on their route to the railroad station, out along the main street, past the whorehouse, the bathhouse, and the synagogue. "Just because we exploded a bomb together. That's nothing to be proud of."

"It was a mistake."

Ekaterina turned around again. "At least there's a bright moon tonight so it's a little less dreary." She pointed to the sky. A flat moon lit the main street like a stage, doubling the form of Lazar Dovitsky and his eight children, who marched up the cobbled street toward the synagogue, discreetly turning their heads away from Osip Blag, the hotel owner, as Blag hesitated before the entrance to the whorehouse. In front of the synagogue Reb Keppel, the *shammes*, leaned forward to chat with Leah and Mendel Feldshpan and Leah's important father, Moishe Kantorovits, manager of the Potocki estate, who, this evening, was proudly showing off his third wife Bella, a strapping youngster of twenty-two.

"I had no idea it would endanger the Jews of Lyesk. It was a mistake in every way. It was even a mistake politically."

He was about to continue when Naomi Benjamin and Leah Feldshpan, having disengaged themselves from their husbands and their fathers, sailed forth full tilt, arm in arm, alighting before the Chodorovs. Kala and Mikhail ceased their conversation and joined the family. "So there I was," announced Naomi, enunciating every word, "flat on my back, unconscious. And my little Pinchas running for the doctor . . . even though he won't be six years old until August . . . and Jacob trying to bring himself to slap my face to wake me up and the first thing I thought of was what my mother used to say: 'Darling, always put on clean underwear in the morning, because you never can tell . . .' " Without a pause, Naomi inquired of Malkeh, "Who is that with Kala?" She leaned forward to receive the answer, her eyes bright as stars, her mouth and, next to her, Leah's mouth, as rapt and ravenous as young beaks.

"A Zuckerman relative," Malkeh replied, recommencing the walk.

"Very handsome," Naomi crooned, strolling alongside Malkeh and Naftali.

"He doesn't look anything like the *shoychet*," Leah observed, taking up her position on Naftali's free side.

"It's the *shoychet*'s wife who's related," said Naftali.

"He doesn't resemble her either. And he certainly doesn't resemble Schlaymie."

"He's out at the old Post House with the Sisters of Mercy," Malkeh said.

"He's working for the Gentiles?" Naomi remarked.

When everyone looked back at Mikhail, he said, "For the Russian people, and we would appreciate any help we can get—volunteers, food, clothing, medical supplies."

"I suppose each person should help a little," Leah agreed. They reached the Chodorov house, where everyone said goodnight, Malkeh promising to send whatever the bakery could spare for the refugees. Inside the house Kala ate up all four pears from the dining-room cut-glass fruit bowl out of frustration. Now that she'd begun to talk about the bridge, she wanted only to continue—to say out loud everything she had kept inside all these months. There had been no one to listen. Sophie had continued to evade her whenever she'd brought up the subject—had seemed in fact to pretend the bridge explosion had never happened. But more than a discussion with Sophie, she realized she wanted to confront and question Mikhail Kossoff.

The next morning—a Sunday, the sky overcast, the air muggy—Kala and Malkeh loaded sacks of flour, sugar, and wrapped baked goods into the cart. Then Kala drove Sir Leslie out to the old Post House, a monumental one-story structure at the junction of Orchard Lane and the high road. Across the facade of the building that Mikhail and his colleagues had taken over stretched a neatly lettered sign: "Northern Aid." All about the courtyard lay stacked forage. In front of the double doors two huge tureens—one of borsht and the other of *shchi*—simmered over open fires. The graveled road, wet from heavy dew, stretched up a long incline toward the north and west. Along the roadway and in the forests beyond, families of refugee peasants camped about their wagons.

Mikhail, in peasant work clothes, greeted Kala with brusque good humor, saying, "I'm glad you've come," before he sent her off to unload her supplies at a side door of the building. A Sister of Mercy came out to help her. Inside, just behind the commissary, Kala caught sight of a makeshift hospital—the bunks hammered together with odd bits of timber and lined with straw. Half the bunks were filled with patients. "Some refugees have come a long way already," explained the sister. "Some have been on the road over a month."

Kala had almost emptied the cart when she encountered a peasant in a tattered coat standing by the door, wringing his hands and calling inside loudly, "Katya! Wife! Come out! It's Dimitri, your husband!"

"Come back later," ordered the sister. "They're being washed now." And without waiting for a reply, she disappeared into the building.

"Katya!" shouted the man.

Kala approached him. "The sister said you can see your wife later."

At this the peasant turned toward her slowly, his eyes wide and filled with misery. "She's inside . . . in the hospital. My wife . . . they took my wife." He faced the building and called out, "Katya! Wife! Our town is leaving soon. You must come out. They say she's too sick to travel, and it's time for us to leave."

"But she'll get well," Kala reassured him. "And you can stay here until she recovers."

"But our town is leaving today. We'll lose our town."

"They'll find you another town," Kala offered without thinking. "They'll find you another town and fix you special papers."

"Another town?" asked the man, astonished. He backed off from the girl. "My house, my fields, my cattle: all gone, like a dream. Could I have been someone else then? And now another town?" He paused, struck by a new thought. "How will the priest know me?"

Stunned by this outcry, Kala imagined herself in his place. What if she were told she no longer belonged in Lyesk but could go to a town which she did not know, where she recognized nothing and no one recognized her? Undone by this notion she held out her hand. "Come with me," she pleaded. "We'll go see the officials and see what can be done."

The peasant let Kala lead him away from the hospital door toward the courtyard. They found Mikhail surrounded by complaining peasants. Several addressed him as "Your Excellency" despite his plain white homespun shirt and trousers. As he listened to their requests, he moved swiftly about, allocating milk rations for the children, stamping food certificates and sending directives and messages to the Sisters of Mercy who worked alongside. When Kala approached, he listened carefully to the peasant's problem, promising he would discuss the matter of his sick wife Katya with the sister in charge of the hospital. "In the meantime," Mikhail urged, "have some borsht. A good borsht will help you." He directed him to the line waiting for the soup.

Once in line, the peasant peered into the faces of the others waiting there, explaining to each that he had seen soldiers, his own countrymen, lay the torch to the cottage his family had always lived in; that he had seen the same soldiers ignite the crops growing on the land of his forebearers. He kept repeating his story, as though if he spelled it out one more time, some clear-sighted person might contradict him.

Fearful she might be interrupting Mikhail's work, Kala began to walk back to her cart, intending to return home. She could see this was no time to discuss personal matters. In a moment Mikhail was at her side, begging her to remain for a few minutes. "Come with me. I'll show you what I've done to protect the water supply."

He led her to a waste field, insisting that she inspect the new toilet facilities he had erected, one for men and one for women. Kala felt odd to be standing among the latrines. Nevertheless—while he gazed raptly at the site, explaining that in this way the campsites and streams would not be fouled—she expressed her admiration. Several men and women passed to and fro, their eyes down. Kala blushed. "Well at least you're helping people now."

"I don't just go about blowing things up."

"Does that mean you've left your party?"

"Left the Socialist Revolutionaries?" He shot her an incredulous glance.

"They condemned the bridge explosion—a nephew of our *shammes* saw it in the Pinsk newspaper. And what's more," she accused him, her voice censorious, "they condemned it because they're in favor of this terrible war."

"Many of us are not," he said, taking a few steps away from her. "There's some disagreement about tactics, not about our final goal. The fact is, we shouldn't have exploded the bridge. We shouldn't have exploded anything. It was all Schlaymie's doing. He gave us the order to destroy the command train. He'd already gone over to the Bolsheviks and he was trying to undermine the Socialist Revolutionaries. My own cousin a traitor!"

"No one could ever count on Schlaymie."

"My own cousin." Mikhail groaned. "You must have thought me an idiot when you heard about my party's reaction."

"Even before I heard it," she said, quietly. "You don't understand what a terrible thing we did. I became a different person. I am a different person. It was not just the threat to the Jews. For all I know, one of the sons of my friend Luka died waiting for the supplies we delayed. For all I know I might have murdered him."

"I wish I hadn't involved you. You've every right to hate me."

"But it's my fault too." She laid her hand on his arm. "Anyway, you're helping people now."

And because she wanted also to be of help, she began to spend several hours a day aiding the Sisters of Mercy in their makeshift hospital. She scrubbed and disinfected the floors and pallets, lifted and fed the patients, hauled planks and unloaded lumber. It pleased her to see she was not the only volunteer from Lyesk. Matryona the midwife also worked in the infirmary, never ceasing to express her amazement at the sudden appearance of so many strange people from so far away. One Sunday she grabbed Kala's arm, insisting that she accompany her to the morning services conducted on a pasture bordering the road. There Father Boris conducted mass for the refugees and the villagers of Little Lyesk.

"You've never seen anything like it!" exclaimed Matryona. "Like a fair it is."

Indeed, as she approached the pasture it seemed to Kala almost as though she had stepped into one of those Bible stories her mother told the children when they were young. Cows and sheep, browsing unconcernedly, mingled with the worshippers. Men and women wore their best clothes. Stiff with starch, the fancifully shaped caps of the women shone in the dull light; bracelets and necklaces clinked and tinkled in accompaniment to the prayers. Even though it was still summer, many of the refugees showed off their best coats. With the help of Matryona, Kala identified the various provinces to the north and west. The men from Lomzha, distinguished by their long mustaches and shaven chins, sported white sheepskin jackets and black shawl-like collars, ornamented with colored beads, while the coats of the Grodno men were of reddish sheepskin with fringes of wool hanging from their cuffs. By contrast, the villagers of Little Lyesk, hanging shyly to the back of the congregation, looked poor and simple, their white homespun and bast sandals signs of generations raised on shallow sandy soil and meager harvests.

"Aren't they strange?" murmured Matryona, linking her fat arm through Kala's. "And proud! You should see the Grodno wagons, covered with their finest cloth, all striped and checked, material we couldn't afford for our best dresses. But those coming in now are the proudest and the funniest."

Matryona nodded toward a group of latecomers who were trickling into the service, pushing themselves through the crowd to the front. The peasants of Little Lyesk began to

[125]

nudge one another and laugh. "Not like us," an old lady muttered anxiously. "Not our faces. Not our caps."

"White Mountain people," murmured Matryona, "from Kholm Province, north country by the sea; you can tell by the fringes." She pointed out that the women wore bangs pulled out from under their kerchiefs, a style she said was ugly and ridiculous. "A bunch of braggarts, they are. What houses they left behind, according to them. What trees! What money! 'And was your land good?' I asked them. 'The best in all the world,' they answered, scooping up a handful of our dirt. 'You call this land? We wouldn't bother to plant in such soil. Now our earth you could eat, like bread—that's what land is!' "

In the middle of the service, Mikhail appeared at Kala's side and begged her to come for a walk with him. Kala excused herself from Matryona and joined the young man on the high road.

"There's a rumor now that Warsaw is about to fall," began Mikhail.

"We've pushed the Germans back twice already," she said. "We can push them back again." She walked sedately, her arms stiffly held by her side. Though it was almost noon, the scrub on either side of the roadway still dripped from the dew, and the wet gravel looked as if it had just been washed. Mikhail's bare arm touched Kala's accidentally and she jumped. After a while the road climbed a ridge of land called Raven's Hill, dividing two long, sweeping plains. Overhead the low gray sky began to break up. Steam rose from the drying roadway. At the crest Kala showed Mikhail a small path leading to a knoll from which the entire countryside could be seen—the land mottled with patches of sunshine and the irregular shadows cast by thick clouds.

"This is my own place," she said. Ahead of them lay the river and the orchards surrounding the village of Little Lyesk. Upriver appeared the houses of Lyesk proper, the spires of the church and the station, the gabled roof of the synagogue. To the north she could see all the way to Lake

Lyesk. A light mist rose from its waters as if from the surface of a pot about to boil. Due south the great forest of Nechaelvo sent up its dark green pine canopy, which shaded gradually into the lighter green of birches and willows bordering the swamps beyond.

"It is beautiful," Mikhail said. He followed her gaze. For some moments they were silent. Then he asked, "Tell me, Kala: if the Germans advance this far—if Lyesk is evacuated —what will you do?"

"I'll go with everyone else in town, of course, on the trains."

"The trains will all be taken up by the military."

"Then we'll take the high road. We'll build another Lyesk —somewhere to the east."

"But not everyone will leave together. Some will take to the road. Some will flee early, to find refuge with friends or relatives—to who knows where. Some will simply hide out close by until the evacuation is finished and the army has withdrawn. Then they'll return to live here under the Germans."

"To live under the Germans?" asked Kala. "By choice?"

Mikhail nodded. "It isn't so farfetched, you know, especially for the Jews. The German government, and certainly the Austrians, are more sympathetic to the Jews than the Russians are. It isn't out of the question that some of the Jews might want to wait for the Germans."

"Of course some may—but not most. If the Tsar thinks we're traitors . . . I may have blown up a Russian bridge, but it wasn't because I loved the Germans."

"Still, what would you do if your family should decide to stay?"

She reproached him with a sidelong glance. "You don't know my mother if you think she would abandon her townsmen. My mother's friends—the people she cares about— are not only the Jews. They're everyone."

"Every Jew has one special gentile friend, Kala," Mikhail interrupted, a trifle impatiently.

"But it isn't a question of just one. We're as close as family to Luka, the village elder—to the landowner Rozumov, to . . ."

"And I'm willing to bet your landowner won't be anywhere near Lyesk by the time the Germans approach."

"Listen, Mikhail," she said, "our town will stay together—even if it means evacuating the land Lyesk stands on and moving eastward. All of us are Russian, we're not German. And it's my mother who will help the town stay together. She has made Lyesk what it is—she more than anyone else." Kala stopped. Turning abruptly, she made her way from the knoll. Mikhail's remarks had shaken her. Uneasily she recalled her father's sly approval of Papa Velvel's advance.

When she and Mikhail reached the roadway, she said, wanting to rid them of the subject, "The Germans have already been pushed back twice. They'll be pushed back again."

Mikhail, too, as if hoping to end the discussion optimistically, delivered a little speech. "If the Germans actually advance this far, Kala, and your family decides to travel east on the road, I'll go with you and help. There will be nothing left of the relief station by then. And I could be of service because I know the way into Great Russia—and all the regulations. I'll go with your town."

"You'll march with our town?"

"Kala," he said, taking her hand, "since October I've thought of no one else but you. When I was able to arrange an assignment to this relief station, you can't imagine my happiness. Seeing you again, like this," he paused and gazed up at the sky, "I understood you're the only person I want to be with."

"No, no," Kala backed away in terror. "You can't mean such nonsense." Into her mind came the image of Ephraim Savich standing at her sister Ruth's bedroom door, telling her not to cry. Kala had no intention of being jilted.

"I love you." He moved toward her.

Startled, she looked into his blue eyes and saw that he might indeed be telling the truth. She found this almost as upsetting as the idea of being jilted. If she allowed him to kiss her, she thought, he might stick to her forever like glue. "No, no," she stammered, walking rapidly downhill. "You've made a mistaken judgment. You don't know me. I'm not the person you want."

CHAPTER TWELVE

On August 4 Warsaw fell. The stream of refugees coming down the high road swelled—carts piled high with belongings and herds trailing along behind, leaving hardly an empty stretch of road from early morning till late at night. Despite the efforts of Mikhail and his companions, gradually the order that they had established at the relief station deteriorated. Milk and sugar, in short supply, were issued only in bowls of semolina for the youngest children, and the lines for food at the gates of the post house stretched out so far that many waited in vain from the time of their arrival to their departure.

In Lyesk, some families quietly hoarded food, packed up valuables, and sent off large packages to relatives. And yet no one wanted to take an irrevocable step which might disrupt normal business. The Germans had been stopped before. Contradictory rumors circulated: at one moment it was said the Russian army would make a stand at the Bug or the

Neman rivers, outflank the Germans, and retake Warsaw; while at the next, someone reported that the Russian troops were fleeing in disarray. Meeting after meeting took place in the town. Malkeh attended each one and at each one nothing was decided.

One afternoon Naftali appeared in the repair shop, locking the door behind him. "Quick," he said, "I have something very important here," he patted his breast, "something you must decipher for me." He carefully removed a handbill from his breast pocket and unfolded it in front of Kala. "Read this."

Kala accepted the piece of paper. She was the only one of Naftali's daughters before whom he did not try to disguise his illiteracy. Companionably she read aloud, "Jews of Russia, hide your goods and await the liberating Germans! Do not let yourself be misled by false promises of the Russian government! Did not the Tsar promise equal rights for the Jews? And how did he keep his word? Remember the expulsion of the Jewish masses from their ancient settlements on the western borders! Remember Kishinev! Gomel! Bialystok! Siedlce! and hundreds of other bloody pogroms sponsored by the Russian government. Join our German forces today! In common struggle we will chase the Asian hordes from Europe's borders."

Dangling the paper between her thumb and forefinger as though it might soil her, Kala dropped it in the waste basket. "Why bring such nonsense to me?"

Naftali immediately retrieved the handbill without replying. He folded it and placed it in his breast pocket.

"I hope you don't show it to anyone else," said Kala, readying herself for an argument.

"Why not? It says the truth."

"You believe such propaganda?"

"It isn't propaganda," Naftali asserted stubbornly. "After all, Yiddish and German are almost the same language. The Germans are much closer to us in their ideals—they're practically our relatives—at least they think of us as relatives."

"They don't."

" 'Join our forces,' they say. 'In common struggle' and so on."

"We're Russians; we aren't Germans."

"We are Jews." He traced his finger along the counter, then blew on his finger. "Kala," he rebuked, "your grandfather dusted twice a day at least—you can't expect customers to respect you if you keep a disorderly shop."

"We're Russians."

"We are Jews," Naftali explained slowly, with exasperation. "If you had any training at all, you would understand that we are more Jews than we are anything else."

"What does that mean?" Kala pushed out her chin. Disputes with Naftali excited her. "Are we three-quarters Jewish and one-quarter Russian? Or perhaps, ninety-five percent Jewish and the rest whatever? No!" She hit the counter with her fist. "We are Russian Jews."

"And the pogroms in Kishinev? Lvov? and all the rest?"

"The Russian government is one thing—it's evil now—but the Russian people. They are a wonderful people. And the Russians of Lyesk . . . they're even better . . . they're our friends. If they're evacuated we go along with them."

"Go where?"

"East, of course, into Great Russia."

"What's the point of trekking into Great Russia? Over there they like us even less."

"Papa." Kala tried to reason. She opened the palm of her hand and spread out her fingers as though by numbering her arguments they might succeed in convincing Naftali. "If we go on the road, we don't become guilty of welcoming the Germans; we don't isolate ourselves from the rest of Lyesk. Just this morning, for example, Rozumov brought Mama a bouquet of flowers from his garden. Is Rozumov Jewish? Not to mention all the others . . . our good friend Luka who treats me like his daughter; Father Boris who came to warn us of the plans for the first evacuation; Matryona—even Ivan Sergeyevich. True, he missed Ruth's wedding but only out of a fearful disposition instead of prejudice against us. These people won't hide in the woods, they won't stay to wait for the German conqueror. How can we turn our backs on our own Russian family and open our arms to German strangers?"

"It happens," Naftali said, "it happens, don't ask me how." An expression of solemn wisdom came over his face as he drew himself up majestically straight. "Lyesk was not always in Russia. Once this town belonged to Poland, and before that to the Lithuanian Empire."

"Hundreds and hundreds of years ago. Once there were savage tribes here too."

"And what does that show? It shows that things change!" Naftali leaned forward, his solemnity giving way to a gleeful, sly shrewdness. "So you want to abandon your birthplace after all your talk about its being so special?"

"Aha! Very clever!" Kala thrust her face to within an inch of her father's. "But what is a town," she went on smugly, "if it's empty of its people? The land and buildings, they'll be burned. And when the Russians win the war, we'll all return together and rebuild everything that needs to be rebuilt— only better, and the fields, the river, Raven's Hill will still be here. Everyone will want you then, Papa: everyone will ask for the best carpenter. 'Bring us Naftali Chodorov,' they'll say, 'to rebuild our town.' Meanwhile we'll go somewhere else and establish a New Lyesk while we're waiting."

Not altogether displeased by this idea, Naftali raised his brows—half ruefully, half speculatively. "If only," he said, "you weren't planning to travel eastward into Great Russia. If only you all were going in the direction of America . . . to Detroit . . . where they manufacture all the cars."

"To Iosif."

"To Iosif." Naftali nodded.

"Mikhail will come on the road with us, Papa. He has offered us his help."

"What will he do—recite poems?" Naftali turned abruptly, unlocked the door, and left the shop, patting the breast pocket in which resided the German leaflet.

No more than ten days later the town awakened to find that the Russian authorities had posted notices informing the populace of the fall of Kovno and the impending evacuation of Lyesk. Accompanying each notice was a photograph of rows of men, women, and children hanging from telegraph poles, their bodies bound in barbed wire—this picture indicating what the citizens might expect should they fail to flee the advancing "Huns."

After ripping off one of the photographs from the side of a building, Kala laid it out on the kitchen table for her family to see. They gathered round and Naftali snorted, "Propaganda!"

"But just as true as the handbill you showed me. Well, now that the evacuation is starting, we'll have to get ready to leave."

"Yes," Malkeh agreed, ignoring the photograph, "we'll have to start. There's a lot to do . . . even though we aren't going very far. We'll hide in the cottage."

Kala stared at her mother. This was exactly what she had feared. "But the Russian government is burning everything."

"No one will come across the river to bother the orchard or the cottage."

"I suppose you've already made that arrangement? I suppose that's one of your bribes? And when the enemy arrives, we'll all come out waving German flags!"

"Kala," her mother replied, "none of our Russian friends will find fault with us for staying."

"Then we are traitors," Kala yelled. "We are traitors and the Tsar was right to put the Jews on trains and send them away from the front."

Naftali glowered at her. "We are not traitors."

"We are traitors!"

"What an odd way you have of looking at things," Ekaterina said.

"Ekaterina," Kala accused, "all you care about is your comfort."

Ekaterina tossed her head. "No one wants to suffer."

"Sophie," Kala invited her sister's support.

"I see no reason to go on the road," Sophie said, "just because the Russian government conducts this war stupidly. You see it differently. Not everyone in the family has to think alike."

"Oh, not everyone has to think alike, but does no one think like me?" Kala cried, and for the first time it crossed her mind she might have to go on the road alone. What would she do without her family—who would she be?

Over the next few days the news from the front grew worse. Hour by hour the echoing wail of train whistles sounded through Lyesk as carloads of fresh troops and horses headed for the front and the same cars returned almost immediately, bearing the wounded. Each day the round trip became shorter. Kala stayed close to home, helping her family dismantle the house and bury the valuables—all the while badgering her mother to join the evacuation. She had not seen Mikhail for almost a week when the young man, pack on his back, appeared at the door of the Chodorov kitchen, announcing that the Germans would be on them momentarily. Wrinkles of fatigue creased his forehead.

"It's like hell," he told Kala when she sat him down with a bowl of soup and a loaf of bread. Wearily he paused between spoonfuls. "There are so many refugees bearing down the high road that everything—trees, fence posts, fields— everything in sight disappears within hours. And the haze from the campfires and the road dust—all orange and red. It's exactly like hell." He put down his spoon and breathed heavily through his mouth as if to suck fresh air into his lungs. "There was no way to help any longer. There was nothing left. I sent the Sisters on and came here, as I promised. Well, I'm glad to see you at least." He appraised the stack of boxes piled near the stove. "What sort of decision has your family made?"

Kala hung her head at his query, her excitement at his presence dissolving. She said nothing.

After a few moments he nodded, sympathetically. "It's all

right, Kala—after what I've seen, I can't blame your family. By any standards, it won't be a pleasant journey."

"But if they don't go," she said in a rush, "that doesn't mean I'll stay here with them. I might not. I'm seventeen. There's something wrong with me if I can't make up my own mind."

"It probably . . . it does make sense for you to stay here. But if you decide to go, I'll come along as I promised, I'll see to it that you're all right."

She had pulled a chair close to him at the kitchen table and now she slid the chair away. "I don't need you to take care of me," she declared. "I've other things to worry about. I have to convince my mother to leave with the town. And she will." Kala raised her head and straightened her shoulders. "Yes, she will. When the time comes she'll start out on the high road and everyone will follow behind—our family and all the rest—the Lavins, the Dovitskys, the Feldshpans, the . . ."

Just then Ekaterina entered the kitchen, sheets and blankets in her arms. "Oh Mikhail, I didn't notice you come in! As you can see, we're moving to the cottage." She bent over Kala and said maliciously, "The more I think about it, Kala, the more certainty I feel that the Germans won't be so bad. Just consider—they have the greatest reputation in all of Europe for their culture and if they bring us one or two philosophers . . . some artists, musicians . . . horse racing."

But Kala's mind was elsewhere, for she was busy lifting up and bodily placing each member of her family on the high road.

In the morning—just before dawn—Kala woke with her mother and the two of them took their biscuits to the front room so as not to disturb Mikhail, who lay sleeping on the kitchen stove. Malkeh stood at the window. Kala came up just behind her. As they watched the first light touch the roofs of their town, Kala heard a strange dull thudding sound as if, she thought, a great horse were trotting along deep within the earth.

"There it is," Malkeh said. "It's begun."

"German artillery. It'll soon be time to leave Lyesk."

"Time to settle in the cottage."

"Mama," the girl protested quietly.

Malkeh gave no sign that she'd heard. "Luka came to the bakery yesterday. He said to wish you goodby. He came to thank me for inviting him and Anya and the children to stay with us in the orchard . . ."

"But he won't stay, will he? He'll go with the others. Mama," she pleaded, "I hate the Russian government. I hate the war. But the Russians . . . and particularly the Russians of Lyesk—they're not the government and not the war—they're part of us. If they have to take to the road, then we have to go with them. Remember that you brought us up not in a *shtetl* but in a town which you yourself shaped so that Jew and Christian could live harmoniously together. Don't just worry about our comfort and safety like Ekaterina. Think about what you truly believe."

"I live what I believe."

"I'll give you time to change your mind," said Kala, and quit the house for the repair shop. Here she finished packing up her tools, separating out those she wanted to carry with her.

As she half expected, she soon heard a knock—a sharp quick tattoo. She opened the door to Sophie and inquired, "Will Mama change her mind?"

"Why should she?"

"Sophie, what should I do? Should I go off by myself?"

Unhappily, Sophie swung on her crutches back and forth across the tiny shop. Stopping in front of the bench, she gazed down at Kala, her eyes as wretched and uncertain as her sister's. "Kala, if you believe in something, do it!"

"That's very well for you to say, Sophie," Kala replied. "It's not you who would be leaving."

Early in the morning the command car of the district came chugging into the square. A staff cavalry squadron and staff motorcyclists followed it. Colonel Sukharov stepped from the command car and informed Captain Varsonevsky there had been a major breakthrough by the Germans the night before. Now the Colonel ordered the Captain to begin the evacuation of the town. All the residents were instructed to assemble on the eastern side of the high-road bridge and to stay off the roadways as much as possible in order to leave a path clear for military units. The Captain sent for Father Boris, Rabbi Hershfill, and Rabbi Benjamin to issue the certificates of emigation, listing the town of origin, the family head, and each soul in the family.

By now the Chodorovs had moved everything but their piano, a few sticks of furniture, and the essential baking implements to the cottage in the orchard. While the women gave their time to baking free bread for their fellow citizens, Naftali, Mordecai, and Mikhail transported the animals and wagons over the high-road bridge across the river. Toward five o'clock a subaltern of the Colonel's arrived with a sack of flour, requesting that Malkeh supply an extra bake to the military forces. It was almost dark by the time the last batch of bread was loaded onto the wagon provided by Colonel Sukharov. When the subaltern attempted to pay, Malkeh refused his offer.

"It's for good luck," said Kala, "and for good luck especially in the coming battle."

The sound of artillery had increased during the day and now the flashes of artillery mixed with the light of the sunset to give an eerie appearance to the western skies. As the Chodorovs and Mikhail wearily walked back to the house to gather up the bedding on which they'd slept, they saw a squad of soldiers spreading hay and woodchips around the buildings of Merchant Lane. A wagon loaded with barrels of kerosene and poles, the ends of which were wrapped in rags, moved slowly up the lane. Without consulting one another, the family proceeded through the rooms of the house—Mikhail waiting outside—like mourners passing in procession. Naftali's hand smoothed the handsome woodwork of the doorways and the mantel, while one by one each person touched the piano—Ekaterina, Sophie, and Kala tapping the keys with one finger, Mordecai patting the instrument's side, and Ruth shutting its lid gently. At the front door Naftali pried off the *mezuzah* with his pocket knife and handed it to Malkeh. Then everyone set off down the back path, through the birch forest to the new railroad bridge.

At the other side of the bridge, Kala brought the procession to a halt. It was almost dark now and she could barely make out the faces of her family as they crowded around her to see what she wanted. Below, the river flowed smooth and strong under the bridge, widening placidly as it proceeded down toward the bend.

"Well . . . goodby. I'm leaving you now." She repeated the words twice to make certain they understood. "I'm off to the high road to join the evacuation. I have my tools with me—I can get along."

"What are you saying?" Naftali yelled out. "If you're running away with that dreamer," his voice shook with anger, "I forbid it."

"Kala, are you certain . . ." Mikhail began, but his voice was lost in the hubbub.

"Kala," Ruth shook her head, "a young man and a young woman setting forth together. It isn't right. It's not God's . . ."

"If you're running away with him," Naftali shouted, "I forbid it! We haven't even spoken with his parents."

"It has nothing to do with Mikhail," said Kala, glancing at her mother, whose mouth remained firmly shut.

"Kala," Ekaterina exhaled crossly, "why are you always so perverse? What an unattractive trip you've chosen! Sophie, tell her she's a fool."

But Sophie said nothing. Through the darkness Kala discerned that Sophie's eyes glittered too brightly, as if so much change were disorienting her, as if the change had stored its unwanted energy inside her large, dark pupils. Unable to bear Sophie's feverish unhappiness, Kala looked away and rallied, "You can all change your minds still. We can load the wagon and the cart at the cottage and be on our way by morning." Her voice trailed off.

[139]

"And you're willing to leave Sophie?" Ekaterina inquired.

"Speak for yourself," Sophie hissed.

Ruth implored quietly, "Kala . . . my sister . . . in a way you're right to feel so strongly . . . but only in a way . . . the family must stay together."

"Do you plan to marry?" Mordecai inquired mildly of Mikhail, who kept staring at Kala.

Then all at once Naftali raised both arms as high as they could reach and clenched his fists as he shook them. "I forbid your running away! I forbid it!"

At the passion in her father's voice, Kala felt flattered. She looked to her mother for some matching response, but Malkeh's bearing and countenance remained impassive, her silence unyielding. Paralyzed and sorrowful, Kala gazed dumbly at her mother.

"Kala," Mikhail finally intruded, "are you certain you want to do this?"

"You have nothing to do with it!" Kala said, turning on him. "It isn't your family. It's my decision—no one else's!"

With dignity Mikhail then went about shaking the hand of each family member, thanking them for their hospitality and wishing them luck during the occupation. Kala watched the young man's leave-taking. When he came to her she thrust out her hand and said in a loud, formal voice, "Goodby! Thank you for helping us, and perhaps I shall see you on the road."

Mikhail shook Kala's hand, holding it a moment longer than necessary, and then slowly moved down the trail alongside the river toward the high road.

"Now, Kala, you can come to your senses," said Malkeh, as if rousing herself from a deep sleep. "It's ridiculous standing here in the middle of nowhere. The family must stay together—that is all we have during these times."

"No," said Kala softly, "there are more important things. Each person has to decide for herself."

"Whatever those important things are," Malkeh went on, her long chin and vast breasts pointing powerfully at her daughter, "you have to realize what you are doing. You are leaving your home. You are leaving everyone who loves you. I don't want you to go."

Witnessing her mother finally unbend, Kala threw her arms around Malkeh's neck and kissed her cheeks passionately. "I'm sorry, Mama, I have to leave." She kissed her father and each of her sisters and scrambled off down the trail toward Mikhail's retreating back. When she reached Mikhail, he turned to offer her his hand. She cast his hand away and then pushed him along rudely ahead of her. But after a few steps she grabbed his smock. "Wait!" she commanded, and turned to watch the family as they climbed up the orchard hill. She strained her eyes to see the back of Malkeh's and Naftali's heads, to make out Ruth's and Mordecai's awkward gait, and to note that for this journey to the cottage Sophie doggedly employed her crutches while Ekaterina pulled along the empty wheelchair behind.

As Kala and Mikhail watched, a sudden blaze of light sent the family's shadows leaping up the hillside ahead of them. Turning to face the river, Kala saw the buildings of Lyesk flame up. In the distance she could hear the shouts of soldiers as the men busily torched the town. The sound of laughter and broken glass floated to her ears over the sound of the river. A steam whistle echoed out from the north and a train moved slowly along the other side of the river toward the station, followed immediately by another train and yet another.

After a while the blaze no longer danced high in the air, but smoldered and flared only occasionally. Kala turned from the town to search out her family on the hillside. She saw them continue to climb. Her mother stopped and gazed in her direction. Mikhail took hold of Kala's arm and was leading her toward the high-road bridge when an unexpected sound reached their ears, carried across the river by a light breeze from the west. After a moment Kala realized she was hearing piano music, sweet sad music followed by a lively march.

"It's Chopin," identified Mikhail.

"Chopin? No, it's our piano," she corrected, incredulously. "They've taken our piano out of the house—and someone is playing. They've saved our piano!"

Listening, she calculated that the music was also reaching her family on their slow ascent through the orchard. Then she smiled at Mikhail to hear such beautiful sounds as she'd never believed possible emerging from the unwieldy instrument Malkeh had cherished for so many years.

CHAPTER THIRTEEN

KALA AND MIKHAIL TURNED AWAY FROM THE SMOLDERING town. On the banks of the river just east of the high-road bridge, they searched for the people of Lyesk. To their dismay they discovered the woods populated with strange refugees. Unfamiliar voices warned them away; large dogs barked and snapped at them; and in the darkness, from out of nowhere, the wet muzzle of a horse nibbled politely at Kala's palm. Startled, she leaped back, then clung to the creature's warm flank in relief. Then she and Mikhail continued ahead, peering into camps where already the campfires were burning low, prolonging their exploration until at last, finding themselves surrounded by a herd of lonely cows—so besieged by the cows they could barely move—they decided to give up and make their own camp on the banks of a stream.

A sharp chill lay in the air. Together they quickly built a fire. When they sat down Kala thought how lonely it felt to be out here in the dark with this strange young man. If only he were Sophie. How cozy it would be to listen to her sister whittle and practice her jokes—to be reassured by Sophie's pealing laughter.

"What's in your mind, where are you hiding?" Mikhail's voice floated over the warm fire.

Kala brought her knees up to her chin and smoothed down her skirt. Looking at her feet she half laughed, half groaned, "Oh, I feel like such a fool."

"Why?"

"Because I'm no more than a mile away and already I miss everybody."

"I'll take care of you."

"I told you before, I can take care of myself."

"Oh, I know you can! I know how able you are. And if you miss your family, that's only natural."

"Only natural?" She glared into the fire. "I suppose you're above missing your family. You're too . . . too," she sought the right word, "too world-weary."

Mikhail picked up a stone and threw it into the flames. "Sometimes I miss them." He picked up another stone, handed it to Kala, and waited while she—not meaning to imitate him—nevertheless launched it into the fire also. "My family isn't as close as yours. Or perhaps," he mused, "they're close in a different way. They're . . . they're complicated . . . more difficult . . . much more nervous, much more high-strung." He tossed his head fitfully, feigning carelessness. "Three quarters of the time my brothers don't speak to each other and my mother and father don't speak to my brothers."

"No one speaks to anyone else? Your mother and father, even your brothers don't speak? What kind of family is that? That isn't a family!"

"It is a family, believe me . . . particularly since everyone," he added ruefully, "always speaks to me."

She turned and took in his handsome profile, the kind and gentle softness of his eyes, the receptive curve of his lips. No wonder, she thought, they talked to him. Under normal circumstances she would want to talk to him too. "And why are you the only one they talk to?"

Mikhail shrugged. "Because I'm by far the youngest. Because," he proposed, "I have the least amount of talent." For a moment he studied the ground. He paused and then suggested, "Because they just like having me around—perhaps I don't come back at them with too sharp and witty a tongue, like their tongues, or with too prickly a disposition. The point is, I don't mind their affection—I rather like it and so quite naturally I'm affectionate in return. On top of that they're every one of them leaders and they realize that by temperament I'm a follower. So they're always saying, all five —my father, my mother, all of my brothers—'Misha darling, come here, come there, do this, do that.' "

"But you're also a leader," Kala suggested out of the realization that even if she did not want him to take care of her, she wished he would show himself more than simply a dreamer, as her father had charged. "For example, at the relief station . . ."

But he had begun to talk about his family and seemed unwilling to stop. "My mother is extremely clever. Her name is Eva. One day you'll meet her. Unfortunately, she's a victim of her class and so she spends all her time collecting art and organizing musicals and refurnishing . . . she'll travel the corners of the world just to locate certain painted chests or chairs. And yet she's clever—and has nothing to do. Every other year she refurnishes the townhouse—that's where she mainly lives—and in between she tries to change the house on our country estate—that's where my father spends most of his time. He comes into town on the weekend."

Kala gaped at him. She knew no one who lived under such circumstances—certainly not anyone who was a Jew. "So you have lots of servants . . . peasants?"

He lowered his head in shame but almost instantly raised it again, his eyes dazzling her with the brilliance of their earnestness. "My family has them, not I. The peasants are my friends. They understand my friendship." He paused, a troubled frown passing over his face. "At least some of them do. They know I can hardly wait for the system to fall, to become transformed, so they can take their place as equals to my family—not only with my family but with everyone else." He sighed. "Of course some of them laugh when I talk to them about the future. They make fun of my politics—they think I'm just young and foolish. Oh, Kala," he seized her hand, "one day I'll take you back with me to Vilna and show you everything."

"And your brothers?" asked Kala, allowing her hand to remain within his. "What do they do?"

"The eldest helps my father with his city affairs—with the apartment buildings, with his bank associations, with his investments. The second is a mathematician and he teaches in Warsaw. His name is Andrei and he wears thick glasses. The third is a doctor and he also lives in Vilna—he has eight children already, just imagine. He's a very good doctor though he suffers from migraines and can do nothing to help himself. He collects foreign art too—seriously, not like my mother." He fell silent. Despite his jaunty air Kala imagined that this tale about his family—even with so slight an amount of criticism—troubled him, for he broke off abruptly and said, "Let's go to sleep. We'll look for the others in the morning."

Gently Kala removed her hand from his and stood up. As they spread out their blankets, she averted her gaze. "Come to sleep, Kala," he whispered. The girl remained standing, bewildered that she had set off from home without considering the possibility of such moments. She'd had enough experience, she berated herself, to know better. She and Pyotr Fomich, Luka's nephew, had marched off into the fields and in the haystacks had examined parts of each other's bodies and embraced. They had stopped just short of making love. But tonight was different from the casual adventures with Pyotr. Having left home, perhaps forever—alone in the forest with this young stranger, she understood the seriousness of even one caress. She kept on standing, unable to think of anything else to do, while her feet grew heavy as if they were filling up with sand. After awhile, hesitatingly she kneeled; she settled and arranged herself a short distance away from Mikhail. She held her breath and she waited. Time passed; she heard the forest moaning and the stream lapping slightly; she heard Mikhail's even breathing and small animals in the brush; she opened her eyes and even believed she heard the stars. But nothing happened. With some difficulty she concluded Mikhail had no plans to touch her. The relief she then felt was mixed with both gratitude and disappointment. Sitting up, she leaned on one elbow. In the dark she listened with intent interest to this creature breathing quietly and deeply by her side. She reached out and touched the back of his head—carefully, so as not to wake him up. She reflected that tomorrow, when she located her townspeople, it would look bad enough to join them without her family, let alone to appear with this odd and decorative young man from Vilna.

The next morning the couple set off in search of the refugees of Lyesk, whom they found almost immediately—camped on the very bank of the river to the east of the bridge where, the day before, Police Captain Varsonevsky had instructed them to gather. Not a step further had they proceeded nor did they show any sign of intending to depart.

"Here's Kala with that same young man," Patch greeted them.

Flustered by Patch's announcement, Kala placed herself on the opposite side of the gathering crowd and said in a loud voice, "Shouldn't we be getting ready to leave?"

"Look who's here! Look who's here!" Stepan and Natasha, Luka's grandchildren, came speeding toward her. "Look who's here, look who's here!" the twins noisily repeated, claiming Kala for their own by kissing her, yanking her hair, and entwining their limbs about her. "Is Sophie coming too? Is Ekaterina? Where's your wagon?"

"I'm all alone," said Kala firmly, daring anyone, including Mikhail, to state differently.

Just then Luka approached. He frowned as he took note of her pack. "Does your mother know you have this plan?"

"Yes. Of course."

"And she allowed it?"

"More or less," Kala replied.

Luka fixed his penetrating eyes on her. "The people of Little Lyesk—we are White Russian peasants—we have no claim on the Germans. But for you, Kala, for your people, you'll be better off if you don't come with us—if you go back to the orchard."

"I've made my decision and I want to travel with your family, if you'll allow that. You know I'm a good worker— and I'll fix watches, too, along the way."

"It won't be like staying home," Luka said. For some moments he appeared to be thinking very hard. At last he cuffed her affectionately on the head. "You are always welcome in our family." He walked away, rolling slightly on his huge thick bowed legs.

"So many are still missing," Matryona said, and Sarah Finkel added for no reason, "We're waiting for others, too."

"I don't know which others you mean," stammered Kala.

"Where are Sir Leslie and Mishka?" demanded Stepan and Natasha. "Will you let us ride on their backs?"

"My own family," Kala addressed her fellow townsmen rather than the twins, ". . . they told me to tell you they're very, very sorry." She shook her head back and forth. "Ruth's condition . . . Sophie . . ."

But already the Lyeskers had turned away to spare her embarrassment. Only Mikhail remained to hear her glum attempts to confess to the ground. "You don't have to apologize for your family." He patted her back. "No one expected them to leave. Quite the contrary—everyone's surprised that you've chosen to go along."

"It's the most natural thing in the world for me. I was born in Lyesk; these are my countrymen." She wheeled about and raced to place herself in the midst of the throng of Lyeskers.

To her surprise she saw that the mood of the camp was

almost festive, as if a holiday were taking place. Across the river, the cottages, the fields, the shops, the buildings that had consumed the Lyeskers' days now rose in thin trails of smoke that wound into the heights of a summer morning— leaving little for anyone to do except picnic, chatter, play with the children, or examine the road. Occasionally a few villagers cast glances across the water as if trying to identify or discern in the smoke their own crops and cottages. "Shouldn't we be getting ready to leave?" she asked them; and when they did not respond she clasped the twins' hands and went in search of Luka's wagons.

She found Luka's wife, Anya, alone at the Fomich camp, reorganizing supplies for the journey. Without an instant's hesitation Anya took the young woman's pack and stowed it in Luka's lead wagon.

"When are we scheduled to leave?" Kala asked her.

Anya smiled vaguely and shrugged as if it didn't really matter.

"But the Germans must be near," Kala urged.

When Anya merely nodded politely, Kala left her to search out someone of authority. Almost immediately she came face to face with Mikhail, who complained, "I've been warning your townspeople they must hurry and start out to escape the Germans. But all they do is smile."

"You haven't tried hard enough." Kala said, after which, somewhat aimlessly, the two of them followed one another through the camp. Finally they came upon a crowd of Lyeskers standing by the high road.

Mikhail addressed them formally: "Are you all ready to go? We should start out in a few minutes."

The people nodded gratefully, but then turned back to the road where extraordinary sights rewarded their attention.

"All of Russia is on the move," marveled Matryona, capturing Kala's arm. "For years it was only our people who suffered from famine and were pushed off the land and had to say goodby and head for Siberia. Now everyone's caught the same disease. Look," she pointed, "when have we ever witnessed a parade such as this?—we can see right into the lives of the whole world!"

The other Lyeskers, even if somewhat less triumphantly, joined the midwife to review for Kala this roadside spectacle where each wagon on the gravel carried the most precious earthly possessions of its owner. Pleased to be welcomed by her countrymen, Kala gazed avidly at the sights pointed out to her. Kitchen utensils, farming implements, tables, chairs, chests, icons wheeled slowly by in majestic view. From each side of one small two-wheeled wagon appeared the ends of an ancient sewing machine; a scrawny pony was barely able to pull the load along. A second wagon contained nothing but a metal roof, a useless item for such a journey, but the Lyeskers conjectured its owners had no doubt sacrificed many years of labor to cover their simple cottage with such noble material.

"Why should anyone want to take along a metal roof?" questioned Luka's wife Anya in a tone of wonder. She had followed Kala and Mikhail to the edge of the high road.

"They didn't want to leave it," suggested Sarah Finkel. "Of course, that's my own opinion. Wouldn't you agree, Kala?"

"They didn't want to leave it," Kala echoed, nervous because the Lyeskers were wasting too much time. She glanced around and observed Mikhail Kossoff approach Father Boris, whose carriage stood nearest the bridge. She watched the young man gesture and shake his head, evidently importuning Father Boris to lead his townspeople off.

"And what kind of chairs are those, Kala?" clucked Patch. He indicated a wagon on top of which stood two handsome upholstered armchairs, upright as if its occupants remained in intimate conversation as they traveled. The owners of the chairs, a husband and wife, each carrying a stick, walked on either side of a fine pair of horses which they urged on, all the while bickering with one another over the animals' rumps and every so often gazing up with obvious pride to make sure the chairs remained secure.

"They want everyone to see those chairs," commented Anya.

"And why not?" nodded Matryona. "I would like to sit on a chair like that one day."

"Even with four chairs, you'd still overlap," said Patch.

"Look!" said Matryona as the Lyeskers heard the sound of voices speaking Polish and discerned the roof of a bathhouse and then made out the rest of a ramshackle structure mounted on wheels and pulled by a pair of emaciated horses. The driver, a pale grim man, stood rigidly upright as he drove. Through the open door of the bathhouse a group of children, sitting in a circle on wooden benches, sang in Polish as if they were at school. Behind the curious vehicle marched a parade of eight Polish women dressed in black, each carrying a portrait of the Virgin Mother draped in dark ribbons, decorated with branches of evergreen and garlands of leaves and withered flowers. As the women passed, Kala, Matryona, and Sarah Finkel greeted them, but the women's heads did not turn; their sunken eyes did not blink. Their voices took up the children's song, a hymn in praise of God. The expression on all eight faces remained frozen, the eyes bright and ecstatic. Matryona and Sarah Finkel spat over their left shoulders and rapped their knuckles on the side of a cart. Kala did the same. It struck her that the mournful procession was a portent and that she would not be able to erase its painful frozen stateliness from her mind.

Mikhail was still appealing to Father Boris when she made her way to his carriage and intruded, saying, "Father Boris, we have to leave!"

"Yes, yes, soon perhaps," answered the priest. He appeared glad for a reason to escape Mikhail. He turned and began to fuss with the back of his carriage to which he had attached an ingenious platform. On the platform stood a dozen wooden planters lashed together. Out of each planter grew slips of fruit trees, which the priest now busily tended. "We have to make certain that wherever we go we'll be prepared to start orchards. We'll want pear trees, apple trees . . ." He was interrupted by one of Luka's grandsons, who ran up calling, "Father Boris, here comes the captain of the police over the bridge. He wants to see you. Here comes Semyon Varsonevsky."

"Ah! Semyon Varsonevsky!" exclaimed Father Boris as the official police carriage came lumbering over the high-road bridge. The townspeople and the villagers crowded around to greet the Lyesk police captain.

To everyone's surprise, Semyon Varsonevsky, in full uniform, sat on the driver's box. Crammed inside, among a jumble of household goods—lamps and chairs, chests, mops and pails—could be seen the pale terrified faces of the Captain's sister with whom he lived and her two teen-aged daughters, staring out.

Surrounding the carriage, the Lyeskers shouted up to Semyon Varsonevsky: "Where have you been?"

"Is everything burned?"

"Where are the Shulevites? the Pyotr Ivanovichs? Irina Ivanovna and her uncle? Iosif and Tatiana?"

"Why isn't everyone here with us?"

"Did you save your own house?"

"Where is your driver?"

Stony-faced, the police captain answered not a single question.

"And Orchard Lane?" inquired Father Boris. "Have any of the trees been spared?"

Semyon Varsonevsky reached into his tunic and brought forth a long brown envelope. "Here are the papers for the city of Lyesk, Father." Puzzled and reluctant, the priest took the envelope. The Captain continued: "Proceed eastward and obey officials as you go. When they put you on the train you will learn your destination."

"At which station?"

"They'll tell you which station. Just obey the officials and proceed ahead."

"What about our flocks, our cattle?"

"Everything will go on the train to your new home," said Semyon Varsonevsky. "Everything—all of you—animals and goods. God be with you."

"But Semyon Varsonevsky," said Father Boris, climbing up one of the steps to the driver's box, "won't you be with us?" He tried to hand back the brown envelope.

"I have my orders," said the Captan mysteriously, pressing his whip on the chest of the priest to force him off the steps.

"Bless you, Semyon Varsonevsky." The priest made the sign of the cross as the carriage jerked forward. Then while the Captain swung the vehicle back on the high road, the crowd, angry at his desertion, sang out its jeering version of a blessing. The Captain did not look back. He whipped his horses ahead, ringing his official bell. The carriage careened along the verge as if it were being pursued, and just before it disappeared the pale white hands of the Captain's sister and her daughters fluttered their farewells out of the windows.

Shamefaced and as though resigned, Father Boris opened the envelope and showed its contents to Kala and Mikhail, who stood close to him. The meagerness of its contents alarmed Kala. There was little to guide anyone: simply an official military order commanding the evacuation of the town of Lyesk; the appointment of an official representative of the emigrants of Lyesk—the name had not been filled in; and a number of blank certificates of emigration entitling the bearer and family to food, care, and available transport.

"And the official?" the priest asked Mikhail.

"It appears that you are the official," replied the young man. "With most of the towns that have come through, only the priest has remained."

"Well, there you have it," said Father Boris to the assembled company. "Yes, we all must leave Lyesk." He sighed and looked up into the sky. "There will be no reprieve."

"And no other people to join us?" pursued Kala, bitterly.

"What do you mean?" asked the priest.

"Where, for example is Stepan Ilyich Rozumov? Where is Ivan Sergeyevich Dovrynin?"

"Ahhh," murmured the priest, smiling, a bit embarrassed.

"They've all escaped like the captain of police," Kala cried out. "And why shouldn't they save their skin? When you think about it, who said we needed them? Who could need Avrom Lavin with his broken watch, or the stableman Dovitsky or Naomi or our rabbis . . . Let them go where they like, or stay, all of them."

Father Boris gazed off noncommittally. "Ah, well," he offered in a kindly manner, and then was silent. But Matryona spoke up, "Little darling, a good number of your people are here. Sarah Finkel you've seen, one of the first to arrive. And Rivkah the bath attendant is over there, and so is Shmuel the Holy One and Nachman the rag collector. You won't be lonely. A good many of your people are coming with us. Even Patch has joined the crowd, though in his case it's for no other reason than that he longs to plague us."

At these words, Mikhail began to exhort the crowd. "The wealthy and the powerful have saved themselves; they've escaped in comfort or are hiding to join the Germans. The poor have been betrayed. They've been shunted from their communities, they've borne the brunt of this imperialist capitalist war." He went on for some time.

The townspeople shifted about restlessly. Kala wished Mikhail would not repeat himself so many times or use such unfamiliar big words, for she judged he spoke the truth, but had failed to convince her friends. The eyes of the Lyeskers glazed over and the crowd drifted away, leaving only Kala. Reluctantly Mikhail stopped speaking.

"Oh, what a fool I was," Kala said, "to have thought everyone would leave Lyesk together—that Rozumov, Dovrynin, and the whole crowd from the bakery would join the rest. But at least my family—at least my mother and father—they should have acted differently."

"There's nothing wrong with your parents or your sisters. You mustn't blame them personally. In fact, by deserting the poor they are simply playing out their role in history—hastening the revolution. They are doing their part for the future. You mustn't be angry at them. They are fine people."

"Fine people?"

"Generous people, hospitable people, kind people."

Kala stared at the ground.

CHAPTER FOURTEEN

T HE NEXT MORNING THE PEOPLE OF LYESK ENTERED THE
parade of refugees plodding eastward toward great Russia. They composed a contingent of roughly four hundred
peasants and poor townsfolk accompanied by horses, cows,
sheep, pigs, chickens, geese, and dogs. Father Boris, with
Mikhail at his side, led the column, Kala and the Fomich
family commanded the rear, and in between rolled some
forty wheeled vehicles, ranging from wheelbarrows to hay
wagons. Once underway, the twins Stepan and Natasha
perched inside one of their grandfather's wagons and chatted
with Kala, who walked alongside. As the familiar fields and
the river disappeared from view, all three craned their heads
for one last sight. Then Kala said, "The trip has begun and
I am one of you."

And, in fact, the journey started out much more comfortably than she had imagined. Though her own resentment
toward the officials and the wealthy Russians who had fled

Lyesk on their own, or toward those Jews and the town's few Poles and Lithuanians who had hidden out to await the Germans had not diminished, she soon discovered that the peasants and the poor townsfolk felt in no way slighted by the absence of the rich and the powerful from their midst. Now there was no one to issue orders, no one to make demands. On the first night a mood almost of gaiety spread throughout the camp. While fires blazed through the forest, while samovars boiled, while the smell of roasting food joined with the sweet scent of burning pine, children in groups of twos and threes rushed through the darkness, calling out to their relatives and friends, and Mikhail Kossoff paid a formal visit to the Fomich campsite—bowing to each member of Luka's family and shaking hands.

In the morning the Lyeskers set off again, this time leaving the cool forests watered by the Lyesk River and climbing steadily to a wide, dry plain that led to the great road between Warsaw and Moscow. Ahead, thousands clogged the way. In the distance, on either side of the road, the rooftops of small villages could be seen. Nearer the road, the unending migration had ravaged the trampled ground. Not a blade of any plant stood growing, not a fence post or sapling remained. All had been carted away or rooted up to be eaten or burned as fuel.

Sighing with boredom at the monotony of the landscape through which they passed, Stepan and Natasha trudged along on either side of Kala. In their excitement to be off that morning they had awakened earlier than necessary; they had rushed about and run in circles, helping Kala tend the Fomich herd; and now they asked her wearily, "Are we almost there? How much longer? When can we get on the train? Look how ugly it is here."

Luka, passing by, said, "No animal does as much harm when he strays in search of food as man."

"Soon we'll be in Baranovits," said Kala.

"And in Baranovits we'll board the train," said Natasha, just to make sure.

"Yes," Kala said.

"And where will we go after the train?" Stepan asked.

"We'll go . . ." Kala began and then stopped—for she had no idea how to answer. The evening before, while the campfire burned down, she had tried to bring up the question of resettlement with Luka and Anya. Luka had rebuked her. When she'd persisted, he'd stopped her, saying abruptly, "It's not up to us. That's for the authorities to decide." Taken aback, Kala had then sought out Rivkah, Patch, and Matryona who shared a wagon borrowed from Luka. Yet not a single one of them appeared inclined to address the problem—not even Patch, who normally enjoyed any kind of speculation. Finally Matryona had echoed Luka, declaring they must leave all such worries to Father Boris and to the government that had given them instructions and sent them on the road.

"We don't yet know our exact destination," Kala now confessed to the twins. "We don't know exactly."

"But I know!" Natasha said. "We're going to our new Lyesk." She enunciated every syllable with an air of great certainty.

"A new Lyesk?" Kala laughed, marveling that the little girl had the same idea as she. "What will it be like?"

"What it will be like," Natasha explained, "is the old Lyesk—only better. You'll recognize it when we get there because it will have orchards and a river and a railroad station. It will have cottages and fields and a big church." Her voice was matter-of-fact, yet her cheeks puffed out with pride.

Stepan, who had been listening to his sister with a doubtful expression on his face, now inquired, "Will it have a bakery?"

"Oh, yes," Natasha assured him. "A very good bakery. Like Malkeh's—only better. And Kala will be the baker."

"And what wonderful cakes I'll bake," Kala beamed, forgetting her unfortunate past record. "Special cakes for you . . . plum cakes, almond cakes, raisin cakes . . ."

And she went on in this fashion until, replete with the promise of so many cakes, Stepan and Natasha grew drowsy, climbed into the wagon, and dozed. An hour or so later they rejoined Kala on the ground. As they marched along, little by little the three of them distinguished a buzzing drone that issued from the west behind the caravan. Kala cast a glance down the road but could identify nothing except other refugees whose heads were also turning in the direction of the odd sound. Far back along the column she detected one person after another pointing into the air and waving. Then Stepan looked up and exclaimed, "An airplane! How terrific! A real airplane!"

"It's going to our new Lyesk," Natasha blithely sang out.

Above them a lone glistening airplane followed the line of the high road with care, as if it could no more stray to one side than to the other. Presently the plane waggled its wings, and at this signal of friendliness and good will Kala and the twins waved and called to it, pleased by the antic object cavorting overhead.

"Look—do you see the two men in it?" Stepan cried. "You can just make out their heads. Oh how terrific! I've never seen an airplane before. How terrific to fly in the air!"

"Still, I wouldn't want to," Natasha declared. "I just like to look at it and to wave at it."

"I might want to. But maybe not. How strange to be so separated from the earth," Kala said, her mouth bunched to one side while she pondered whether it made sense for human beings to venture into the bright sunlight inside so frail an object—an object held together with nothing but wires and struts and with only a tiny pair of wheels to cushion its return to earth. Then she noticed a black cross painted upon the tail of the plane and two more on the undersides of the wings. "Germans!" she said.

A minute later the air throbbed with a thunderous noise. The refugees continued to advance, peering ahead apprehensively. Then in the east a black cloud lifted up from the roadway. Once more Kala and the children heard the buzzing of the airplane, its drone rather faint, and then the column stopped short as if it had met an obstacle. The buzzing grew louder, drowned by an explosive sound not far away.

A wild movement of people and animals came rippling down the high road from ahead. "Bombs!" the word rose above the din.

"Clear the roadway!"

People, horses, wagons, cows began to move in every direction. A handful of refugees tried to turn their teams around; others, abandoning their horses, flung themselves into the ditch, where they were run over by horses and wagons that toppled off the road. Still others set off across the fields full tilt. Shouts of terror filled the air, along with the sound of crunching wheels as wagons collided. Cattle lowed, dogs barked, horses whinnied in shrill distress. The droning buzz of the airplane grew louder, and at the next explosion Kala, standing in the roadside ditch, found herself holding onto the harness of one of Luka's teams of horses, trying to calm the animals to keep them from overturning the wagon or kicking it to pieces in their terror. She glanced around for the twins and when she realized they were still at her side, clinging to her dress, she looked around for Mikhail and did not see him.

The bomb had exploded no more than a hundred yards away, missing the road. In the fields, two wagons lay on their sides next to the crater. With her heart pounding, Kala ran toward the screams of the wounded and discovered the first victim, an elderly peasant from the Potocki estate. His wife, children, and grandchildren surrounded him, splattered with his blood and gazing in amazement at his body pierced by shrapnel. When she understood the man was dead she raced on to the two overturned wagons. Under the sideboard of the first, a three-year-old girl lay crushed. The child's mother sat on the ground next to her, wailing and throwing dirt on her own head. Half in the crater and half out, a bay mare, her eyes rolled back, bled from a deep gash in her belly while a peasant with a long-handled knife slit the creature's throat. Bright blood, spurting out of the belly and throat, splashed into the smoking hole in the ground while dazed men,

women, and children sat on the ground near the crater, gazing in. Some were wounded, others merely shocked. For a
moment Kala paused, hypnotized by the expression of terror
on the face of the mare, still alive as her blood spewed out of
throat and belly. It was a horse she knew well. In Lyesk she
had regularly stopped in the fields to stroke her forehead and
to offer her sugar and other tidbits she kept in her pockets for
the animals she favored. Her stomach wrenched; an old man
had died, an innocent baby, and now this nice horse. She
turned her attention to the human beings around the dying
animal.

Quickly she ripped strips of material from the wagon cov-
erings. She tied tourniquets, fashioned bandages, and prepared splints. At one moment when she needed help with a
very bad thigh wound she called out. Someone took hold of
the tourniquet so that she could staunch the bleeding with
more rags. Looking up she gazed into the blue eyes of
Mikhail, who helped her tie off the wound. Glancing around,
she realized that everyone was helping—that all the people of
Lyesk were joining together to care for the wounded.

By the time the chaos had been sorted out the sun began
to set. Of the Lyesk contingent, two had died—the old man
and the infant—five had been seriously injured, and ten had
received superficial wounds. Moreover, the bombs had
stampeded the herds and a number of cows had fallen into a
gully, injuring themselves so that they had to be destroyed.
In their shock, the people of Lyesk pulled their wagons together at the very edge of the road and made camp for the
night.

Wanting to be alone—to try to make some sense out of
what had happened—Kala walked out across the ravaged
fields. She stopped and gazed to the west where, at the edge of
the horizon, the treetops blazed in the setting sun. Mikhail
appeared out of the low bracken and fell in step with her.

"Why did it happen? It makes one realize how fragile, how
delicate life is; and how tragic to waste it. Kala, I want to

[161]

travel with you. I'm lonely without you—particularly up there at the head of the column with only Father Boris to talk to."

"You want to travel with the Fomiches?" she asked.

"No, not with them," he said impatiently. "I'm not in love with the Fomiches. In our own wagon. We can get hold of a wagon now."

"You're making a joke. You're not serious."

"I'm utterly serious."

Kala folded her arms across her chest like her mother. "Why, that would offend everyone," she said.

Undaunted, he went on, "And if it offends people, it will do them good. It will help them understand that the world is changing and that they too must change or else be destroyed."

"Mikhail, why must you always make speeches?"

"And if you and I . . . as revolutionaries . . . intend to realize ourselves . . ."

"Mikhail," she objected, "I never said anything about being a revolutionary. And certainly not in that manner. Certainly not by sharing a wagon."

"I see," he said, a little bitterly. His shoulders sagged and the vitality appeared to seep out of him. "I understand," his head nodded up and down, as though by persevering it might bounce away all his disappointment. "I understand very well and if I can't change your mind we are still close friends and I will tell you something I would have much preferred to tell you in our wagon."

"What is that?"

"That I'm a coward."

"Mikhail!" she exclaimed, remembering he had made a similar confession once before—in the tree house, with the bomb between them. She recalled wanting to comfort and reassure him, but now she felt assaulted by his admission. Grimacing, she demanded, "Why do you tell me that?"

"So that you'll know . . . that when the German airplane bombed us, I ran into the fields and I hid."

"But Mikhail, everyone tries to protect himself. The

bombs had hardly landed before you were there—helping with the wounded. That's the only courage that's necessary."

"Oh I was there afterward, of course. But at the crucial moment when I could have been protecting you or someone else, I was running into the fields."

She shrugged and quickened her step. It disturbed her that he worried about the exact amount of courage he lacked or possessed—like someone who lived on a different planet. She wished he acted a little more like other people. Ordinary people like Luka and his family, she reflected, did not question trying to save themselves, nor did they find it necessary to make a special effort to save others. "Saving your life has nothing to do with cowardice."

"That's your opinion," he said as they headed back toward camp. "Still, you're right. My fears aren't very important when you think about the deaths."

In the morning—with Mikhail and Father Boris leading the column—the diminished Lyesk caravan entered the Warsaw-Moscow highway. Here they joined an even thicker flood of refugees, police, soldiers, enemy captives, road menders, and cattle that choked the road. At intervals all such travelers were swept to the side by a deafening rumble and honking horns as military trucks and motorcycles charged through toward the front. At one such instant Kala found herself thrown to the verge of the road, with Sarah Finkel landing on her lap. "Baranovits used to be so close," said Sarah Finkel as she dragged herself upright. "How much longer before we get there?"

"How much longer before the train?" the twins repeated again, and, just as before, Kala replied, "It's a short trip. Only a few days. Not much longer."

But hour by hour the pace of the column slowed, sometimes stopping altogether as the refugees bunched up at each other's heels. The dust of the march, suspended overhead, choked the throats and noses of the refugees. Kala, checking on the depleted herds, remarked to Luka, "What's worst of all is the way the animals suffer. The cows are crazy with

[163]

thirst. Look how they wander off, searching for water." And, unhappily, she ran up and down among the Lyeskers, raising her voice and trying to joke, "In a day or so we'll be strolling around Baranovits with a fish market like you've never seen before. Just in a day, maybe two days. I've been to Baranovits with my sisters," she tried to boast, "and in all your life you've never seen such an extraordinary fish market—salmon, perch, cod, pike, smoked whitefish."

"But we don't actually want fish," her companions remarked. "We first want water." And they licked their dry, cracked lips and talked of the wells of Baranovits, where they would fill their bottles, drink at length, and water their herds before mounting the train.

"A few more days," Kala promised, hugging the twins before she darted from one edge of the road to the other, trying to glimpse ahead. "It's a short trip. It will soon be over. A few more days . . . and then a train ride from Baranovits into the very center of Russia, where we'll build our new home."

But at the outskirts of Baranovits she found the entrance to the main street blocked by a barricade of wagons manned by armed soldiers who brandished their weapons, shunting the parade of homeless people south along several narrow country tracks. A swelling sound of voices, monotonous and plaintive, moved down the ranks of the Lyesk people. "The trains! The trains!"

"Further on," replied the soldiers.

"The trains," murmured the refugees.

"Further on," repeated the soldiers, their long, dark shadows reaching out along the ground. "To the east, to Bobruisk, to Rogachev and Roslavl!"

Obediently the refugees turned away from the city. The twins demanded, "Where is our train?"

Appalled that the entrance of Baranovits had been blocked, Kala called, "Luka, you have to talk to the soldiers." When he did not respond, she pleaded, "You are the elder."

"Here I'm nothing to them," Luka said.

"You are our elder."

"This is not my place."

Frustrated and angry, Kala stepped to the middle of the road, stared at the guardians of the city and slowly began to walk toward the soldiers, intending to plead that her fellow travelers be allowed to replenish their supplies of water, to argue that Bobruisk was too many miles to the east, to implore that the soldiers allow the people access to the city and to the trains. She had barely gone ten paces when Mikhail put himself in her way.

"It won't do any good," he said. "I've already talked with the soldiers. They're in a nasty mood, preparing for the Germans who are expected within hours. There's nothing to do but go on."

"At least I can try."

But he barred her way again, this time taking her arm and gently forcing her back toward the column of refugees. "There's no way we can board in Baranovits. The trains here are being used for troops. We have to go on to Bobruisk."

"If you can talk to the soldiers . . ."

"They're in an awful mood, you don't want to get near them. It's a bit easier for me because I have a military pass— I'm part of the relief forces."

"With your pass," she said somewhat vindictively, "you could enter Baranovits, couldn't you?"

"I imagine I could."

"And you would be allowed to get on a train?"

"Yes, I suppose."

"Then why don't you?" She looked at him and observed how lined and exhausted his face appeared: he had never recovered from the weeks of toil at the relief station. "Why don't you?" she repeated less belligerently.

"Because I don't want to—because I'd rather be with you and the people of Lyesk. We're going on to Bobruisk."

"Do you think we'll make it?"

Mikhail surveyed the Lyesk caravan. "Our people are in decent shape. We can find water enough for our use at the bottom of wells in the country past Baranovits. And if we're careful to boil the water—and if the war doesn't catch up—we ought to get to Bobruisk and onto the trains in about three weeks."

"Three weeks," she mused, noting that though Mikhail's homespun peasant blouse and trousers were beginning to look ragged, the red sash belt and the red bandana which he alone wore still gave his costume a jaunty pride. Chastened by his desire to remain with the Lyesk caravan and by the earnestness of his declaration to her, she admitted that his presence brightened things up. She moved toward him so that their sides touched. She had the sense of having fastened onto his body. When he put his arm about her waist she said, "Then we'll go on to Bobruisk."

CHAPTER FIFTEEN

DAY AFTER DAY THE JOURNEY DRAGGED ON. ALTHOUGH the intense heat abated, the autumn proved to be unnaturally warm, the breezes balmy. The normal rains held off. The green of the birch leaves darkened, coated with gray dust; there was no sign of a change of color to mark the season. The moment Kala began to walk each morning, past and future disappeared, her mind numbed by the crunch of gravel under her feet, the incessant rumbling of the wagons, the choking dust and the boredom. Every day repeated the day before.

Then one evening the warm breeze brought the smell of new forests—an unfamiliar smell of a foreign land. After supper she wandered off into the woods, further and further from camp. She inhaled the soft air, seized a small sapling with her right hand and spun rapidly round and round it, wanting to feel dizzy for a moment, free from cares. Behind her she heard footsteps and then Mikhail's voice, "Kala!"

When she heard her name, she realized she had expected

him to follow her all the time. Without turning, she stopped and waited. In a moment he reached her, cupped her face in both his hands, bent over and kissed her. She returned his kiss. Then side by side the young couple wandered on through the strange forest, parting to go around a great pine, following one another single file through a narrow gully and up a winding path until they came upon a clearing, a meadow in the midst of the woods. When Mikhail came up to her, he circled her waist with his arm. He said, "Kala, I love you."

"I love you very much, Mikhail," she answered, surprised to hear herself utter such words. Her arms twined about the young man's body and soon she felt as if she were floating—either in a stream such as the one that gurgled nearby—or else in the warm breeze that stirred the branches overhead. After a few minutes he released her and drew back.

"We'd better stop," he said.

"Stop?" she challenged. "Why should we stop?"

He took a breath and seemed to agree he had come up with a foolish remark for he went right back to her, pressing her body against his—the pair of them kissing, nibbling, tasting. With arms and legs entwined they enfolded and bound one to the other until Kala had the sense that, standing in the middle of the meadow fully clothed, she and Mikhail had fused into a single two-headed wonderful animal to whose powerful appetites she abandoned herself. They ran, danced, leaped; yet remarkably they stood on one spot. At last it was she who said in a choked voice, "We have to stop."

"Yes," breathed Mikhail, "we have to stop." But already they were crumbling to the soft couch of grass, where they touched the parts of one another's bodies and groaned and sang out. Then Kala forgot everything except for the flesh that hardened and entered into her. The pain surprised her when it arrived, gathering within it all her doubts and fears but then disappearing in a wave of joy and pleasure that washed over her, flooding her insides and seeming to mold her body and spirit to Mikhail's.

Amidst their jumbled clothing they lay together, naked, in the middle of the forest meadow with the dark trees towering over them. Mikhail fell asleep, rolling slightly away from her. Wakeful, Kala wished she could tell Sophie she had come to care for the young man, that they had embraced, and the lovemaking had worked—the parts had actually fit. Kala raised herself up and, in celebration, pranced about a nearby tree.

When she lay down again she carefully placed herself so that her side touched Mikhail's. She fell asleep and woke once in the night, her body released and peaceful. In the early morning he was awake before her and he took her in his arms. The dawn sky gleamed, milky and rosy. They searched out the stream and washed. Overhead the birch leaves trembled slightly in the early morning breeze. Dark pines rose here and there. They smiled at one another—as if in wonder, in utter amazement—while the rays of the morning sun exploded around them. But once they had dressed and straightened their cloths—had tied their laces, fastened their buttons, smoothed their garments, and finished readying themselves to face the world, a disheartening awkwardness descended on them and each found it impossible to meet the other's gaze. Neither could think of a single thing to say.

"We ought to talk." Mikhail forced his voice so that it sounded deeper than normal.

Kala shrugged. "What is there to talk about?" she asked matter-of-factly, annoyed that the universe had suddenly grown so different from the one in which she'd lain down with Mikhail.

"But after last night . . . this morning," he stammered, "even more than before, we are together . . . we are pledged."

Kala gazed at him. Cross-legged on the earth he looked at ease and as graceful as if he were seated in an armchair. Frowning, she turned away, stared at the ground, and for the first time contemplated the fact she had welcomed this man's body into hers without the ceremony of marriage. "How are we pledged?" she spoke slowly.

His back stiffened slightly, his ruddy cheeks flushed with embarrassment at her question. "Well, at least I am pledged to you."

Regretting her words, she reached out and took up his hand. "The problem is, Mikhail, what we did together . . ." she sighed, "it's not official. We aren't married."

Abruptly he withdrew his hand from her grasp and stood up. His voice became stern and formal with just a trace of sarcasm in it. "I'm willing to marry you if you think it's necessary."

"I didn't say that," she threw back quickly. "You don't have to marry me. I don't even know that I ever want to be married."

"Well, marriage," he offered weakly, "it's just a convention."

"I don't know that I ever want to be tied to anyone. What I want . . ." her lips turned down in an expression of self-deprecation and wistfulness, "at least right now, I want our people to survive . . . to stay together and reach the new Lyesk Natasha talks about."

The young man hung his head and picked at the earth. "Tell me, Kala, when the fate of your townspeople is decided, what will you do? Will you stay with them?"

"Of course. That's why I'm here."

"But when they've found a place . . . when they're settled," he went on, still digging at the earth, flinging little handfuls this way and that, "I want you to consider leaving them. I want you to come with me. I know that's asking a lot but it's time for the revolution. We're losing the war, the country is falling apart. The Party will need us all."

"Your party doesn't need me . . . because I'm not a member of your party."

"You could be easily," he urged. "And you ought to be."

She reached down, picked up a handful of pine needles and flung the needles like a spray over Mikhail's head. She grinned. Then she said, "I pledge myself to some kind of justice, if not to your party."

All the next day—still startled by the memory of their love-making, inflamed and excited—she found herself looking forward to another tryst in the woods with Mikhail. Cautiously she considered traveling with the young man instead of remaining with the Fomiches. She set the idea aside; but every fifteen minutes or so, back again it came. Then that evening, as the caravan made camp on the fields of an abandoned farmstead and the Lyeskers lined up to draw water from the well, the one-eyed Patch appeared at Kala's elbow.

"Young lady," Patch said, pulling her aside to the back of his wagon and drawing himself upright, "you are a representative of our race. The others watch us and ask, 'Is this the way Jews act?' You can't just do whatever you find pleasurable."

"How is that?" asked Kala.

Sternly Patch focused his good eye on the young woman. "Unfortunately everyone knows how friendly you are. People take advantage. Remember that you are Malkeh's and Naftali's daughter."

Kala snorted and poked her face into Patch's. "What a busybody!"

"Certain men take advantage," he persisted, his loud voice catching the attention of the people around them. "And I already heard this one stand up at your father's *shabbas* table and recite a verse—I still remember the words—'They spit black dirt on us.' For such a man to repeat words like that—with his high-flown manners and the fancy red scarf he wears around his neck—how can you trust him!"

"Of course I trust him," Kala exploded. "How dare you! Do you think you are my parents?"

"I'm a friend of the family's—no more, no less. No one else here has eaten as many Friday night suppers at your house. When I think of how much of your family's chopped liver and how much of their flanken has gone into this stomach—I want you to behave. Remember, miss, you are nothing without your family—you are nobody."

"I am myself," said Kala, "and a member of this caravan."

She looked to Luka and Anya, waiting for them to insist on her right to belong, but they avoided her appeal, busying themselves by gathering buckets for water. If they disapproved of her actions, Kala thought, instead of putting themselves at such a distance, she would have preferred that they spank her with a bridle. Abandoned, it now struck her how much less the Fomiches seemed like her family here on the road than they had in Lyesk.

From the back of a nearby wagon, Rivkah poked out her head. "If your mother only knew," Rivkah spat at the ground, "lying with such a man all night—without a wedding, without a *mikveh* bath." The bath attendant withdrew into the wagon.

Kala turned away from her accusers and walked in a daze toward the deserted farmhouse. A weight pressed down upon her. She searched out Mikhail and said, "People have already noticed we were away from camp last night."

"Really?" Mikhail's face lit up with interest. "They commented on it, did they? Well, let them talk. If we feel strongly about one another, then we ought to act on that feeling."

"But, Mikhail," she interrupted, "why do you want to displease the very people with whom you intend to make your revolution?"

"Because we have to show them that true feelings are more important than ceremonies, more important than business transactions—which, in general, is what marriage has become today."

"And what if I conceive?" The question sprang from her unawares and unnerved them both.

Gradually Mikhail composed himself. "We'll be more careful in the future. I'm certain you and I don't want our babies now. We want our babies after the revolution."

"Our babies," she repeated. The idea, so unexpected, filled her with anticipation—made her feel lightheaded. A moment later she remembered Patch and Rivkah's nasty scolding. Her mood dampened, she pursed her lips and said, "I don't care what people think, but anyway, Mikhail, it's best if we stay away from each other, at least for a while."

"You do care what they think," Mikhail contradicted her, the expression on his face both stricken and indignant. "You're embarrassed by your own feelings." Distraught, he looked around, his eye lighting on the crowd of Lyeskers at the well. "There's nothing for it," he said grimly, "but to wave to you from afar and tend to my job." He strode off toward the well, thrust himself through the Fomich family, and confronted Luka who had just hauled up a bucket of water. "Stop!" he commanded.

In his hand Luka held a tin cup which he proceeded to dip into the bucket to ladle up some water for Stepan. He ignored Mikhail.

"You don't want to endanger your own family, do you?" asked Mikhail, taking the cup from Luka and pouring the water back into the bucket. "I've told everyone before—this water is so low in the well that you must boil it."

"Your Excellency," murmured Luka, tipping his hat as he eyed the young man warily.

Mikhail's face lost all color save two minute patches of red at the cheekbones. "I'm not Your Excellency," he protested. "It's simple hygiene, medical knowledge."

"Your Excellency," Luka repeated—this time more humbly than Kala could bear. Stepping forward to save the two men from one another, Kala led Mikhail away.

She got him to a bank on the side of the road behind the wagons. Here she let go of his arm. "You told me you grew up with peasants in Vilna but your manners are so . . . so . . ." she hesitated, "so grand."

He drew himself up and gave her an injured glance. "There's nothing grand about me." Putting his finger up his nostril he rubbed vigorously to illustrate her error.

"You had a much better manner toward the people when you were at the relief station."

"At the relief station," he explained ruefully, "I was too busy to talk."

"My townspeople feel . . ."

"Kala, sometimes I get tired of your Lyesk peasants, you know." He exhaled with exasperation. "They seem so slow and so hidden. And then, of course, the peasants near Vilna like me. Yours don't seem to." He scratched his head. "Maybe it's my accent—do you think it could be as simple as that? No, it's more serious. If we stayed together," he said hopefully, "I'm certain I could learn. If you won't travel with me, then why don't I join Luka's family and travel with you? I'm as much a peasant as you are."

Kala laughed. "Oh, well, Mikhail, I don't see you becoming a peasant. Not ever. We can walk along together during the day but at night, for now, I think it's better if we remain apart . . ."

Two, three or four days later—sooner than many had expected, for they had lost track of time—the Lyeskers noticed road markers indicating the approach to the city of Bobruisk. Reaching the gravel bank of the River Berezina, they made camp across from the town and lit a great bonfire. They broke into two groups, one on either side of the fire, in order to thank God for having brought them this far together with the loss of only eight persons—four to the German bomb, three to illness, and one man who fell under his wagon wheels in a drunken stupor.

As usual, the Christians gathered around Father Boris and the Jews around Shmuel the Holy One. Suddenly the frenzied voice of Patch interrupted the service: "Stop! Stop! What month is this?"

"What month?" murmured the congregation in bewilderment. The question circulated from mouth to mouth, at last reaching across the fire to Father Boris who, after a quick calculation, sent back word that it was the middle of October.

"The middle of October," wailed Patch. "What happened to *Rosh Hashonah*?" he demanded of Shmuel the Holy One. "What happened to *Yom Kippur*? Why didn't we remember to observe?"

[174]

"Oh my God, we've lost the High Holy Days!" moaned Rivkah.

A shocked silence fell over the Jews of Lyesk. Across the fire they could hear Father Boris's nasal voice intoning the Orthodox prayers. Stricken, Shmuel the Holy One gazed around him, apologetically seeking his congregation's averted eyes. Slowly, one by one, the Jews dispersed, each to a lonely place by the slow-moving river to contemplate how serious their plight had become. Kala walked rapidly down the bank and squatted just at the verge of the water, her shoulders hunched protectively. She could not believe they had let the New Year and the Day of Atonement pass without some sign, some recognition. According to her father, lightning should have struck them all, she thought; yet here they were across the river from Bobruisk, almost intact. Only at this moment did she become aware of what a chasm had opened up between her and her past. She had to concentrate before she could summon up the image of her father's eager black-clad figure marching confidently toward the synagogue with the other Jewish men. As for her mother's jutting chin, her memory had all but erased it. Even the beloved figure of Sophie had curiously dimmed, leaving no more than a hint of that complicated humor shining from her eyes, that lilt of laughter which Kala carried in her own throat.

Then, having conjured up her family, Kala began to worry about them. She fretted over whether or not the Germans were treating them as well as Malkeh and Naftali had predicted. She tried to guess the birth day, the sex, and the name of the child born to Ruth and Mordecai. She speculated on who was feeding the Chodorov animals.

That night the Lyeskers found it difficult to sleep—so close were they to the trains, and so anxious. In the middle of the night the twins pummeled Kala awake. "Get up, get up!" they whispered loudly. "There's no fun to just sleeping—let's do something. Let's play games. Let's count the stars. Only don't just sleep, Kala—we're almost to our new Lyesk!"

[175]

CHAPTER SIXTEEN

IN THE MORNING FATHER BORIS, LUKA, AND MIKHAIL SET OFF across the river for the railroad station to arrange for transportation. Half an hour later, hounded by the frenetic questions of the twins, Kala took Stepan and Natasha and walked with them into town. A line of petitioners for places on the trains stretched down the station platform and wound up the main street. Around the station camped a crowd of strange-looking people, waiting also for train spaces. So tattered and wild did they appear that at first Kala thought them a special group of indigent peasants, the inmates of a poorhouse or a prison. Shortly, however, she recognized the distinctive "fringes" of hair, the bangs worn by the women of the prosperous Kholm province, the beaded white sheepskin jackets of the Lomzha men, the reddish sheepskin jackets with fringes of the Grodno men. All these clothes, so brilliant and impressive when the refugees passed through Lyesk at the end of summer, had turned almost to rags, the colored beads lost, the gay borders frayed beyond recognition.

"We are the leavings," said one old peasant. "Many have died. Some of the others have gone on alone, the stronger ones, while we wait to be sent off this way and that—who knows where?"

Gradually the enthusiasm of the twins subsided. Solemn and subdued, they followed Kala about the town. Unable to find Luka, Father Boris, or Mikhail, Kala and the children marched back across the river, where they waited to hear the news.

A few hours later Father Boris assembled everyone. "It's hard to explain," he began. "We've been assured places on the train—eventually—for all of us . . . with the exception of our livestock. The officials are very clear on that point—the government cannot transport livestock. That means, of course, we will have to sell our horses, cows, our sheep—and at a market price that is shamefully low." He paused to give his audience time to understand. "But I have even worse news. The spaces on the trains are awarded by lottery. Some of us will be sent north, some east, others south."

An unhappy silence greeted this information. Mournfully, Father Boris, his strong-lined, wind-burned face, framed by long white hair, shook his head and walked back and forth in front of the Lyeskers. "No provision has been made to keep the town together," he said. "Not a single provision to keep the town together. There you have it."

"We'll go on all the same," the words escaped from Kala's lips. "We'll stay together."

To her surprise Father Boris then loudly echoed, "We'll go on."

"We'll go on and we'll keep our livestock," Luka added.

It was the old Luka, Kala thought, and she saw that the entire Lyesk caravan suddenly awakened. People shouted, "We'll go on!" or else, "Shall we go on?" Several persons voiced specific hesitations. Sarah Finkel expressed her fear of winter on the road. A stout Rozumov peasant argued that soon the journey would begin to weaken them, pointing out, "Look how much we depend on the relief stations already. And even so we've lost eight people." Matryona dismissed his charges, claiming no one had died because of the march itself: except for the bomb, all would have died anyway. Mikhail interrupted to warn they would have a more difficult time getting on the trains the further they went. Kala contradicted him to declare, "We are what is left of Lyesk. We have come this far together. It would be terrible to give up now. We all heard Luka."

At last it was determined by a show of hands that the townspeople and the livestock would continue on the road together. The Lyeskers, inspired by their decision, clapped one another on the back, embraced, and shook hands vigorously. As Mikhail came up to Kala, she shrank slightly into herself, fearful that the opinion she'd expressed lacked practicality and that he would reprimand her. But instead he said, "It was a wonderful meeting! It was wonderful! You understood before anyone! This is exactly what it means to be comrades. We'll march together to Rogachev, and if there's nothing there, we'll go on to Roslavl!"

The second morning out of Bobruisk, a cold wind from the north blew across the road, abruptly ending the Indian summer. Upon reaching Rogachev on the River Dnieper—the next city to the east—the Lyeskers found the margins of the water frozen and the birch forests blazing with reds, yellows, and golds. The stationmaster at Rogachev advised them to proceed via Dovsk and Cerikov to Roslavl, the major embarkation point for refugees into central Russia, emphasizing that the Lyeskers must travel as quickly as possible since a half million more refugees were expected from the west before December—a number that would surely overwhelm the countryside and make any further transportation impossible.

By the time the caravan had passed through Dovsk, Kala understood that their luck had run out. The winter wind caught up the sandy soil of Mogilev Province, scouring the

faces of the Lyeskers and picking its way through every opening in their clothing, so that even the most warmly clad shivered from morning to night. Luka's lead wagon carried a
metal can in which the embers of the night fires glowed all
day long. Around this can the family clustered, placing their
hands on the hot metal or close to the flames. Together Kala
and Mikhail aided their fellow travelers, who increasingly
found themselves in trouble with lame horses, broken axles
and wheels, illness, or simple exhaustion. Gradually Kala gave
up her hope that the people of Lyesk would be able to stay
together and found their own settlement. Now her prayers
asked only that they would get to Roslavl alive and find
places on the train to wherever the authorities might send
them. As the days went on, great drifts of sand lay across the
road—sudden flurries blinding the refugees so that they wandered off onto fields and into gullies. Soon it became less and
less possible to keep track of the Lyeskers who fell by the side,
so many having simply given up the struggle. Relief cars and
trucks occasionally chugged down the road to pick up the
worst cases, but Kala suspected that many who dropped behind were never found. In the night the young couple slept
next to one another surrounded by members of the Fomich
clan, huddled in one wagon or another, but now there was no
question of passion between Kala and Mikhail—merely a desire for companionship and warmth.

Two days beyond Dovsk, the last of the cows were slaugh-
tered and eaten. After that, every afternoon a contingent of
the heartiest Lyeskers scrabbled over the frozen fields, digging up potatoes and cucumbers. Even the children helped,
but they suffered most from the cold. Whenever they could,
Kala and Mikhail carried the smallest children under their
coats. Despite years of tough work, Kala's hands swelled,
cracked, and bled; her knees grew so stiff she could hardly
unbend them at night. Only Mikhail's prodding elbow and
small grim smile offered some hope to her that the journey
was worth continuing.

By now—though Mikhail continued to caution the townspeople to boil their water and food—they voraciously ate whatever they could find, barely making a pretense at cooking. Every day Kala heard more and more complaints of severe cramps and diarrhea. The days grew colder still. The refugees bound bandanas around their faces, but the sand coated their skin and their teeth grated when they chewed. Everywhere along the roadside lay abandoned carts and dead horses, their purple flesh torn to pieces by bands of wild dogs. Clouds of black ravens swirled above the carrion, cawing to one another, announcing the feast.

Then, several days beyond Cerikov, Kala began to see white crosses planted on either side of the road: Orthodox graves mixed with Catholic and decorated with icons of the Mother of God or with embroidered belts or bright towels or kerchiefs left as mementos. Here and there the crosses carried messages in crude wrting: "God's Blessing," "She Who Intercedes," or merely "Infant," "Infant," "Infant." There were many more small graves than large ones. Endlessly crossing himself, Father Boris explained to Kala why the graves had been placed so close to the roadway: without a proper burial and the singing of a Requiem—for which there obviously had been no time—the dead could find no rest unless the passersby added their prayers for the souls of the departed.

Late in the night that preceded the Lyeskers' arrival in Roslavl, Anya stuck her head into the back of the wagon where Kala and Mikhail slept. She shouted for everyone to waken. In a moment they had gathered by Luka's main wagon, where Luka and three of his daughters-in-law were trying to hold Stepan and Natasha as they writhed convulsively about on the ground near the fire. Though it was a cold night, sweat streamed from the children's foreheads. Their eyes bulged as though they were seeing ghosts; a bubbly froth welled out of their mouths.

Horrified at the sight, Kala asked, "Have they been bitten by one of the wild dogs?"

"No, no," said the children's mother, a pale, gaunt woman who moved back and forth between the twins, seeking some way to relieve them. "It was the green potatoes in the dirty water. I warned them again and again. They were so hungry . . . they couldn't wait."

All at once the convulsions ceased and the children became conscious, complaining of cramps and painful tenderness in their stomachs. "Water, please, I'm so thirsty," they demanded, almost in unison—after which they began to chatter deliriously, calling out for their mother and for each other, asking how much longer they must wait before they could ride on the train.

Mikhail had asked that broth be boiled in order to lave the twins' digestive tracts. When the liquid was ready, he held Stepan and fed him while Kala fed Natasha. But whatever the children swallowed went through them quickly, expelled in loud explosions. Waste mixed with blood streamed from their bottoms: "Their blood is passing from them with their dirt," gasped the twins' mother.

"Keep on," ordered Mikhail. "We must wash them out."

The Fomiches hovered around the children, toweling them off with rags dipped in water. The children's bodies burned with fever and shivered violently. By morning they had grown very weak. Reluctantly Kala relinquished Natasha to the embrace of her mother and Mikhail transferred Stepan to his grandmother. The young couple stood with the rest of the family, praying with Father Boris. For the first time in a week the fierce wind died and a weak sun glimmered behind a high gray cloud bank. From a long way off the deep baritone of a bell tolled. As if he had been waiting for this message, Father Boris moved toward the twins. He rendered the last rites to each of them. Within an hour the children died— Natasha first, and then Stepan, an instant later.

Kala knelt amidst the women of the Fomich family. She did not join their wailing. From a great distance she seemed to walk endlessly with Stepan and Natasha while they described their new Lyesk and asked how long before they took the train. The Fomich women continued wailing. After awhile the twins' grandmother, Anya, instructed Luka and

Mikhail to search for coffins in the nearby village of Sumyaki. Anya ordered the women to get up, to clean the bodies
and dress them properly. Kala began to help but the twins'
mother pushed her away, asking to perform the task alone.
Then Kala noticed how little flesh was left on the twins'
bodies and at this sight her grief broke through and she
began to sob, unable to stop herself until Luka and Mikhail
returned with coffins.

It was because of Father Boris and the passion of his plea
that the Sumyaki priest allowed the twins to be buried in a
corner of the town cemetery, high upon the crest of the hill,
within the bounds of the cast iron fence. "They will be safer
here," Father Boris assured Luka.

"Their graves must be clearly marked," Luka said. "They
were my favorite grandchildren."

As if comforted by this idea, the twins' mother drew a
single quick breath. "At least they won't have to stay like the
others—on the side of the road."

"Or in a battlefield ditch," murmured Anya, referring to
the children's father.

Father Boris prayed and the people of Lyesk sang. Soon
darkness started to fall. When the graves had been filled in,
the eyes of the mourners began to stray down to the road
where the ceaseless parade of refugees continued on toward
Roslavl and the trains. Pointing ahead, the Sumyaki priest
indicated that from this hillside they could see all the way to
the River Oster and even to Roslavl, barely visible on the
high opposite bank over a dense white haze. Amidst the
opal smoke, purple smudges could be seen erupting in show-
ers of brilliant sparks above the river bank.

"The city must be on fire," murmured Patch.

"No," the priest explained, "it's the bonfires of the
refugees."

"A sea of bonfires in Smolensk Province," Matryona intoned.

"Yes," acknowledged the priest proudly, "you have arrived
in great Russia now. You are in the first true Russian town."

"Where Jews are completely forbidden," Patch hissed to Kala. Then he addressed the strange priest. "Is there space on trains?"

"There is space, but you have to wait."

"And can an arrangement be made," Matryona inquired, hope rising in her voice, "so that people from the same town can be transported together?"

"People from the same town?" The priest appeared puzzled. "There's a lottery here, as elsewhere, you know. Perhaps two or three of you. A family," he allowed as consolation, "goes together of course . . . but large families have to wait longer."

Hanging back from the others, Kala remained within the cemetery until she was alone. In the distance she heard the sound of a steam whistle and gazing westward she could see, high on the river bank, small red and blue lights glimmering from the train station. Kneeling by the fresh graves, she took up two clods of dirt and ground them between her fingers, letting the dirt trickle down over the mound which covered the twins. The journey was almost over, she thought. Here lay new Lyesk. In Roslavl the people of Lyesk would sell their animals, leave their carts, and take their separate places on the trains. She tried to tell herself it was just as well the twins had never reached the very end. Who knew what suffering lay ahead? She rose and walked in a daze toward the cemetery gate. Mikhail stood patiently waiting for her. She reached out and took up his right hand, pressing it to her lips. "You have stayed with us—with Lyesk—to the end of the journey, just as you promised. Thank you."

That night the dysentery that had killed the twins spread through the Lyesk camp. Along with Mikhail and Father Boris and side by side with Matryona and Rivkah, Kala moved methodically about the camp trying to ease the pain of the victims. In the morning Luka approached Kala. Around them stretched the marshy meadow on the western banks of the river, where the refugee caravans had made their camps. Between the camps loomed the shapes of hundreds of

[183]

abandoned carts, wagons, wheels, and shafts. Gray waiflike creatures wandered about, prying up firewood, loose iron parts, bits of harnesses or wheels, whatever could be used. Stray horses stumbled here and there in a trance of hunger, as if they were searching for the wagons they had once pulled, or for their former masters. "The government is purchasing mounts in the Muchin Yard in Roslavl," Luka said. "Will you help me take the horses there?"

"Of course."

Looking away, Luka added, "I'm asking you because you're better with horses than the other women."

Kala lowered her head. Sadly she accepted that Luka had chosen her because he did not want any member of his family to witness his final humiliation. After all, she was not a Fomich.

As the late autumn sun glimmered, Kala and Luka herded the Fomich horses across a shallow ford, breaking the thin ice that had formed overnight, and wound their way up the cliff of the opposite bank into the town of Roslavl. The horses' breath steamed in the morning chill. Kala could see that Roslavl, once a pretty little town, had now succumbed to the legions of refugees from the west. Every building had been altered in some way to accommodate the refugees or to protect itself from them. Through a side street Kala glimpsed the marketplace beyond, jammed full of people trading their possessions. In the courtyard of the hotel, proudly named Hotel Petrograd in crude letters, a mass of refugees waited for lottery numbers that would give them passage upon the trains. As Kala and Luka proceeded, urging the frightened horses through the crowded main street, a gleaming coffin of new wood coming in the opposite direction caught Kala's attention. Red and green and blue streamers, strangely brilliant amidst the drab gray crowds, fluttered from the sides of the coffin. Four young girls shouldered the coffin's weight, the oldest barely fifteen.

"Who has died?" called out Kala. "Who has died?" she was forced to repeat to catch their attention.

[184]

"Our sister," replied the youngest, a black-haired child of eleven.

"Shshshhhh," murmured the other girls. All four wore dresses embroidered gaily in red and green and blue.

Kala stopped to watch the girls pass. She noticed that no adult accompanied them. The memory rose within her of walking with her sisters down Merchant Lane to bring bread and cake to the Jewish refugees at the train—a memory so vivid that for a moment she thought she stood on the hillside above the Lyesk railroad, looking at the station's gabled wooden tower while Ruth pointed out that so picturesque a structure lent a special character to their town. From there it seemed to her that Ruth, Ekaterina, and Sophie—Sophie miraculously walking without her crutches—had come to Roslavl and were just now disappearing down this main street, the gaily decorated coffin on their shoulders. Then all at once it became clear to Kala who lay inside the coffin. It was she herself who lay within. Hastily she turned away and ran after Luka's horses.

In Muchin Yard there were no shouts, no loud bids, no vendors as there had been in the market. Here there were only sad-looking men and women waiting with their animals for a turn to stand before the government inspectors and army purchasing agents. Without a word Luka joined the line. Kala took up the very rear and did not look at him again—not during the government inspector's perfunctory appraisal of the horses, or at the moment he was given a recompense of a few roubles, or when the animals, one by one, were forced to earth and the government brand applied.

The elder and the young woman proceeded silently back to camp. That evening Luka Fomich shut his eyes and could not be induced to open them the next dawn. He died at midday. The afternoon of the funeral, Luka's oldest daughter-in-law, the mother of the twins, took Kala aside and explained that though Luka had listed Kala as his daughter on the forms submitted for places on the train, each extra name made it more difficult for a family to get an early placement.

Willingly, Kala removed her name from the Fomich allotment. Within several days she received an independent lottery number, which she showed to Mikhail.

"At the railroad," she told him, "they promised that within three weeks all of us will be accommodated—some off to Riazan, some to Kazan, some to Orenburg, some to heaven knows where."

"Kala, I want you to come with me to Petrograd."

The young woman shut her eyes and shook her head. "I don't want to, Mikhail—I'm too tired to go to Petrograd." The dense smoke of the fires and the smell of dead horses caused her eyes and nose to run. "What I want . . . is to go home." She let herself utter these words though she knew there was no way to travel back across Russia through the war zone, past the trenches and the battlefields. "I want it all to be as before."

"As before? No, it must be changed—overturned completely so that such things cannot happen. Certainly now you have to agree. Come with me—you'll meet my comrades."

"Listen Mikhail, it will be hard enough for you to get to Petrograd alone—even with your pass."

"It won't be hard. And you know as well as I do that you can't go home. But for Petrograd . . . I can simply add your name to my pass."

"How is that?"

"As my wife."

"I'm not your wife and you talk such foolishness," she said with finality.

"But you could be my wife," he pointed out. "It's not out of the question." And informing Kala he would soon be back, he trotted off in the direction of town.

Presently she forgot that he had gone—so burdened was her mind with the failure of the journey. The tears fell noiselessly down her cheeks. They had not yet dried when she caught sight of Mikhail galloping toward her, his cheeks freshly barbered, his reddish locks and mustache trimmed, a bright new kerchief knotted about his neck. In his hands he carried a large robust-looking bunch of carrots tied like a bouquet with a shiny red ribbon. Bending down on one knee he offered her the carrots, raised his intense blue eyes toward her and demanded, "Darling Kala, will you marry me and be my wife?"

"What are you saying?" Stunned, Kala stared down at him. "Get up this instant. Get up—don't be a fool."

"Darling Kala, will you marry me and be my wife?"

"Get up. There's something wrong with you after all." She tried to pull him to his feet. "What good is marriage—and you of all people to suggest it!"

"If I was contemptuous of marriage before," Mikhail declared, refusing to budge, "I look at things differently now. Ever since . . . ever since Bobruisk I've been examining all sides of the question. To survive such horrors as we have, we need the strongest commitments. Not just to one's party—though the Socialist Revolutionary Party is very fine. Not just to the revolution. Kala, please marry me now, here, before all your townspeople go off."

Kala sighed, glancing down at her torn and filthy skirt, her blouse and jacket hanging in shreds. The thought of Mikhail's virtue and his steadfastness touched her. "Marriage," she tried out the word, "it sounds so fancy. What will it prove? And how can you speak of marriage in this place where we've all become a part of death?"

"Kala Chodorov," Mikhail persisted, "you've seen how unsure I am about so many things—but of two things I'm certain. I love you and I love justice. Don't you see," he continued, "that marriage is a commitment to life. It's an act of defiance. A revolt."

"Marriage a revolt?" Kala asked. "Marriage isn't a revolt . . ."

Putting his hands over his ears, Mikhail refused to listen. In his loudest voice he repeated, "I love you, Kala Chodorov, and I want you to be my wife."

The wedding took place a week later, at dusk, on the immense marshy meadow where the Lyeskers had set up their camp. Partly because this was the first true festive occasion of the journey and partly as a final farewell, the townspeople roused themselves and cleared away the junkyard of the evacuation—the carts, wagons, carcasses, mounds of refuse—to produce a wide clear grassy space by the edge of the river. Under the supervision of Shmuel the Holy One, they constructed a *chupah* of wagon wheels, draped with boughs of pine trees, all standing on a stage made of abandoned carts. They sewed clothes for the bride and groom. They located two gypsy fiddlers. They sent Patch out into the environs of Roslavl and in a remote hut Patch located a rabbi. After finding the rabbi, Patch went forth again and successfully rounded up four Jews to join the six surviving Jewish men in the Lyesk caravan to make the *minyan* for the wedding.

At five o'clock a circle of bonfires were lit and Patch's four Jews arrived, one trailing after the other in their long black coats—each one smiling faintly, as if with embarrassment, at never having been introduced to the bride and groom. In turn the Jews of Lyesk peered at these unknown Jews with a curiosity mixed both with gratitude for their presence and a mild resentment that they were strangers. But the rabbi turned out an altogether different matter; the rabbi met with instant approval. With his long white beard, his gentle intelligent manner, his air of accepting everything that happened in the universe and everything that would ever happen, he appealed to every Lyesker, Jew and Christian alike. No matter whether or not they understood the Hebrew of his service —from the moment he opened his mouth they listened to him carefully, at first with respect and then with fondness and finally with hope.

"Nowadays," murmured Patch, "you never see a rabbi like him."

"You're right," agreed Matryona—though in fact she had had little acquaintance with rabbis, "nowadays such rabbis are very rare."

Inside the shelter of the wagon wheels and the pine boughs, the rabbi addressed Kala and Mikhail: "Within this sanctuary," he said in his calm, sweet voice, "man and woman complete one another in companionship. Under this canopy, man and woman dedicate their bodies and souls to God's creation. Here today, stripped of all goods and ambitions, you two children come together to join your flesh and spirit, creating a new house in which God can find comfort and nourishment. May God grant that out of this wedding canopy hung with simple boughs of pine, and out of this sacred oath of marriage will issue a lifetime of joy and many loving children. We give thanks unto Thee, O Lord, for Thou hast answered us and art become our salvation."

Kala and Mikhail said together, "Behold thou art consecrated unto me by this ring, according to the Law of Moses and Israel."

Turning her head briefly, Kala glimpsed Matryona among the spectators and noted that the midwife winked at her in the exact same way she had at Ruth's wedding. Reassured by Matryona, she was slightly disturbed to catch a view of Sarah Finkel weeping, but then heartened to witness Rivkah grinning as pleasantly as it was possible for Rivkah to grin—especially considering that Kala had had no ritual bath. The rabbi spoke out the seven benedictions. In a low voice meant only for Kala's ears, Mikhail promised his bride that the revolution would give meaning to their lives. Then Kala and Mikhail each blessed the fruit of the vine and sipped from the single glass that the rabbi provided. The glass was placed gingerly down and covered with a swatch of tarpaulin. Mikhail lifted his foot high and stomped it into pieces with one blow. At this Father Boris exclaimed very loudly, "There you have it!" and the gypsy fiddles started up.

Kala, deciding it was a beautiful wedding, wished with all her heart that her family had been present.

PART TWO

"COMRADES!" THE MESSENGER PAUSED TO CATCH HIS breath after climbing the six floors to Kala's and Mikhail's garret chamber. "There's a curious fellow with a suitcase down below asking for Kala. He's all dressed up in a suit and tie, a bowler hat, an ivory-handled cane."

"I think it's my father," exclaimed Kala.

"The old guy complained about the scuff marks on the floors."

Terrified, Kala dressed hastily and ran down the long flights of stone stairs. Three years had passed since her departure from home, and in that time she had obtained only snatches of news from Lyesk. The war had made all contact difficult. Only after the treaty of peace with the Germans, signed in March of this year, 1918, had she been able to communicate freely with her family. Since February she and Mikhail had been living in Moscow at the Morozov Palace on Triokhsvyatitelsky Lane, headquarters of the Left Socialist

Revolutionaries. In her first letter Kala had written, for Ekaterina's benefit, that the Morozov Palace rose six stories into the air and under the Tsar had housed a wealthy linen manufacturer—a count—and his family. In a simplified fashion she tried to explain to the Chodorovs the events that had led to her and Mikhail's move: the Bolshevik take-over of the revolutionary government in October 1917; the exclusion by the Bolsheviks of all other revolutionary parties except for the Left Socialist Revolutionaries; the advance of the Germans on Petrograd in February 1918 and the resulting displacement of the government from Petrograd to Moscow. She made no mention of the political disagreements that had developed between her and Mikhail over the last few years, or of her growing disillusionment with the Revolution.

Now, as she raced down the grand staircase to the second floor of the palace, Kala caught sight of the dapper figure of her father. He was examining the decor of the reception salon with the interest and detachment of a visitor to a museum. For an instant she regretted that it was her father rather than her mother or Sophie who now appeared before her. In the next second she ran across the broad parquet floor and threw herself upon Naftali. Awkwardly he returned her embrace, responding to her frightened questions with a pleased and slightly smug expression on his face. "Fine. Fine. Everyone is fine. The whole town is fine. Only the animals are getting older."

"Papa, here's Mikhail, my husband."

Naftali raised his head toward Mikhail, who had just descended the stairs, and proceeded to peer at the young man as though not quite able to place him. With a certain formality the two men shook hands but then Mikhail leaned forward, said, "Welcome, Papa," and kissed both of Naftali's cheeks— an intimacy which appeared both to satisfy Naftali and unsettle him. Turning away, he righted the matter by flourishing his cane in a wide arc. "I don't deny that this is a beautiful palace," he said, "but the chandeliers are dusty, there are handprints all over the mirrors, there are scuff marks on the floor, and the furniture needs polish. Have the Russians lost all pride?"

"You're absolutely right, Papa," Mikhail answered. "We've let certain things go—just for the present. On the other hand, you look fresh and all spruced up."

"I stopped by the public baths at the station."

"But it's a long difficult journey from Lyesk to Moscow. You must be tired. Let me find you a decent bed." And Mikhail set off down the hallway, leaving behind Kala, who kept on repeating, "And is Mama really all right? Is Sophie? Ruth?"

"Fine. They're fine."

"Do they look the same?" she inquired, her heart beating swiftly. She led her father to a corner of the salon where she dusted off two chairs with her skirt, bombarding him with more questions about the family.

"They're just the same."

"But things change. Everything does. Papa, do you think I've changed?"

Puzzled, Naftali studied his daughter. "Was your hair longer before?"

"No Papa, it was shorter."

"Have you put on weight?"

"No, as a matter of fact, I've lost weight."

"Were you cross-eyed?"

"Cross-eyed? Not that I can remember. That was someone else."

"Well then," Naftali concluded, "you look the same."

"But you, Papa," Kala hesitated and ventured, "you look . . . thinner."

"Well, of course." He gazed down at his stomach. "People don't eat as much as they used to—that goes without saying. No one even wants to eat as much. I suppose you know that the bakery is the only building in Lyesk the Russians didn't burn down. Your mother saved it." His gaze narrowed shrewdly and he winked at his daughter. "And after all, what did it cost us—a case of kvass, a dozen bottles of vodka, nine silver plates, and a few roubles. I wish she had saved the house too."

"And the orchard?"

"Oh, they didn't burn the orchard—but we expected that. I can't tell you how many people we were able to hide and how grateful they were—Lavin and Dovitsky and the Zuckermans and Reb Keppel, and Rabbi Benjamin, and who knows who else. And what's more, there was a big delicious crop of apples to eat while everyone waited."

"Then it's just like before," Kala mused. "Mama runs the bakery?"

"Just like before," corroborated Naftali. He paused and changed his mind. "Except that the bread is different. The German recipe is about one-half sawdust. That's because the Germans chop down the trees just as fast as they can and they send the lumber back to Germany . . . so we have a lot of sawdust around. They're still fighting in the west, you know. They take all the wheat from the Ukraine and send it to Germany, where everyone is starving . . . so there isn't much flour. Otherwise . . . to the best of their abilities, the Germans are good to us, they appreciate us." Naftali waved his hand in the air in praise of the Germans.

"Well, thank God for that."

"Oh, they're intelligent—nothing gets past them. For example, they've selected Mordecai and me as foremen for German projects in the district. You should see Mordecai and me—we ride all over in an official carriage with rubber wheels. And they've made friends with Malkeh—or else it's the other way around—Malkeh has made friends with them; and Ekaterina . . . would you believe she no longer goes to school?" He gloated. "The Germans have given her a job. She has a position as a secretary and translator for the authorities at the telegraph office in the railroad station. And sometimes she works out at the new airfield."

"The new airfield?" Kala's mouth dropped open.

Proudly Naftali shut his eyes. "We have an airfield with an airplane."

"So it's true . . . everything's really all right?"

"Fine. Everything is fine."

"Then if you don't mind my asking, Papa—why exactly did you take so dangerous a trip and come to Moscow?"

"Why?" Naftali shrugged. He brushed the lint off his trousers. "Because your mother told me to check things out—to look you over—to see what you're up to. And when I learned you had moved into a palace . . ."

"To look me over?" Kala laughed. "You came all this way just for that? Well, tell Mama," she smiled, "that I still have lots of work inside me, just as she used to say. I've repaired five times as many watches in Petrograd and Moscow as I ever did in Lyesk. Just recently I even fixed the watch of one of our party's heroines, Spiridonova. Have you heard of her? She just came back from Siberia, where she spent eleven years in prison."

"I've never heard of her. Don't they have anyone better than you fixing watches?"

"I also repair the printing press. And I pass out leaflets and go out to the villages to organize the peasants."

Purposefully Naftali removed a furled white handkerchief from his breast pocket and gave a small snort in it before replacing it. "And why are you still struggling so hard," he demanded in a slightly exasperated tone, "when the Revolution is supposed to be over?"

"Yes, the Revolution is over, it's true, and the Tsar no longer rules; but nothing at all remains simple." Kala sighed, reflecting sorrowfully that everything had seemed less complicated, less unwieldly before the Revolution. The day the Tsar had been overthrown she and Mikhail had marched up Nevsky Prospekt with their comrades—a great crowd of peasants, workers, soldiers, Cossacks, Jews, Moslems, Tartars, and Poles, all united. But then coalitions had formed, parties had splintered, friends had become enemies and enemies, friends. Threats to the Revolution had risen from the right, from the left, and from the center. One provisional government had followed another until the Bolsheviks had seized power, sharing it only with Kala's party, the Left Socialist Revolutionaries. And now the Left Socialist Revolutionaries were sparring with the Bolsheviks, who had proved determined to maintain peace with imperialist Germany and to sacrifice the welfare of the peasants to the needs of the city workers.

What among all this could she excerpt for her father? "Papa, we had a Jewish wedding, Mikhail and I. Shmuel, the Holy One, built a *chupah*; a wonderful rabbi—as pure as our own Reb Chaim Pearl—married us; and Mikhail broke the glass on his first try."

"I know. We heard. Patch made his way back to Lyesk."

"Patch?" Kala queried excitedly. "How did he make his way back? And Matryona . . . is she there too? What about Sarah Finkel . . . Father Boris?"

"No, only Patch," Naftali replied uneasily. "And he didn't stay long. He got into the habit of wandering. For that matter, you know who else recently left Lyesk, and after all these years? Reb Keppel. He took a position in Pinsk." Naftali stood up, smoothing his trousers carefully, and strolled toward a large wooden chest that rose some seven feet into the air.

Kala followed her father. "I was with Luka when he died, and I held the twins in my arms all their last night . . ."

"I know. Patch told us," Naftali said abruptly. He ran a practiced hand over the elaborately scrolled woodwork of the chest. "I'm building a new house." He introduced the topic hopefully—as if to cheer her up. When he failed to cheer either of them, he turned momentarily irritable. "It's only half built—I can't understand why your mother couldn't have saved the old house—it's not so easy to finish building when you can't get enough lumber, or the right sort. Still, it's only a question of waiting a bit and when I'm finished it will be a grand house with room enough for us all—for you and your husband and your children too. Which brings me to the most important subject. Your mother wants to know," he turned his head away from Kala—either out of fastidiousness or chivalry or both—"are you pregnant?"

"No."

Naftali grimaced. "Then what have you been doing for the past three years?"

"I already told you. I've been working for the Party."

Naftali leaned toward her. He whispered, "Your husband, he's all right? Your mother and I were wondering . . . I mean, with all his pretty manners?"

Kala blushed. "He's perfect," she declared. "There's nothing wrong with him."

"Well then," Naftali tapped his cane onto the floor in front of her, "in that case your mother wants you to come home, if only for a visit, to see the doctors or the wonder rabbi if it comes to that. It isn't natural. Three years and not a child in sight. Look at your sister Ruth. She has three children already—unfortunately all three of them girls who look like Mordecai! But I thank God for your brother Iosif. Look how many children Iosif has produced."

"Ah, yes," Kala murmured, twisting her wedding band uncomfortably round and round her finger and at last understanding the true object of her father's journey. "Iosif must have at least ten children by now."

"He has three," Naftali corrected. "And almost as many automobiles. He's doing his part. Last year he sent us a jar of beans through the Red Cross—actually they were jelly beans. And a few jars of face cream—if anyone should need it for her skin. He also sent us several letters—short letters, notes actually, he was never much for writing." Naftali raised his brows and appeared to gaze across an enormous distance. "I believe that one day soon, when we least expect it, Iosif will show up to take us all to America with him." Now he turned and focused upon Kala. "And when he comes, or when he sends for us, I want us all to be together, ready. I can't come running here to Moscow every week to gather you and your family up. Tomorrow we set off for Lyesk. We'll cross the border at Luninyets—it's simple to cross there, it's all swamps and mudholes—no one on either side even bothers to patrol."

"Papa, I've been wanting to come home—you don't know

how much. But for the moment we can't leave Moscow." She regarded her father. It seemed to her he could not have arrived at a more inappropriate time. It was July 4. The Fifth Soviet Congress was meeting and the Left Socialist Revolutionaries planned to confront the Bolsheviks the next day. Her party, Kala thought, would need all of its members for this crisis.

"I'll wait a day or two," Naftali said. "I'll take a little look at Moscow and then we'll start back."

"But Papa, it isn't as simple as that. Our party's in a struggle with the Bolsheviks. Things here at the Morozov Palace are a bit touchy."

"Things are touchy everywhere. Now here's your husband —what's-his-name—and I want to sleep. I'm tired. Have you found me a good bed?"

"In the Countess's sitting room," said Mikhail, lifting Naftali's suitcase. Kala and her father followed him down a long passageway where Mikhail turned a door knob and opened a door. "Unfortunately, it may be a bit crowded here as they've stored furniture in the room."

They entered a small sitting room, where a large amount of gilt furniture had been piled together. Naftali shook his head. "Everything here is disorder," he clucked. "Such fine expensive commodes, tables, chairs, abandoned, neglected . . ." he turned to his daughter and Mikhail, "while if you come home with me you will see how well the Germans organize everything. Our streets are clean, our buildings free of fleas. Once a week the poor get baths and fumigation."

"Yes, Papa," said Mikhail, smiling. "But here the poor rule themselves. Give us time. Once we go back to war, your German imperialists will have little time to clean the streets."

"Let's not go into all that," objected Kala.

Naftali raised his brows and wagged his head. "First you want peace and then you want war and soon you'll want a revolution against the Bolsheviks, your own allies. And if you think, young man, it will be so easy to beat the Germans, I'd advise you to examine the workmanship of the German trenches we've constructed in Lyesk."

"Papa," Kala moved between her husband and her father, "there's no reason to argue like this. It's bad enough our party and the Bolsheviks are squabbling . . ."

"Let them squabble," Naftali said. "I'll have nothing to do with either of them. And you, young man, just remember that whoever is in that Kremlin over there, he knows you're a Jew. Now I want to sleep. It's way past midnight. Go."

As Kala and Mikhail mounted the staircase, the voice of Naftali echoed down the hall. "Kala!"

Kala returned. Through the door of the sitting room her father's arm protruded, his suit draped over it. "Press this, daughter," he demanded in an urgent whisper. "Press it carefully and bring it back first thing in the morning."

Kala thrust her father's suit into Mikhail's hands and then went about the palace searching in closets and cupboards. When twenty minutes passed and she was unable to find an iron, she climbed to her chamber where she and Mikhail smoothed out the suit as best they could and hung it up for the night. They undressed for bed—Mikhail asking questions, one after the other, about Malkeh's health, about Sophie, Ruth, Ekaterina, Mordecai, about the bakery, even about the piano.

"Everything's the same." Kala beamed.

"Your father looks wonderful—so trim. I'm sorry I baited him about the Germans."

"It's all right, he likes to argue."

"What's terrible is, he's just arrived, and now, tomorrow you have to convince him to leave."

"Tomorrow?"

"If we lose the vote in the Congress, there's bound to be fighting."

"But he wants to see Moscow."

Mikhail shut his eyes and pinched the bridge of his nose. "Kala," he began deliberately, "there's a plan. Our party is serious this time—and I won't be around to help protect your father. I've been ordered somewhere else."

"Why wasn't I told? Where will you be?"

"Somewhere else. So it's best if he leaves Moscow by to-morrow afternoon if possible."

Kala walked across the room and settled herself within the wide embrasure of the window. She said nothing.

"Kala, I'd rather talk with you next to me. Come to bed."

"Not yet. Not just now." A chill ran through her body. She wished with all her heart she were in Lyesk. Though it was July, the thick walls of the palace retained the winter's damp cold. She looked out the window, guessing it was late—perhaps two hours past midnight. Around her the curiously white summer night's sky of Moscow ranged with the glow of an opal. Below, the rooftops of the city—their bulbous domes, cupolas, and turrets—blossomed like odd assorted flowers beneath the moon. How strange, she mused, to live in Moscow at the top of a building—so great a distance from the ground and so far from fields, from the high road, from rivers unencumbered by man-made embankments: and how much more strange now that her father also occupied a space in the immense labyrinthine city. She turned and looked at her husband. "If we lose the vote, where will you be, where will they send you?"

"I've promised secrecy. Only some of us were told. Kala, come to bed," he pleaded.

Filled with foreboding, she shook her head and stared at the moon and the milk-white sky. "Will there be a terrorist act?"

"I think so. Spiridonova has given her approval."

"Spiridonova! How could she! The Party has stopped using terror. If we go back to war—and it sounds like that's what you want to do, Mikhail—if the Left Socialist Revolutionaries resort to terror, we'll just destroy everything we've worked for."

Mikhail sat upright in bed, cross-legged, wearing only a pair of drawers. His mouth stern, he tried to explain to Kala the necessity for fighting both the Bolsheviks and the Germans. "They threaten what we've worked for. Each of them. Our party's made the decision. And I agree."

"And I don't agree," Kala said quickly. She rubbed the windowpane with her finger, miserable at the prospect of new violence. She pictured her father asleep, as if on a holiday, on the rose-colored chaise longue she'd made up for him, and she longed to be rid of the endless plotting and enmities of Moscow. Then she berated herself, thinking that if only she possessed a bit more of Mikhail's steadfastness, if only she had his loyalty and strength, her enthusiasm for the Revolution might not have faltered. But as it was—despite the camaraderie, the glory, the excitement, and the hope—for the moment, all that she could recall of the February Days, the July Days, the October Days, were hoarse shouts of terror when the crowds fled from barricades of armed men, leaving behind only a few dark forms on the pavement. Uncomfortably, she stirred with a different kind of concern. "Mikhail, you won't go looking for heroism again?"

"Of course not," he assured her. "This isn't a personal matter. But if it were, courage isn't all that bad. Cheer up, my darling. Listen to this poem." He raised his head and in his musical Russian recited:

"*But what can we lose if we try one*
groaning, wide, ungainly sweep of the rudder?
The earth swims. Courage,
brothers, as the cleft sea falls back from our plough."

"Where did you find that?" Kala asked warily.

"On the streets—it's no more than two months old. Do you want to hear another poem?" he asked, grinning, his voice hopeful.

"No. One poem is enough."

"One poem. That's nothing."

"I'll hear it some other time."

"Oh well. Some other time." Mikhail lay down and stretched out his limbs. "Some other time, if I don't forget the poem." He yawned ostentatiously, making room for her beside him. "It's possible," he offered, "that at the Congress we'll win the vote."

"But we won't," Kala accused. "We won't win. You know the meeting's been stacked against us two to one." Again she pressed her nose against the glass of the window. It saddened her that her father had arrived in Moscow at such a moment. "Mikhail," she said in a low voice, "you used to be against war."

But Mikhail was already sleeping. After a while Kala crossed the room, blew out the candle, and crept into bed. She tried to push all thoughts of politics from her mind and to substitute the news her father had brought her—that everyone in her family was well; that the animals remained in good health; that Ruth had borne three daughters who resembled Mordecai; that Lyesk had been rebuilt and was thriving. She tried to forget the differences between her and her husband. Presently a small contented smile settled determinedly on Kala's face.

CHAPTER EIGHTEEN

In the morning Kala awoke to find her husband gone. Glad to be distracted, she renewed her search for an iron. She poked into cupboards and asked among her comrades, one or two of whom mentioned they had noticed an iron not too long before but could not place exactly where, while two others claimed they had not laid eyes on one since before the Revolution. She woke Naftali and returned his suit, unpressed. "I'm sorry, Papa, very sorry, but these are difficult times."

Her contriteness appeared to mollify her father, for he accepted the suit without grumbling and soon emerged fully dressed, his ivory-handled cane in his hand. Ready for breakfast, he followed Kala to the palace kitchen where the party personnel ate at long communal tables, joined by many of the poor from surrounding neighborhoods. "And that's the way it should be," Naftali told his daughter. "The poor should always eat at your table—even if you only offer this dishwater gruel. That's very much in accord with the Jewish commandments for charity." Then without wasting any more time on moral problems, he proceeded to question her about her marriage.

"What about his family?" he asked. "Don't they want to know about your dowry? It's still there, safe in Lyesk. Has his family met you? Do they help you out? Don't they wonder why you have no children?"

But she could not concentrate on Naftali's demands. She had read her orders for the day in the palace hall and was trying to figure out an arrangement to make for her father. At one o'clock she had to report to the Congress at the Bolshoi Theater to act as a messenger, and afterward to return for guard duty. Until then she was free. "Mikhail's family," she replied to her father's question, "is in Vilna. I've never met them but we communicate a little. Mikhail wishes nothing from them and of course they respect that." Abruptly she stood up, having decided that nothing ominous could take place before one o'clock. "Come, Papa. Let me show you Moscow."

They stepped out from the coolness of the palace into a heavy humid summer day. As they walked along, Naftali tapped his cane, pointing at the disrepair of the old buildings and frowning at the mass of ugly newer houses. Appearing utterly at home by his daughter's side, he exclaimed over the ornate churches that stood on every other corner and at the beauty of the Church of Vassily Blageenyi in Red Square. Presently they reached the river. From here Kala indicated the Kremlin, its bronze and pink bricks reflected in water so thick and languid it just barely flowed under the heavy bridges spanning it. Scattered along the banks of the river, people teetered about—some empty-handed, others selling meager wares of chocolate and biscuits and candles and pancakes to workmen, sailors, and soldiers who passed along.

At her father's bemused expression, Kala explained, "Aristocrats, most of them. And some of them great merchants and their wives. These are the ones who survived the violence."

Wandering along the river, offering the contents of their parcels, the former rulers of the city wore an assortment of ragged finery—soiled and crooked melon hats with stains upon the crowns and straw boaters, high collars in the old style, moth-eaten feather boas and silk shawls, torn and dirty lace, worn-down boots. Now and then they turned in surprise when a tramway or an automobile passed.

"The world has passed them by," said Kala, depressed by the sight of these lost souls. "The Revolution went ahead without them."

"All ages," noted Naftali, compassionately, "they are all ages: old, young, middle-aged."

"One day the sky fell on their heads." She and her father chose an empty bench by the river and sat down. She tried to think how best to approach the subject of his departure. "Papa, it's not a time for you to be here. Mikhail had to go off this morning, and I have to spend this afternoon and the next few days at the Congress." She laid a hand on his forearm. "There's a crisis. I think it would be wise if you return home today. So does Mikhail."

"I don't intend to leave until you leave with me. Your mother expects you. I didn't come here just to sight-see. But now that I'm here—I've just begun to see Moscow . . ."

"We'll follow you later. For the moment, it's dangerous here. There might be fighting after the Congress."

"Dangerous? No, it's sad. Look at that poor creature." He indicated a woman wearing a skirt over a pair of trousers and a torn red knit shawl. The woman paced twelve steps back and twelve steps forward in front of them, her head bowed as she concentrated upon her felt slippers sliding over the cobblestones of the walkway. "And if it's dangerous, that's all the more reason you ought to come back with me. Besides," Naftali added smugly, "there won't be another train until tomorrow evening because it's the weekend."

"Papa. What am I going to do with you? I can't just let you go around by yourself. There might be a riot—these things happen—and I'd never find you again."

"Then you'll just have to take me to your precious Congress," Naftali concluded. He gazed unhappily at his clothes. "I'll have to go there in my rumpled suit."

"Your rumpled suit?" Kala muttered absently, calculating it might be best, after all, to keep her father by her side so that she could guide him if an incident occurred. It would not be difficult, she thought, to get him admitted to the Congress as a party aide. "Papa, I'm sorry that your suit is rumpled."

"Oh, it's all right you didn't iron it, but at least you could have hung it up. It looks as if you slept on top of it." He followed Kala back across the bridge. "So this is Moscow." He peered about. "I would have liked it better in the old days."

An hour later they neared the square on which the Bolshoi Theater stood, joining a throng of delegates who shouted and laughed but who sobered at emerging upon the square itself to find that the theater had been cordoned off by Lettish troops, a regiment solidly loyal to the Bolsheviks. Quickly the delegates lined up at the steps to the entrance, where two tables had been placed for officials to examine credentials.

Kala took her place in line and, as a party functionary, managed to obtain a pass for Naftali. She scanned the square for some glimpse of Mikhail and then gave up and announced to her father, "Well, here we are," as they stepped through the high doors of the theater. Gilt ornaments, damask and velvet hangings, brass fittings, gold ropes, and elaborate tapestries surrounded them. "Magnificent, isn't it?" she boasted, slightly belligerent, but with an air of wonder. "Would you ever have guessed that you and I would wander about inside?"

"What beautiful mirrors," Naftali responded. "Mirrors everywhere." He examined himself with interest in three or four.

Today, in addition to the gold and tassels and the velvet, the crystalline glass of the mirrors reflected a drab mob of peasants, soldiers, sailors, and laborers. In an attempt to show their nonchalance at so grand a setting they stood in the spacious halls with legs wide apart, their thumbs hooked into belts. Others squatted in small groups in corners as if they occupied a country field; still others seated themselves in clusters up the wide circular staircases.

Kala, whose first job was to distribute the agenda, seated her father in the back of the party box. The reporters and the diplomats had just begun to arrive, entering the first tier of boxes reserved for their use. Very near the stage a prominent box had been accorded to the Germans—a sign which Kala identified as a deliberate provocation by the Bolsheviks. She recognized the German ambassador, Count Wilhelm von Mirbach, the main target of her party's hatred, then observed he had wisely left his uniform and medals at the embassy. He and his aides, all dressed somberly, sat up very straight without touching the backs of their seats—as though they were riding horses.

At last the Congress chairman, Sverdlov, sounded the bell for quiet, and Kala climbed up to join Naftali. Sverdlov sounded the bell again, but the delegates in the orchestra continued to mill about, embracing, shouting greetings, and arguing heatedly over the previous day's events, when the Left Socialist Revolutionaries had protested the presence in the square of troops sympathetic to the Bolsheviks. After a time the audience settled down, allowing the chairman to utter various procedural announcements before he launched into his own speech as Secretary of the Soviet Executive. When he had finished, several other speakers rose up, spoke out, and uneventfully quit the stage. Then the Left Socialist Revolutionary Maria Spiridonova, Secretary of the Peasants' Section, was introduced and the hall erupted in loud cheers and applause.

"Ah," exclaimed Naftali, "a lady!"

"Mikhail's heroine. At the age of seventeen she murdered a general."

"Quite an accomplishment," Naftali remarked.

"And was raped by the Cossack guards and ever since has contributed nothing but grand gestures. She used to be my heroine too," Kala went on bitterly, but then experienced a twinge of conscience for attacking this woman whom she had so admired during the early days of the Revolution. Yet Spiridonova now favored the renewal of terror against the Bolsheviks. "Nothing but grand gestures and squabbling. I'm sorry I fixed her watch."

"Still," said Naftali, clucking, "she looks like a lady."

With her simple black dress and plain white collar, her hair drawn back, and her solemn, pale expression, the speaker looked almost as if she had stepped out of a cloister. She had the fine features and mannerisms of a well-born lady, particularly when she lifted the pince nez from the ribbon around her neck and placed it precisely upon the bridge of her nose. The noisy welcome continued for some time. Nervously the speaker waved her hand through the air to silence the audience. She glanced down at her notes and laid them on the podium. The chairman rang his bell. Finally Spiridonova reached into her handbag and produced a small silver object with which she pounded the podium.

"A revolver?" asked Naftali, wonderingly.

"A gift from the Party for her brave actions," replied Kala. "Last year when they let her out of prison at Chita, she became mayor of the town and blew up all the prisons."

"Just have to build new ones," Naftali commented; yet he looked with more sympathy at this attractive lady than he had at the other delegates.

Spiridonova began her speech quietly, detailing the history of the coalition between the Bolsheviks and the Left Socialist Revolutionaries. The delegates, mostly male, listened intently to her words—an audience of beards and mustaches, of large sweating bodies packed together, who stood up or applauded enthusiastically whenever the frail and modestly clad speaker paused. As Spiridonova continued, the tone of the speech changed. She began to talk of the village requisition squads and the Bolshevik war against the peasants, a subject which clearly inflamed her. She laid aside her notes and flailed the air, attacking Bolshevik policy: the capitulation to

Germany, the re-imposition of the death penalty, and, worst of all, the oppression of the Russian peasant. Half the audience applauded and cheered, and the rest became increasingly silent and offended.

"The woman is having a fit," Naftali whispered to his daughter. "Her imprisonment must have affected her mind."

Higher and higher rose Spiridonova's voice until it reached a piercing note with the accusation: "The Bolsheviks have betrayed the Revolution!"

Boos and hisses, cheers and applause filled the auditorium, resounding and echoing off the walls. Kala decided that all was lost.

"Lenin . . . Lenin . . ." Spiridonova pounded the podium on every syllable with her small silver pistol, "Lenin has set the proletariat against the peasants. He has reintroduced class warfare into the villages. According to Lenin, fellow peasants, you are no more than dung." The uproar grew. "When peasants are humiliated, oppressed, and crushed," each word she punctuated with a further assault upon the counter before her, "crushed simply because they are peasants—then you will find the same pistol, the same bomb in my hand as I once bore against the vile oppressors of the old regime!"

She raised the pistol high in the air and turned, presenting to the massed audience the profile and spectacle of a woman of fine blood and education who had martyred herself for the sake of the Russian peasant.

With sick heart Kala watched the battle lines form in the auditorium below: the Bolsheviks against the Left Socialist Revolutionaries. Arguments and fist fights broke out all over the hall. "Cossack whore!" came a shout from the gallery directly below Kala's box. Naftali leaned over and looked down. "Is that Schlaymie, the *shoychet*'s son?" he exclaimed to Kala.

"It's Schlaymie the fool."

"What a foul mouth he has. And to think his parents sent him to *yeshivah* in Baranovits!"

In the gallery, a mass of writhing bodies converged upon

Schlaymie. Spiridonova gathered up her notes and disappeared from the stage.

A number of officials stepped forward in an attempt to quiet the uproar. One by one they retreated until finally a short, well-knit figure in a dark suit paced out of the wings, his hands clasped behind him, his head bowed slightly in thoughtful fashion as if he were strolling through his back garden. At center stage he turned to the audience, his lifted head and lifted eyebrows expressing surprise that he was not alone.

The audience hurled at him, "Kaiser! German lover! Tsar!" and yet there appeared to be a diminishing of the turmoil.

The figure smiled and slowly raised his right hand in the air. The auditorium quieted. The delegates, even the opposition, eyed the speaker with an air of expectancy.

"Who is that little man?" inquired Naftali.

"Lenin."

"The small man wearing a suit is Lenin?" Naftali stared down at the stage. "Lenin is . . . bald?"

"Hair or no hair, he knows only how to listen to himself." Kala glared at the leader of the Bolsheviks, who opened his speech by ridiculing Spiridonova and her party. Next Lenin launched into a methodical and lengthy defense of the Bolshevik position—daring the Left Socialist Revolutionaries to walk out of the Congress if they disagreed. To emphasize his remarks, he hunched his shoulders forward, head inclined, and advanced upon the audience as if he were going to dive at them, his thumbs moving up to his armpits where they lodged. Then he executed a series of backward hops, his fingers spreading from his armpits like wings.

"Now he's dancing about," murmured Naftali. "Your leaders, daughter, seem to be afflicted. As for the rest of the people," he nodded toward the audience, which seethed with anger, "they too have taken leave of their senses."

"And who can blame them? Certainly not I. Politics can drive anyone mad."

"What's this? Lenin's going away. Lenin's leaving the stage," Naftali half wailed—as if, having just set eyes on Lenin, he regretted losing him so soon.

Without so much as a moment's delay the Left Socialist Revolutionary leader Kamkov took Lenin's place and at once brought the entire auditorium to its feet by a frenzied attack upon the Bolsheviks and the German imperialists. At the finish of Kamkov's harangue, Kala watched with acute embarrassment as her fellow party members massed under the box where Count von Mirbach sat and raised their fists in the air, chanting, "Down with Mirbach! Away with the German butchers! Crush the imperialists!" Kala stared down glumly, ashamed to have her father witness such a disorderly spectacle.

Lettish troops filed in to escort the German ambassador and his staff from the hall, and the chairman dismissed this first session of the Congress.

When the auditorium had emptied, Kala hurried silently with Naftali back toward the Morozov Palace. She had not encountered Mikhail at the Congress and his absence made her almost certain that at this moment he and his companions were preparing some unknown, some extreme provocative attempt against the government. The only thing to do now was to get her father to a safe place.

Suddenly Kala grew aware that Naftali had taken hold of her hand. Not since she was a very small girl, and then only rarely, had she felt the dry, tough, splintery skin of her father's palm clasping hers. "Don't upset yourself," he said. "It isn't worth it. It's the same all over. Wherever you go in the whole world, politicians carry on."

CHAPTER NINETEEN

AT THREE O'CLOCK THE NEXT AFTERNOON, KALA STOOD ON duty at the porter's lodge in the courtyard of her party headquarters. The palace had been placed on full alert since the evening before—a cannon and a machine gun stood on either side of the gate, while men were hastily boarding up the windows of the facade. All the same, no one in the courtyard understood the plans of the party Central Committee: on the one hand, the leaders of the Party had barricaded themselves within the guarded palace and were issuing orders as though a state of siege existed; on the other hand, they had sent the ordinary Left Socialist Revolutionary delegates to the next session of the Congress as though nothing unusual had occurred.

At three-thirty a muffled explosion sounded out from the direction of the avenues. Soon came the sound of shouting, and down the lane an old man trotted, pushing a handcart inside of which a few sorry vegetables careened about. "The troops are out," he yelled in passing. "There's fighting down by the river."

Several people ran up the lane. "A bombing!" yelled a schoolgirl.

"The troops are out!"

From the porter's lodge Kala's Duty Commander—formerly a law professor in the Ukraine—a short, burly, genial man with a wide, pale orange face and a thin layer of hair over a pale orange scalp—shouted, "Shut the gate! All sections remain on duty. Rifles will be issued to everyone!"

Six members of the Military Committee immediately began to pile sandbags around the front door. Squads manned the two gun emplacements and, except for a cooing of doves from the eaves, all normal sounds of the city ceased. The Duty Commander disappeared into the palace to receive further instructions from the Central Committee. Upon his return he summoned his workers. "Duty Section!" he said. "Hostilities have officially broken out between our party and the Bolsheviks. There are battles all over the city and we can expect action here momentarily." He beamed. "Each of you must face the enemy bravely, for each is responsible to defend the Revolution." He then commanded that rifles and ammunition be brought out to the courtyard.

The six members of the Military Committee entered the palace and returned, bearing stacks of rifles and ammunition belts. The Duty Commander proceeded to distribute the guns, bestowing each rifle with a smile and a nod of congratulation, as though he were conferring certificates or diplomas. When he held out a weapon to Kala, she shook her head, furrowed her brow, put her hands behind her back, and walked away. Nonplussed, he trotted after her. "Kala, what's this?" he called. He followed her to a corner of the courtyard and back, the rifle and ammunition belt dangling from his fingers. "Kala," he coaxed, "take your gun and ammunition. Kala," he prompted as though she'd fallen asleep, "pay attention and take your gun."

"What would I do with a gun?" she objected.

"You've been trained."

"Only at target practice."

"I know you're no schoolmaid."

Hands still tightly clasped behind her back, she said, "Why should we fight among ourselves? Doesn't the Revolution have enough outside enemies. The Bolsheviks—in spite of their faults—were the first to honor the people's simple needs after the Tsar fell. And now suddenly they're the enemies of the people."

"They are the enemies of the Revolution," the Duty Commander confirmed. "They've betrayed us to Germany. They've cruelly ignored the hunger of the Russian peasant—as you know better than others. You yourself confronted the Bolshevik requisition squads in the villages."

"Take the gun, Kala," begged Gregori, a fourteen-year-old peasant boy, Kala's relief on her watch duty. "It's an order—it's what we must do." He looked to the Duty Commander to settle the matter.

The Duty Commander laid down Kala's gun and ammunition, took hold of her arm, and led her over to the lodge. Once inside, he gazed at her with great perplexity. "You of all people—to refuse to take a gun . . . when your husband is such a loyal comrade."

"Mikhail has nothing to do with it. Who began this fighting?"

"The Bolsheviks attacked us."

"Attacked us?"

"Because we assassinated the German ambassador, Mirbach."

"That's murder." Kala recalled Count von Mirbach sitting vividly and invulnerably in the Bolshoi Theater surrounded by his aides, each in a straightbacked military posture. To steady herself she put her hand on the Duty Commander's shoulder. "So we began the fighting."

"Not exactly." The short burly man regarded her courteously and seemed to Kala to grow shorter, her arm descending with him while he shrank.

"Do you know where Mikhail is?"

"He's somewhere with our fighting troops in the city. We're battling everywhere. The entire project has been wonderfully successful. You have no reason to refuse a gun."

"You're right," said Kala, all at once subdued. "I have no reason to refuse your order." She walked ahead of the Duty Commander to the courtyard, took up her rifle and shouldered it. Continuing her watch, she reflected that now there would be another civil war, this time among the revolutionaries themselves. Her loathing for politics overwhelmed her.

After a few hours the young peasant boy, Gregori, took over from Kala and she rushed into the palace. She found her father seated comfortably in an ornate yet sturdy armchair in the Countess's sitting room, leafing through an elaborately illustrated travel book. "Papa," she began, then put her hand to her mouth, unwilling to reveal that the same people who had joined to establish justice throughout Russia were about to start shooting one another.

Naftali looked up from the travel book, indicated a brightly colored picture of tropical vegetation and azure skies and marveled, "Here in Moscow—I almost know how to read."

"Papa," Kala went on, "that nastiness we witnessed in the Bolshoi Theater—it's come to a head. Here at party headquarters we're preparing for battle. I want you to leave right now and go to the station. There's no reason for you to stay. Come!" she commanded, taking up his suitcase. "I will get them to let you out the gate." She tried to give him his hat and cane.

Naftali rose and replaced the hat and cane upon the table where Kala had found them. He then sat down and crossed his legs. "I am going nowhere without you."

"But there might be fighting. There probably will be fighting. There is fighting."

"Let them fight. I'll have nothing to do with it. When you and Mikhail are ready to come with me—the sooner the better—then we'll go. I have all the necessary papers in my pockets."

Thwarted, she returned to the courtyard. Here she found the Duty Commander standing on top of a pile of sandbags and reporting to the members of the watch that their party had seized the Central Post Office in addition to other strategic areas of the city, that their party was winning over the Bolsheviks—he rubbed his hands in satisfaction—and that General Muraviev, Soviet Army Commander on the Volga, was marching his army toward Moscow to support the Left Socialist Revolutionaries. The wide flat expanse of the Duty Commander's orange skin shimmered with pleasure. "General Muraviev, the defender of Petrograd against Kerensky!" he identified proudly. "Former Soviet Commander of the Ukraine—I know him well!"

Nothing happened for hours. Kala was once more placed on guard duty and once more released. On her way to the kitchen for tea, she looked into the Countess's sitting room, where she found her father sound asleep in the armchair. As she drank her tea, a flurry of rifle fire sputtered from this direction and that—after which the sound of a heavier gun boomed. Then there was silence and Kala managed to doze briefly before she was awakened for the next watch. On her way to the courtyard she joined a group in the entranceway reading a statement issued by the Central Committee to the Bolshevik-controlled government: "The Central Committee of the Left Socialist Party takes full responsibility for the assassination of the imperialist German ambassador and the Left Socialist Revolutionary Party unilaterally declares a renewal of the Socialist struggle against imperialist Germany. Nevertheless, we wish to emphasize that this act in no way reflects upon our loyalty to the democratically elected Soviet government. We merely seek to correct the illegal acts of certain officials and to demonstrate that the shortsighted response of the Bolshevik Party to our protest has forced upon us a limited course of self-defense based upon the principles of the Revolution."

Kala read the notice. It struck her, then, that all words had lost their meaning and that with this conflict between her party and the Bolsheviks the Revolution had descended into chaos. Slowly she walked out of the palace and in the courtyard found her Duty Commander equally upset by the proclamation, though for different reasons than her own.

"Equivocations!" his voice quavered. "To be restrained by equivocations! How can we fight when our leaders insist they have no intention of overthrowing the government? We could be masters of Moscow at this moment!"

"Do you really believe that?" Kala asked him.

"Yes, yes, we took them completely by surprise—sending our delegates to the Congress as though it were just another day. Now if the Central Committee would only make use of their advantage . . ." He stopped short and ran into the palace. Presently he returned, the cheerful shimmer gone from his orange, now pallid and yellowing, skin. In a dismal voice he informed the watch that although the Left Socialist Revolutionaries had trained their guns upon the Kremlin, the Central Committee was allowing only one shell an hour to be fired, out of fear of retaliation upon the delegates now being held hostage at the Bolshoi Theater. "Such an ineffective bombardment," he protested, "will only encourage the Bolsheviks."

"Why are you surprised? We're good at ineffective gestures," Kala remarked.

Ignoring her, the Duty Commander continued, "And now our lookouts report that the Lettish infantry is dragging a cannon up the Levanka Heights and that the next thing we know they'll start shelling us from there." Growling, he demanded more sandbags placed around the courtyard and gave instructions about seeking shelter should a bombardment actually begin.

Toward dawn a full heavy fog rolled out over the city so that Kala could hardly make out the buildings across the lane. Anxiously, she peered into the lane, hoping that Mikhail would return, and fearing he might be wounded or dead. At daybreak the Duty Commander assembled the guards. His face sagged with fatigue, and in his dejection he could barely make himself explain that the Left Socialist Revolutionary armed forces, demoralized by the conciliatory attitude of their own Central Committee, had lost the Post Office and almost all the strategic territory they had won the day before. "Worst of all, Spiridonova stole away from the palace during the night without informing anyone. She has surrendered herself at the Bolshoi Theater to share the fate of the hostages."

A groan rose from Kala at Spiridonova's act of self-sacrifice. "It's an omen of defeat," she said.

And indeed, a half hour later, a dejected band of Left Socialist Revolutionary soldiers returned to the palace and deployed themselves around the courtyard. To Kala's joy, Mikhail was among them. But she had no time even to greet him, for he had no sooner arrived than a shell whistled over-head and exploded nearby. Kala found herself on the ground as shrapnel and paving stones clattered about her: the Lettish cannon had begun to fire. To her right she heard a bellowing cry from a member of the Military Committee who lay on the ground, blood spurting from his shattered left arm. While his companions rolled their cannon forward, seeking some target through the closed gates, Kala crawled to the wounded man, seized his good arm and dragged him toward the palace door. A second shell from the heights burst, damaging a building across the lane; a third hit somewhere behind the palace. The palace gunners wheeled their piece this way and that but their view of the enemy on the heights was blocked at every angle, either by the palace itself or by other buildings. The Lettish shells, seeking the correct range, began exploding here and there in the neighborhood. As Kala cleared the palace door with the wounded man, a party of medics rushed forward to care for him. Then a great crash sounded over-head. The building shook, windows and mirrors shattered, and one of the great chandeliers above the staircase fell to the landing. Almost immediately a shout came echoing down the hallway, repeated by one voice after another, "Surrender! Surrender! The Central Committee's capitulated by telephone! Lay down your arms!"

In the confusion that followed, Mikhail joined Kala in a search for her father. At the Countess's sitting room they discovered the door open—Naftali and his belongings gone. Back in the corridor they found themselves pushed this way and that within a milling crowd that surged about to shouts and orders. Mikhail suggested that they split up: he would search the upper stories and she the lower. Kala caught sight of her comrades feverishly throwing their rifles and pistols to the floor before marching toward the front entrance with their hands held high in the air. As they passed, she asked if they had seen her father. Some merely shook their heads; some were too upset to answer, the tears streaming from their eyes. In despair the young woman ran from room to room, finally stopping to scan the grand staircase. Here Mikhail joined her. On impulse they followed after the Duty Commander and three other men who had just forced their way back into the palace. They sprinted through a door and down some steps to the cellar of the palace. In the darkness Kala bumped into someone and excused herself. "Shhh!" the men whispered. "Make sure the upper door is closed." A man slipped past Kala up the stairs and closed the door. Then Kala made out a line of light at the far end of the cellar, shining under another door. For a moment she feared that from behind the edge of light a troop of Bolsheviks would emerge to capture them. The Duty Commander drew his pistol and crept forward. Swiftly he thrust open the door to reveal Naftali, wearing only his white shirt, his white underdrawers, his shining high-laced black shoes and his bowler hat. Two oil lanterns stood on either end of a table covered with a sheet on which lay his trousers and his jacket, carefully smoothed out.

"What's the meaning of this, don't you have any manners?" In his hand, poised over his trousers and jacket, Naf-

[221]

tali held an iron, hot embers glowing in its chimney. "Imagine bursting in on a man without knocking!"

"Who is this madman?" asked the Duty Commander, his pistol wavering about in his hand.

"He's my father—and Papa, this is my Duty Commander. Papa, if you put down the iron, my Duty Commander will put down his pistol."

"Why should I put it down?" cried Naftali. "I had too hard a time finding it. I had to come all the way down to the basement."

"Is that really your father?" the Duty Commander asked with a look of bewilderment. He sheathed his pistol. "All the others are surrendering. We're going to wait down here for nightfall when we plan to escape. Your father is welcome to join us."

Kala stared around the room at the men who had crowded in, shutting the door behind them. They were busy stripping off their uniform jackets and putting on working men's jackets and shirts they had carried down with them. "Papa," Kala said, "it might be wise of us to surrender. Almost everyone has surrendered. I think they would let you go."

"I have no intention of surrendering," Naftali replied. "I haven't even finished ironing. When everything has quieted down, there's a perfectly good coal chute in the corner. We can make our way up through it to the street and take your belongings." He indicated two good-sized rucksacks that stood next to his suitcase, explaining somewhat smugly, "When the shelling began, I went to your chamber and took everything—clothes, bedding, even a little blue vase that stood on the table next to your bed. Why should we leave it for the Bolsheviks?" He held up his suit to scrutinize his ironing, folded the suit, removed his shirt and tie and placed the clothes carefully in his suitcase. Then he dressed himself in a peasant smock and trousers belonging to Mikhail, peered into each of the men's faces to determine if Mikhail's face was among them, and inquired of Kala, "Where's your husband?"

"Mikhail?" Kala asked. "He's right here. Don't you recognize him?"

"I haven't seen him that often."

Overhead the clatter of boots and the sound of shouts slowly diminished, then ceased and the faint light faded at the far end of the coal chute where it connected to a small back lane. "Are you all right, Kala?" Mikhail whispered.

"No. Of course I'm not. The Party brought all this on itself," Kala began. But it was impossible to carry on an argument in the crowded cellar. As she sat in the dark listening to the restless movements of the men around her, her bitterness toward the Party's politics gradually dissipated. She was moved instead by the close presence of her comrades, whose breaths and coughs filled the silence. She was grateful to them for the warmth with which they had always accepted her—for the fact they had welcomed her into their family and had shared with her their hope and excitement for a just future. Then, once more, gradually, her disappointment with the Party came drifting back. "We weren't even honestly interested in taking power," she said to Mikhail. "All we wanted was to register a protest. And we did it with murder."

"We spoke to the Bolsheviks in their own language."

They said no more. It was clear to each of them that their positions had not changed. Finally the midnight bell tolled and Kala's and Mikhail's companions set forth, one by one, through the coal chute at intervals of half an hour. The Duty Commander, the last among them, embraced the young couple lengthily, wishing them good luck. When he had disappeared up the coal chute, Kala asked, "What will happen to the Party now?" She lowered her chin, staring absently at her boots with the sense she had lost some precious connection.

"The Party will survive. If that interests you," Mikhail declared.

"It doesn't want to survive. If it did, it would give up violence."

"We'll take everything I packed," Naftali interrupted. "No reason to leave it here. We can use it all at home."

Briefly Mikhail objected, reasoning that so much luggage would prove cumbersome to their movement, but Naftali drew down his lip and refused to listen. Giving up, Mikhail crawled through the coal chute up into the coalyard and Naftali handed him the suitcase and the two rucksacks. By good fortune an upended wheelbarrow lay next to the chute, and in a moment Mikhail was wheeling their goods along while Kala and Naftali marched on either side of him. Just as they turned onto the lane alongside the palace a squad of Lettish infantrymen overtook them from behind. "What are you doing out so late?" the squad leader demanded.

"Going to the market, your excellency," replied Naftali, his voice—to Kala's astonishment—having taken on the exact broad accent of the peasants of Lyesk.

"The market! At this hour?"

"If you don't get there early, you don't get a good stall."

"Go ahead," said the soldier, shooing them on their way.

"Where are we going?" asked Kala, after they had turned a corner.

"To the station, of course," replied Naftali. "Our plan is to leave Moscow on the next train."

"It's no use," murmured Mikhail. "We'll never get through the guards."

"Don't be foolish," said Naftali. "I have everything we need." He paused in the corner of a courtyard, where he removed two sets of blank identification papers from his trouser pocket. "I bought these at the baths, first thing, when I got to Moscow. I knew you would be coming back with me one way or the other. It's just a question of your filling in the right blanks and transferring your identity card photographs. After that, leave everything to me. I can tell just by looking who to bribe." And he urged the pair of them to the train station, repeating as he hurried them along that there was no reason to stay in Moscow—that there was hardly anything in the city to eat, that half the buildings were falling down, and that the palaces would always remain undusted. Inside the station he led his daughter and son-in-law to an obscure corner far from the gates, instructing them to stay in one spot while he went off and tried to procure space on the crowded train. "Take care of your identification papers," he added. As he left, Kala and Mikhail, without glancing at one another, took positions at opposite ends of a bench.

For a few minutes neither spoke. Then Mikhail said, "I don't think it's right for us to go. Let's just put your father on the train."

"And stay here and be arrested?"

"We could hide out."

"And then what?"

Mikhail moved toward Kala on the bench. "This is ridiculous. People will overhear us." He moved still closer. "I know you want to go home—you've been wanting to for a long time. And perhaps that's what we ought to do for the present. At least the Bolsheviks can't get at us there."

She nodded gratefully. "We'll be safer in Lyesk." She slid the last few inches separating them, and they went to work filling out their papers.

When Naftali returned, half an hour later, he found the young couple asleep in one another's arms. He had to wake them up to board the train.

Just before they reached the Russian-German border— across the swamps from Luninyets—Kala and Mikhail started to argue again.

"Enough! Enough carrying on!" commanded Naftali. He raised his hand to stop them. "And now no more talk about revolution—left, right, socialist, or whatever. We're almost to the border and the Germans don't want to hear such talk— they can't abide it—they have a horror of revolution just like everyone else in the world except for the Russians. Only the Russians are so foolish and grand. So far as anyone outside the family is concerned the two of you have been working for the relief organization, Northern Aid."

"Then what shall we talk about?" Kala challenged.

Brushing off the edge in his daughter's voice, Naftali benignly proposed, "Why, any number of things. Ekaterina, for example, and whom she might marry—in spite of her picky airs and the dozen suitors she's rejected. Or about whom Sophie might find for a bridegroom, considering her legs. We'll talk about important things—important subjects. We'll talk about suitors and marriages."

CHAPTER TWENTY

On A MOONLESS NIGHT NAFTALI LED KALA AND MIKHAIL through a series of mazelike paths across the swamps that formed the border near Luninyets. He pushed ahead without hesitation though he had been shown this route only once—on his way to Moscow—by a local peasant. As they reached the railroad town of Luninyets, Naftali produced from his pocket another set of identification papers and a railroad pass for each of them—papers which he'd obtained from friends in the German command before leaving Lyesk. At Kala's grateful exclamation, Naftali stopped short. "You and your sisters," he said. "You think I can't do anything. You think that just your mother is capable of everything. But when it's necessary . . . I can do a lot."

"You can do a lot," Kala hastened to agree.

Shortly after dawn they entered the railroad station, and a few hours later they boarded the train to Baranovits amidst a frantic, jostling crowd. As they mounted their carriage, word spread that the Tsar had been executed by the Bolsheviks somewhere in the south—near Ekaterinburg. The three travelers, shocked, sank into a corner of the stifling railroad carriage. "And all his family," repeated Naftali. "The children too."

Who was the enemy of the people now? wondered Kala. She gazed at her husband and saw bewilderment in his deep blue eyes. She reached out and touched his arm. Exhausted, she fell asleep when the train started up—jouncing, swaying, and rattling its way north and west toward home. She dreamed that the freezing dust storms of Cerikov enveloped the summer streets of Moscow; that the living were dead and the dead living. Luka and the twins came rushing at her bearing a Bolshevik banner; Mikhail lay still alive but half-buried by the side of the road in a shallow grave at Bobruisk. Once when she woke briefly and moved her head to make certain Mikhail was safe, she heard her father begin to speak, his voice oddly metallic amidst the rumbling of the carriage. "The first thing your mother will want to know," he said, his eyes wide open as he stared through the darkness, "is why you have no children. She'll mean for you to go to the doctor or to the wonder rabbi. And she's right. By your age she had borne four children—three of them already dead—each of the babies dead except for Iosif—there was nothing we could do for the others, but at least they had been born. What is a marriage, Kala, without children? When you think it over it's something peculiar, something perverse. And then, of course, every Jew has a duty to keep on producing children in order that our people survive."

The carriage rocked back and forth and Kala's head nodded—bounced along by the train, which all by itself seemed to her to take in, to acknowledge her father's words. She let her eyes fall shut again; and she slept.

The next morning, after they had changed trains in Baranovits and had gone on, passing off the main line, the train stopped in the middle of a birch forest to take on water from a tank fed by a nearby stream. The passengers stepped down to stretch their legs and to check on where they were. "We're not far," said Naftali. "We'll be in Lyesk in just a few more hours."

Kala looked around and sniffed the air. This was the countryside of her childhood: she could see shadows and sunlight dance about the forest floor. Soon, she thought, she would walk on the streets of Lyesk; she would climb through her own fields, wade in the river, enter through the door of her house and embrace her mother and sisters. It was a warm summer's day; yet a cool breeze ruffled the birch leaves. With joy she shouted, "I'm going home!"

"I'm glad you're happy," Mikhail said.

But when she, her husband, and her father arrived in Lyesk, a forlorn and shoddy railroad station greeted them. The gabled tower had not been rebuilt and the station house consisted of little more than a big shed with a corrugated iron overhang to shelter the public from rain or snow. The red and gold sign was gone and the name of the town was printed in German, with a small parenthesis below in Cyrillic letters to recall Lyesk's former rulers. Scanning the crowded platform, Kala recognized not a single person among those who waited. Every face announced its difference, every person appearing more impoverished and somehow sadder than the people she'd known before. "Who are they?" she asked her father. "Where do they live?"

"Mainly they are Poles and most of them live in Lyesk," replied Naftali. "If you ask me, these are the worst of the lot. When they could make no living in the kingdom of Poland they came east to fill up the empty land and take the jobs of the evacuated Russians. We even have Polish peasants in Little Lyesk now, though still not a large migration, and they've scarcely seeded the land they live on—if they've planted twenty percent, that's a lot."

"What have they planted?" Mikhail asked.

"Who knows? Nothing has come up." As he spoke, Naftali led them to a corner of the station house. "Stay right here," he said and then disappeared between two German guards

[229]

through a door. When he did not instantly return, Kala paced down the platform. She passed a handful of German soldiers who stood listlessly about, their uniforms worn and wrinkled; and she was reminded that for their country the war continued on the western front, with fighting in Belgium and France. She looked at the men a second time, pitying the boredom of their stance. Her eyes then lifted to the road that climbed from the station to the town. This was the same road, she thought, down which the Stationmaster, Ivan Sergeyevich Dovrynin, had driven in his droshky to meet the important trains; yet at its summit, the buildings—raw with a mixture of new and old boards—belonged to some other town. She paced back to Mikhail and remarked wryly, "Well, you can't say this is the same place as before."

Just then Naftali emerged from the station house with a young blonde woman. Kala stared. The woman stared. The two sisters ran toward each other, stopped short, and then kissed noisily. Stepping back, Ekaterina surveyed Kala. "You haven't changed," she summed up. "You've been to Petrograd and Moscow but you haven't changed."

Kala blushed. She glanced down at her frayed blouse and mended skirt, her worn boots. She felt ashamed and then annoyed. "I am different," she shrugged. "For one thing . . . you remember Mikhail . . ." Mikhail came forward and he and Ekaterina embraced quickly. "But you, Ekaterina," Kala fixed her eyes with admiration on her sister—particularly on her sister's white-blonde hair which, instead of covering half her face, was coiled into a smooth chignon on top of her head. "You look so adult."

"I'm seventeen."

"You look so grown-up. Your face," Kala grinned, "you're letting it show." She pointed to the lovely angles of Ekaterina's cheekbones and her chin.

"I am grown-up," Ekaterina said, raising her head. "I earn wages."

"Your clothes, Ekaterina . . ."

Ekaterina nodded with approval. "It's the new dressmaker. Her patterns and her styles all come from Paris."

"The dressmaker's French?"

"She's Polish."

"And our own dressmaker, Dunya?"

"Oh Dunya," Ekaterina sighed. "We all miss Dunya, but it's the same story with her as with the other Russian refugees. We're sure she's trying to get back across the border like all those who fled with you—Ruth says she sometimes imagines Dunya standing at the guardhouse, unable to enter. Officially no one gets in—the Germans are too afraid," her glance traveled pointedly between Kala and Mikhail, "of revolutionaries."

"There are no revolutionaries here." Naftali's frown warned Ekaterina. "Your sister and her husband have been working for Northern Aid. And Ekaterina," Naftali offered over his shoulder as he took Mikhail and walked away to engage a cab, "if you want to hear about my trip to Moscow, you can come up to the bakery with us for a few hours."

"I can't just leave my work at the telegraph office and come up to the bakery." Ekaterina's lower lip jutted out. Recognizing her little sister again, Kala took an eager step forward. "I can't just leave, I've got too much to do." But then she smiled and informed Kala she had arrived just in time for a fair. The Northern District Military Commander was coming to Lyesk and on Sunday the local military command would be giving a parade and a band concert in his honor at the airfield. "There'll be stalls and prizes and games and dancing, and I've been put in charge of all the stalls and the invitations." Ekaterina sucked in her breath; her eyes sparkled. "It's our first real entertainment since before the war. Mama says it's almost better than extra flour and sugar." She checked about to make certain her father had gone out of earshot. "And I'll show you the airplane. I know how to fly."

"To fly?"

"Not exactly. I've gone up and come down at least five or six times with two of the officers. Sophie is the only one who knows. While you were gone, Sophie and I have become best friends." She slid Kala a sidelong stealthy glance. "I promised that one day I'll take her up with me. Now don't mention to Papa about flying—here he comes with Lyesk's new coachman. Just wait till you see how slowly that horse staggers along."

A few minutes later Kala, her father, and Mikhail started up Station Hill. A swaybacked horse pulled them—the animal driven by a sour, unpleasant man who spoke only in Polish and who made no effort to help them with their luggage. As they climbed Station Hill, Kala tried to picture Ekaterina flying an airplane all the way to Paris.

"The coachman takes whatever business he can from Lazar Dovitsky," Naftali remarked.

"Lazar Dovitsky runs a stable," Kala explained to Mikhail. "He's one of our friends."

The carriage reached the town square, where Kala contemplated the buildings to discover she could not identify a single one. Even the location of everything had been moved—with only the church and the city offices rebuilt on their original foundations. Through the buildings she glimpsed the countryside, the high grass of the fields waving, the green blades signaling at her that Luka and the twins were dead. She forced herself to remain silent.

"In my opinion," Naftali said while they rolled through Merchant Lane, "the street looks a hundred times better now than it did before the fire. All those old buildings were ready to fall down anyway."

"Yes, it's a lot trimmer than before," Mikhail said. "It's cheerier. It's brighter." He glanced anxiously at his wife. "It's cheerier, isn't it, Kala?"

Kala squared her chin and sat up straight. She wanted to agree that the new facades—though pieced together from scrap lumber and possessing a patchwork aspect—nevertheless looked sprightlier and more substantial than the hovels lining Merchant Lane before. She opened her mouth to offer some charitable remark and prove she did not mean to carry on about anything so trivial as buildings, but her tongue refused to shape any words. Worse still—to her humiliation, a tear threatened to form at the corner of one eye.

The next thing she knew the horse drew slowly to a stop and the coachman shouted in Polish, "All out!" For an instant Kala sat frozen: the ride had seemed much too short. She wondered if, on top of all the other differences, the distances and the size of the town had shrunk. Then, stepping from the carriage she saw the bakery—she saw it utterly unchanged—with its proud and festive porch, its Dutch door open. On the porch—as if no exodus, no fire, no change of rulers had taken place—Avrom Lavin, Mendel Feldshpan, and Moishe Kantorovits sat drinking tea. Upon catching sight of the newcomers they rose, greeted Naftali, and gazed with surprise at Kala and her husband. Choosing not to pause for them, Kala raced straightway into the bakery and jubilantly threw herself upon Sophie so that they spun round together in the swivel chair behind the cash register. Laughing, she kissed her sister again and again. Hungrily she took in Sophie's long black hair, her high cheekbones, her vivid color, her dark blue eyes. "Sophie, my Sophie," she exulted, "you look exactly the same!"

"You too look the same," Sophie echoed, in pleasure.

A few feet away Malkeh waited. Kala went up to her, startled by the air of magisterial grandeur that surrounded her mother. She realized she had forgotten, or had let herself forget, the range of intelligence in Malkeh's gray clear eyes, the magnetic force of her presence. She and her mother embraced, and in her fervor Kala put aside for consideration at some other time the new worn lines in Malkeh's cheeks and around her eyes. "Mama!" she exclaimed. "Mikhail and I are home! We're home!"

At this, Naftali, Avrom Lavin, Mendel Feldshpan, and Moishe Kantorovits came in from the porch, and Ruth emerged from the back of the bakery, a baby in her arms

[233]

and two small girls, barely walking, holding onto her skirts. As Kala's arms encircled Ruth and the children, the two small girls began to cry. "Don't cry," Ruth scolded them, "don't cry—it's your Aunt Kala." They cried even louder. Their tears had not subsided before Naomi Pearl Benjamin and her cohort, Leah Kantorovits Feldshpan, entered the bakery at a trot. Everyone embraced Kala and Naftali and shook hands cordially with Mikhail. "So you've been to Moscow!" chorused Naomi and Leah.

"Even Papa's been to Moscow," Sophie added.

"And now I've come back. Malkeh," Naftali demanded, "bring some cake!"

"There isn't any cake," Ruth murmured. She and Malkeh brought the travelers weak tea and lemon and three thin slices of black bread. The little girls continued to hold Ruth's skirt in their fists. Kala noted that they possessed large brown eyes like their mother's and that their other features resembled Mordecai's—by some great misfortune even their large peach transparent-looking ears. But what was most distressing by far was that the look of serenity on Ruth's face—that expression of Ruth's belief on which Kala had counted, which Kala had loved even when it had exasperated and baffled her the most—had altogether disappeared. A struggling, almost fierce expression had taken its place, and Ruth's brows—once so wide apart and placid—had darkened and moved closer together.

Naftali ate a slice of black bread, took a sip of tea, and with both hands urged the bakery's customers to draw near the front table where he'd settled in. "I have much to tell you about Moscow," he began. "I have a thousand impressions. Here in Lyesk you may think we're unfortunate because we can't have cake. But in Moscow the bourgeoisie are allotted one-eighth pound of bread a day."

"The workers get half a pound," Kala interjected.

"In Moscow," Naftali ignored her, "there's even less food than here. Because there's no land. Everyone is hungry. You can walk from north to south, from east to west, and the whole city is full of the sound of stomachs grumbling. Sometimes you see children with eyes popping out and bloated bellies."

"Otherwise is Moscow wonderful?" a woman inquired.

Naftali gazed into the near distance, reflecting. Then he shook his head contentedly and went on, "Half the buildings are full of holes, the government employs madmen only, and the normal population is threatened day and night by rude ruffians in uniforms who carry guns." He took an appreciative gulp of tea. "But the sights . . . oh the sights!"

"The sights . . . ?"

"The Kitay-Gorod Market for one. In that market you can put two hundred of our markets and still have room for two hundred more. The shops in Red Square for another. Not a lot of merchandise in them but whatever there is . . . is exceptional. I saw nobility selling peanuts, sunflower seeds. I saw the famous churches . . . have you ever heard of the Church of Vassily Blageenyi? Near the Kremlin I saw," he counted on his fingers, "Arabians, Turks, Mongolians, Finns, Lapps, Chinese, not just Poles and Lithuanians like here. I saw the Moskva River, a fine river, a stately river . . . a little lethargic."

But already some of his listeners had grown impatient and were turning away—among them Naomi and Leah, who had posted themselves behind Mikhail. Peering over Mikhail's shoulder they inquired after the health of his family in Vilna and remarked that simply to look at Kala's husband was a pleasure, particularly in these years when all handsome able-bodied men were off fighting, either in Germany or Russia, or else they were dead.

"But not my husband, the rabbi," Naomi informed Kala. "He isn't fighting. Wait till you see him. These days instead of aping the Russian aristocracy he's busy imitating the Germans. He makes Avrom Lavin cut his suits so they look like uniforms and he carries a swagger stick even though he doesn't own a horse. "But my Pinchas—nine years old and smarter every day—you should see him."

"I saw the Moskva River and across the river, the Kremlin," Naftali said. As no one paid much attention, Naftali cleared his throat. "I saw the Moskva River and across from it the Kremlin." When still no one paid enough attention, Mikhail cleared his throat on behalf of his father-in-law and Kala sternly clapped her hands.

"Kala, why are you clapping your hands?" wheezed Avrom Lavin. "Kala, Kala," he waved his gold watch in front of her face. "It always works now—ever since the new watch repairman fixed it. He's a Polish veteran, lost his legs in the German army, decided to stay. His wife's a dressmaker. To have a real watch repairman in Lyesk—what a relief that's been!"

"It's a relief to me too," Kala said.

"Not a single word against Kala's repair." Malkeh entered the conversation. Though her voice was low and unemphatic, all heads pivoted toward her. Several of her customers jumped as if they had something to hide, while others appeared momentarily relieved of their worries. "We are more than blessed this afternoon," Malkeh said. "The children and Naftali have come home. And there is other news—good news for all of us." She paused, the barest pleased smile on her lips. "Major Kleist has decided not to cut down the eastern corner of the birch woods—and not only that," she turned to Mendel Feldshpan, "the Major's decided to keep your leather machinery in Lyesk, Mendel, instead of taking it from your factory and sending it on to Germany."

"So I'm still a leather manufacturer," Mendel mused.

"For a time," Malkeh said. "Meanwhile, don't fool yourself that such a thing was easy for the Major to arrange. You know as well as I . . . Lyesk has failed to supply its ration of lumber and tools for shipping back to the homeland. I told him you were grateful, Mendel."

"I am grateful," Feldshpan agreed.

"And I found out, in the course of talking, that the Major's boot size is eleven and a half, medium width. He's not a greedy man, Mendel—just a pair of boots and a saddle is all he wants. It turns out his youngest child has a pony that needs a saddle with bells."

"I visited the Bolshoi Theater," Naftali said.

"And considering our good fortune this afternoon, when you go home—you, my friend Mendel and you too, my good friend Moishe, I want you—and everyone else—to look and see what you can spare for the refugees. We're gathering a few packages to send to the border."

"Not the refugees again!" moaned Feldshpan.

"Why not the refugees?" Malkeh demanded. "Or else they'll starve at the border, just waiting to get back home."

"Either the refugees go in one direction," Avrom Lavin said, "or else they turn around and go in the other direction."

"In the Bolshoi Theater I saw the Soviet Congress," Naftali muttered.

All at once Mikhail pushed back his chair with a violent gesture and stood up. "My father-in-law has been to Moscow. You must listen to him!" he shouted passionately. "My father-in-law—he alone—is responsible for our safe return to Lyesk. Without his courage, without his wits, we would still be stuck on the other side of the border or in jail."

Kala gazed appreciatively at her husband and Dovitsky the stableman called out, "Hooray for Naftali!" But then Mendel Feldshpan added, "And now the Tsar and his children are dead," and a lively discussion started up.

"The Tsar is dead and I saw the Congress of his enemies," Naftali declared. "The fact is, I saw Lenin himself. I saw Lenin."

At the mention of Lenin, Malkeh, Ruth and Sophie looked in Naftali's direction. Briefly he acknowledged their interest, then dismissed it with a sharp nod as if, with Malkeh having usurped the center of the stage, he now required a larger audience than his family, a better and more powerful response. "Lenin," his eye roved discontentedly about, lighting on Malkeh who stood with folded arms filling the doorway to the bakery ovens. He stared at his wife as though unable to wrest away his gaze and finally it was she he addressed, his voice turning querulous and plaintive. "Lenin is . . . Lenin is bald."

Someone in the bakery giggled.

"Yes?" Malkeh inquired of Naftali.

"Lenin is . . . bald." Stubbornly Naftali sealed his lips. "That's all I have to say."

With this remark Kala witnessed her father shrink down and return—almost, it seemed to her, with relief—to his old place on the fringes of the family. Glancing away from him, she cringed, thinking there was nothing she could do—no way to change the fact that Malkeh drew importance out of her husband and gathered it to herself.

Toward the end of the afternoon Mordecai entered the bakery. After a few minutes he and Naftali moved to a back table. There they lit up and sat puffing on their pipes, clouds of smoke soon enveloping them and hiding them from concern and comment. Kala, peering through the haze, could scarcely believe that this Naftali was the same man who had reprimanded the Duty Commander for bursting in upon him with a drawn gun and had helped her and Mikhail escape Moscow. "Lenin," she heard Naftali murmur to Mordecai as the two men disappeared in their pipe smoke, "under his cap, Lenin is bald."

When the smoke was at its thickest, Malkeh closed the bakery though it was somewhat earlier than the usual hour. She sent Mordecai with Mikhail and Naftali to the bathhouse and Ruth and Sophie home to start dinner and arrange sleeping accommodations for the newcomers. "Kala and I need some time to be together so we can catch up."

Flattered, just as she'd always been when her mother singled her out, Kala looked on while Malkeh cleaned up. But instead of talking about Kala, as the young woman had expected, Malkeh said, "Ruth has become very religious."

"Ruth has always been very religious," Kala replied. She leaned back in her chair and basked in the bakery's whitewashed walls and ceiling. She watched her mother clear the shelves and wipe the counters.

"But this is entirely different. Do you remember what a careful little mother she was to you and your sisters . . . how she fussed over you?"

Kala laughed. "We were always doing something wrong."

"Or something right," Malkeh corrected. "Yet now that Ruth has her own children, she doesn't give them half the attention she gave you. Sophie takes care of the little girls as much as Ruth does—maybe more."

"Oh, it's all right to share those duties," Kala allowed, curiously happy to be gossiping about her sisters with her mother. "There's nothing wrong with that." She breathed in deeply, renewing her acquaintance with the old scent of cinnamon and yeast, her eyes keenly taking in the bakery's Dutch door, its thick beams and side-paneled front windows. She had the sense that her mother had raised her to the status of the eldest daughter. Indeed, so taken was she by this rendezvous with Malkeh, enriched by the odor of apples and yeast and the sharp smell of Naftali's pickle barrel, that she let her mother scrub away, forgetting to get up and offer her some help.

"Oh, of course. It's fine to share those duties," Malkeh said. "But the point is . . . what I want to tell you is that Ruth has become fanatic. She takes food to the poor scholars in the House of Study—which is very good, of course, it's what I want her to do—yet once she gets near the House of Study she forgets everything—her children, her husband. She doesn't want to come home. Sometimes we have to send for her, and there she is, standing in a corner, reading some commentary or other."

Kala was silent, thinking this was the wrong confidence for her mother to reveal. She wished Malkeh had shown more restraint. It troubled her to hear her mother complain—especially about Ruth. Then she noted the threads of gray littering Malkeh's hair and observed that the muscles of her back, the flesh of Malkeh's shoulders, her arms, her breasts, seemed slightly to droop.

"Ruth was always religious by nature," Kala said, wanting

in some way to improve matters and at the same time not to think about the new fierceness in her sister's face. "And if the scholars let her read the commentary with them . . . ."

"Oh, she never sits down with the men. I think they pretend she isn't there. Our new *shammes* tells me that as she passes out the food or stands by the door listening, the men turn to her and ask questions—over their shoulders. I think she's more learned than they. Even the *shammes* says so. But it bothers me to think of her like that . . . so . . . so extreme—fanatic." Malkeh glanced out the window. "And there goes our Sophie, riding by."

"Sophie?" Quickly Kala shifted her head. "Where is she going?"

"To the barracks. We bake for the army, of course—which is why we're better off than most—and on these fine evenings I let Sophie harness Mishka and ride the cart to the barracks. She takes her time going and coming—just to deliver bread—so that I can't help but worry about her. Yet it's her only outing and Sophie deserves a chance to get off by herself." Malkeh made her way across the room and sat down, a trifle heavily, across from Kala. For a space of time she gazed at Kala in silence, as if simply to appreciate their being together. She laid her hands on top of Kala's hands on the table. "Are you happy, my daughter?" she inquired.

"Very happy, very happy, Mama," Kala replied. "Very happy," she repeated and grew even happier as though, following this genuine expression of Malkeh's concern, every confidence she now released to her mother would have room within Malkeh's ample presence to wander about, to take short naps, to emerge refreshed.

"With Mikhail?"

"Oh, with Mikhail . . . I never imagined in my best dreams I could be this lucky."

Malkeh nodded. Her hands pressed down, very slightly, on the back of Kala's hands. "And does your work with your party satisfy you?"

Astonished—never having expected her mother would so much as allude to her connection with politics—she said, "My work?"

"It isn't that I have sympathy for the revolution. But if your duties with your party follow your conscience—that's of very great importance."

"I thank you, I thank you, Mama."

"Without work, life loses its meaning and its sweetness." Malkeh glanced away. At the same time she pressed down harder on Kala's hands. "Mikhail is good to you . . . considerate? Is there a reason you have no children?"

Eager to explain, Kala began, "We made a conscious decision." She took a deep breath. "A complicated decision. Until our country's political conflicts . . ."

Malkeh interrupted her with a benign smile. "The world continues to go around, my daughter. No one has ever waited for politics to straighten out before they have children. If they did, no one would ever have been born. There must be some other problem."

"No other problem. We're just very careful. Mikhail takes responsibility seriously. He wants children when their lives will be less upset, when conditions in our country have improved. I still consider myself Russian."

Malkeh untied her apron. Carefully she pulled it over her head and folded it on her lap. Her fingers smoothed the starched fabric. "You can tell me if you are trying to protect him. I know your loyal nature."

"Protect him from what? From you?"

"He was a student in St. Petersburg," Malkeh went on, unperturbed, "before he met you. A radical. In cities like St. Petersburg and Moscow a young man can pick up any number of diseases. I don't say that he has. I don't even mean to suggest he is sterile." She stood up, lightly holding to the back of her chair. "But suppose if, after you've seen the doctor and the wonder rabbi, he cannot give you children, then could you see your way to asking for a divorce?"

"For a divorce? From my husband? When I've just explained that he's the man I care for more than anything in the world?"

"If he cannot provide you with children."

The color drained from Kala's face. Gradually it returned, and when she spoke again her manner was as ceremonious as her mother's. "You find him different because he was brought up in a different class. I think he's perfect."

"You'll never convince me until you have children."

CHAPTER TWENTY-ONE

"GOOD NIGHT, GOOD NIGHT," CALLED THE FAMILY. WITH encouraging nods, Naftali, Malkeh, and Mordecai ushered Kala and Mikhail into the half completed parlor, where a borrowed double bed had been set up for them. "Welcome home—it's your own home," Naftali sang. "The bed is comfortable—it belongs to Reb Pearl," he chanted. "Sleep well—sleep long—no need to rouse yourselves in the morning."

Then the door of the parlor was shut. Offended at first by such bald prompting so soon after Malkeh's challenge in the bakery, Kala's mood improved as soon as she cast her eyes on the double bed. The prospect of comfort and privacy after so many days and nights on crowded railroad cars filled her with glee. All the same—as eager as she was to come to Mikhail as well as to try out the bed—she dawdled while he undressed. She studied the parlor's unfinished floor and the rough boards that served for its temporary walls and approached the

Chodorov piano which stood protected from the weather, bundled up in blankets and oilcloth. Recalling that Lazar Dovitsky had once suggested that this piano looked like a cow, she untied a corner of the oilcloth covering and scrutinized its mahogany veneer. She poked at the piano keys and ran her hand along the smooth finish of the wood. After a few minutes she sent Mikhail a sidelong glance. "You know what? Mama wants us to have babies."

"What?" Mikhail had been taking off his boots. Carefully he put them to one side.

"Mama wants us to have babies."

"Is that right?" the young man commented. "We've just arrived and she's already told you that? How many did she say she wants us to have?"

Pretending he intended no sarcasm, Kala mildly inquired, "How many do you want?"

Mikhail stretched out on the bed. He clasped his hands behind his head. "Twenty. Thirty."

"No Mikhail . . . I'm serious."

"Well, in that case I'd like five. Yes, I'd like five." He sat up all at once, as though the chance mention of children—in particular five children—had disarmed and claimed him. "Yes, when the time is right I'd like five girls with brown hair like yours or black like Sophie's. I might even want a boy." His eyes widened. At once sober and bemused, he considered this possibility. "Who knows—out of simple vanity I might even want a boy who resembles my own family—who looks like my father or perhaps one of my brothers. A Kossoff with a brilliant mind like theirs."

"That makes six children," Kala said.

"Six children." Mikhail closed his eyes, a languorous smile on his lips. "And we're the parents."

Frowning, Kala scrambled onto the bed. "But what if we can't have any children? What if it isn't possible? We've tried not to—how can we find out?"

"Well of course we can!" he threw back in a voice as appalled as though she were disparaging his character. "Neither of us has had any terrible disease. We're healthy." He looked her up and down. "And I've never laid eyes on anyone as healthy as you. Just look at the muscles in your arms! When the time is right, then we'll have six children, each with a beautiful name."

Kala glanced covertly at the lower part of her husband's graceful naked body. Everything was there, she thought. Everything was in order for his siring children. Her pulse quickened. Jumping up, she blew out the lamp and bent to kiss Mikhail's forehead, his eyes, cheeks, nose, mouth, and chin. She pulled off her clothes, then tried to hide under a corner of the sheet. "I feel shy . . . in my family's house," she whispered, "though actually," she peered around the room, "it's almost like sleeping outside."

"It is like sleeping outside." He had started to nibble on her ear and he stopped to follow her gaze. Through the cracks between the rough planking of the walls they could see the street and the dim buildings beyond, with lamps glowing golden here and there, indicating the life of the town. In the distance they heard a rumble of thunder, muffled by the humid evening. "So you're shy? What a nice idea!" His arms tightened around her. He kissed her shoulder near the base of her neck and let his lips wander, circling around each of her breasts. Then with one hand caressing her hair, her scalp, he moved on top of her and they sank into one another, bathed by the moist warm air.

Afterward, as they lay in each other's arms, he said, "Before we can allow ourselves the joy and the glory of children, we must be able to give them—oh I don't mean an absolute— but a relatively peaceful, a relatively honorable and stable life. When that's possible, then you and I—we'll devote ourselves to our seven children."

"Not six?" she asked suspiciously.

"Seven," Mikhail drowsily muttered.

"Why is the number going up?"

He did not answer and they fell asleep and were awakened in the middle of the night by loud claps of thunder and the clatter of rain on the metal roof. Flashes of lightning filled the room with bars of light. Uneasily they shifted about. A heavy mist drifted in through the wallboards, dampening their skin and cooling the room. Kala propped herself up on an elbow and tried to see through the boards out onto the street but all the golden lamps had been put out. The town lay dark under a barrage of rain. She imagined the streams of water coursing down Merchant Lane and the sensation of mud as it spilled over her bare feet and clasped her ankles. At least, she thought, it would be the mud of her own town. At her side she heard Mikhail utter a long, unfamiliar sounding sigh. "What are you thinking?" she asked him.

"Of our three good years together—and of the next step that's necessary."

"Which is?"

"Returning to Russia."

"Mikhail, we just left," she protested. "We got here today."

"I know. But by the time we get back the turmoil will have calmed down and the Party will need every one of its comrades—even us."

"Everyone's in hiding."

"They'll come out of hiding. All of our former allies will gather together again—the moderates, the Mensheviks, perhaps even the Bund. We can't leave the Revolution half finished. We'll find our strength in the countryside."

"What strength in the countryside?" Kala inquired, recalling that in the villages outside Moscow where she'd worked she'd observed what little difference the names of the parties made to the peasants. "Can't we abandon politics for awhile? I just want to do plain, practical, everyday work. Can't we just stay here and help people as we did during the evacuation?"

Mikhail lay back on the bed. He sighed, less heavily this time. Surprised, she realized that her suggestion had tempted him. Slowly she rubbed her knuckles against the fine reddish blond hair that formed a soft mat on his chest. Outside the rain had let up and a fresh breeze rattled through the boards.

She sniffed in the rich scents of her childhood and ado-
lescence, the fresh smell of damp earth and hay, the sour odor
of stale cooking. As her husband's breathing deepened into
sleep, she struggled with the idea that they must complete the
Revolution. The Russian nation, she mused, was much too
large and grand a battlefield for her: there one could work all
one's life and still injustice would not be diminished, whereas
within this poor western province where she had been born
and her beliefs had grown up, the idea that land, bread, and
peace belonged to the people seemed more attainable. If only
every small village could have its socialism—without parties,
without theory, without argument—how wonderful! She
smiled and imagined her family and Mikhail, herself and
their seven young children wandering in the birch wood and
strolling gaily among the banks of the river on their way to a
socialist picnic. But could Malkeh give up her power? Could
Naftali give up his fine coats and derby hat? Could Ruth give
up her Judaism and pledge her first allegiance to the masses
and to the future? Knowing that none of this was likely, Kala
fell asleep.

Shortly after dawn, she slipped from bed and made her way
back to the stable where she greeted Sir Leslie, Emmanuelle,
and Mishka. "Hello! Hello! Hello!" she shouted, running
from one to the other. All three looked considerably older
than when she had last seen them. The war had cut their feed
and she could feel their ribs and make out the shape of their
skulls. Their eyes bulged out in an almost comical manner
and they were rude with their muzzles as they searched her
clothing for hidden snacks. "You don't look as though you've
been through hard times," she said to them, "you look very
good to me." She went on hungrily drinking in their faces,
ready to confide her thoughts and describe where she'd been
the last three years, when she saw they did not know her. She
took Emmanuelle's head in her arms and kissed her forehead.
The wide-set black eyes, brimming with liquid darkness,
hardly blinked. "The most beautiful cow in the world," she
said.

[247]

She filled a jug of water and brought it to the front parlor so that she and Mikhail could wash. When she found her husband still asleep, she grew drowsy herself, lay down next to him, and dozed.

By the time the young couple awoke, dressed, and stepped over the threshold into the uncompleted kitchen, they discovered the whole family gathered for breakfast, perched on crude benches around an old table covered with a layer of oilcloth. Recalling the ceremony with which she and Mikhail had been ushered into the parlor the night before, Kala was certain she now beheld a glint of anticipation in every eye—an eager speculative light that quickly faded when she failed to bear with her three infants—a boy, a girl, and a newborn calf. Self-consciously she grinned at the Chodorovs and placed herself next to Mordecai, squirming beneath the disappointment she imagined. She looked round the table—at Ruth, whose face appeared harsher than the night before; at Mordecai, whose ears, repeated three times more in his three small daughters, seemed to have swelled while he slept; at Ekaterina, with a mouth like a rosebud, a nose like a lily, eyes green as stems, and even her hair coiled like a geranium on top of her head; at Naftali, shamefully reduced and yet content; at Sophie, and finally at Malkeh, the true ruler of them all. This was hardly, Kala reflected, the raw material with which to build a socialist state.

After breakfast Malkeh announced to Kala who, alone in the kitchen, was scrubbing the pots and pans, "I've sent a messenger this morning to the doctor. He and his wife have gone on holiday for ten days and I've made an appointment for you and Mikhail when he gets back."

"Mama!" Kala protested. But her mother was already out the door on her way to the bakery and it was now Mikhail who trotted into the kitchen, his head straining forward so that he might kiss his wife goodby before going off to the orchard with Naftali. "Mikhail," Kala greeted her husband, "let's not stay here!"

"But we just arrived yesterday, and it's nice here." His

hand waved round at the kitchen where only a small section of the finished flooring had been laid and the thin wooden frames of the windows held brown paper rather than glass. "It's like a campground or a shed. What's more, I like the idea of working in the orchards with your father . . . just plain good healthy work for once."

"Mikhail, there's nothing for us to do here. Besides, this won't look like a campground much longer." She pointed out that Naftali had already decorated the kitchen oven with picturesque old smooth tiles and had built an oak sideboard with glass-fronted cupboards along one wall to house the family's most precious objects, formerly displayed in the dining room—wine goblets, a *menorah*, the Sabbath candelabra, and framed photographs. "If we stay here, they won't let us lead our own lives."

"Still, they're very kind. And the air is so good." Mikhail inhaled deeply.

"Then on top of everything else, my mother wants me to go to a doctor about having babies. No matter what I say to her, she suspects there's some physical reason we don't have children."

The young man wagged his head and smiled a trifle patronizingly. "If it pleases your mother, why not see a doctor? There's nothing terrible in that." His smile widened. "Why in Vilna three doctors used to look at my tonsils every year."

"What if he finds something wrong? And it's not only me she plans to take on this visit to the doctor—you too have to go along."

Mikhail stopped smiling and blanched. He drew himself up with an injured air. "Actually, you and I ought to go to Vilna pretty soon. I want to see my family and it's time you met them. We can stay here another week or so and then be on our way. Not that my parents will particularly suit your taste, but at least they won't bother us about having children. And in Vilna we'll get the latest news from Russia."

That evening before supper Mordecai spoke up, his manner shy and kind, to suggest that Mikhail settle into Lyesk by taking a position as soon as possible. "If Malkeh talks to Major Kleist . . ."

"Thank you, Mordecai," Mikhail said a bit stiffly. "The fact is, I can't see myself working for the Germans."

"I mean something suitable for a graduate," Mordecai said.

Mikhail thanked Mordecai again, adding, "I'd have problems working with an invading army."

"Boundaries have been known to change," Naftali said.

Mikhail turned to his wife. "Earlier today I went to the birch wood, Kala—just to look at where you and I first walked. I knew, of course, that the Germans had cut down a large number of trees but I wasn't prepared for the devastation I saw—raw stump after raw stump."

"But they had no choice, they've run out of lumber of their own," Mordecai said, ducking his head and clearing his throat. "And you have to keep in mind, they've been very good to us. Whenever there's a special project they make the Jews foremen."

"Our Major Kleist," Malkeh agreed, "is a generous if somewhat casual fellow. He's done his best to help the Jews of Lyesk."

"Yes, he's brought us culture, style, a feeling for the larger world," said Ekaterina, "and he's raised my wages twice. And not only that—just to reward me for how well I set up the stalls for this Sunday's fair and band concert—he gave me a five-year pass to the horse races at Grünenwald in Berlin. A five-year pass, just imagine!" she exclaimed as the family headed toward the kitchen table.

"Kala, sit here, sit here," Sophie patted the bench by her side.

Ekaterina scratched her elbow with irritation. " 'Sit here, sit here,' " she mimicked. "Now that Kala's home, I suppose everything will be different. I suppose the two of you will keep on acting like children. Oh well, I wouldn't be surprised if in a few weeks' time I'm offered a job in Berlin. And in Berlin I'll start my real life. I'll walk up and down the

Kurfürstendamm and sit in the cafes with all the artists and the intellectuals and the people of wealth and power."

"Why go to Berlin, Ekaterina," Mordecai asked, "when you have such a fine job here?"

Ekaterina regarded Mordecai haughtily. "Because I feel German."

"I feel Russian," Kala said.

"Well, of course you do," said Mikhail, "because the fact is, we are Russian."

"We're Jewish," murmured Ruth.

"Naturally we're Jewish," said Naftali, "but that doesn't mean we can't work for the Germans."

"And in two weeks' time I'm invited to an evening of chamber music with violins, violas, and cellos at Major Kleist's house."

"An evening of cellos, violas, and violins!" Sophie clapped her hands and laughed and was joined by Kala. While the two girls roared and hooted, the rest of the family tried to ignore them. Ashamed, Kala forced herself to stop. "And what about you, Sophie?" she asked, attempting to sober them both.

"What do you mean?"

"Are you Russian, are you Jewish, are you German?"

"Oh me," said Sophie grinning, "if you really want to know—I might be Polish."

CHAPTER TWENTY-TWO

OVER THE NEXT FEW DAYS MIKHAIL BECAME MORE AND
more enamored of his work in the orchard and
more comfortable and content in the company of his in-laws
—though, as it happened, he saw little of any of them aside
from Naftali. Tired out by the unaccustomed physical labor,
he exclaimed, "How wonderful to work here!" and promptly
after supper marched off to his bed in the parlor and fell
asleep. Other members of the family soon followed his example, leaving only Kala and Sophie leaning toward each
other in the kitchen, grinning broadly and unable to tear
themselves away from one another's jokes. To Kala the fact
she could still evoke from her sister spontaneous and long-
lasting laughs—that she need not be satisfied with the puny
short nervous laughter of others—filled her with well-being
and delight. She confided to Sophie that while in Great Russia she had found it difficult to make anyone laugh. Even
Mikhail, she related, kept a poker face when she clowned.

Sophie then confessed that she too, left behind in Lyesk, had failed to provoke any noteworthy glee. It was therefore in an effort to make up for lost time that the two girls sat up in the night imitating whoever came to mind, chortling, waving their hands, giggling, guffawing, and hiccuping until at last Malkeh in her nightdress entered the kitchen, a single braid hanging down her back to her waist, and scolded, "Kala, your husband's in bed. You belong there with him. Go to Mikhail. Sophie! You have work to do in the morning."

The next night Kala and Sophie sat up again and in the morning Ekaterina complained that no one was getting any sleep. But this time, with a reluctant smile, Malkeh allowed that even though everyone looked tired out, there was something to be said in favor of Kala and Sophie laughing together as they had laughed before the war.

On the third night, finding themselves all laughed out, Sophie brought Kala into her bedroom. She opened a bureau drawer and brought out a squat white jar.

"Sophie, what's that?"

"Face cream." Sophie grinned. "Special face cream that came in a Red Cross package Iosif sent. Feel my cheek—how it's improved." Her grin widened. "I used to think there was something wrong with Iosif that he sent it but now I think he meant to bolster our morale." She unscrewed the top of the jar, dipped in a finger, then rubbed the bridge of her nose and Kala's nose.

Kala put her hand to Sophie's cheek; then she tested her own. She found it hard to tell which cheek felt different. "What about Mama? Does she use it?"

"Not Mama."

"Does Ruth?"

"Heaven forbid—Mordecai would sooner plaster it on himself. Ruth—I think she threw away her mirror and I bet she tries to roughen her skin. Besides she never goes anywhere except to the House of Study."

Kala groaned. "Why does she spend so much time there? Why doesn't she want smooth skin? What does she want after all? Yesterday at supper—did you see—it was only Mordecai who fussed and clucked over the children and wiped their faces and told them not to cry."

The two sisters stared miserably into the jar of cold cream. Then Kala said, "Remember before—she certainly spent a lot of time over us. We never knew what she was thinking about but at least she looked serene. Now she looks like she's contemplating some horrible talmudic puzzle that she can't figure out. Why is she so grim and distant? It can't all be just because she married Mordecai instead of Ephraim Savich." She waited for her sister's answer, hoping for some relief.

"I don't know," Sophie replied slowly. "I wish I did." She got up from the bed where she had been sitting and swung through the room, back and forth, on her crutches. "You know, Iosif wrote us that Ephraim lives in Detroit. He's started up a lumber business. All these years he hasn't married—not that being married to Ephraim Savich would be so marvelous."

"Not that it would be marvelous at all!"

"Mordecai is better."

"A hundred times better."

"A thousand times better."

"Ephraim would have been worse."

Tormented, the sisters kept on repeating, "Ephraim would have been worse." At last Sophie rescued them by bringing out her new mauve silk suit with a short fitted jacket. "It's the most elegant outfit I've ever owned. I could wear it anywhere." She laughed. "Ekaterina could fly me to Warsaw or to Paris."

"Think of it—Ekaterina up in an airplane!"

"She's had good luck with the Germans. But you, Kala, you're the one's who's been the luckiest of all. You've been all over Russia—in Bobruisk, in Petrograd, in Moscow—and not just as a tourist. You've been able to work for what you believe in, and in the company of someone you love."

Unwilling to be the luckiest member of her family, Kala said, "No, no, I'll bring you lots of luck. You'll see. The first thing is, you'll meet someone; then you'll fall in love . . ."

"I already have," said Sophie in a quiet voice. "I've fallen in love. I've been waiting to tell you."

"In love . . . who with . . . well, there you are, it's just as I said . . . how wonderful!" Kala burst out, then stopped abruptly, shocked that love had descended on Sophie while she was out of town. She looked out the window, where high in the sky a quarter-moon dangled. Warily she sized up the moon and found it lacking. What would love contrive for Sophie, who needed her pony Mishka for a journey of more than a half mile? Would it break her heart as perhaps it had broken Ruth's? Would it expose her to unknown dangers, threaten her body still further, or alter the affection, the allegiance between them? Reprimanding herself for this last, she reminded herself she had abandoned Sophie first. Then she recalled the young boy, Hershel, pushing Sophie's wheelchair through the town. She smelled the pungent odor of the barnyard mixed with the moist summer grass and heard the hoarse sound of frogs from the river bottom. Hershel had grown up. "Is it Hershel?" she hopefully inquired.

"Hershel?" Sophie sounded annoyed. "Why should it be Hershel?"

"Because he always cared so much for you. I ran into him in town yesterday. He stands straight and broad with a nice thick red beard, all bristly and curly." Kala's hand fluffed around her chin and she gave Sophie another hopeful glance. "Do you remember when his hair was parted in the middle and he used to wait across the road so he could see you first thing in the morning? Do you remember how he used to search for lilacs to bring you because you love lilacs? I don't think I ever came across a boy who cared for anyone the way Hershel cared for you."

"And now it's Palestine he's mad for," Sophie added without a pause. "That's all he talks about day and night. All he wants is to emigrate to Palestine. He doesn't realize I wouldn't do him much good there. He needs a woman with the soul of a pioneer and sturdy limbs to go with him and dig in the soil. Maybe someone like you. Besides, Hershel's grown up good-looking and I've fallen in love with someone very plain."

"Very plain?"

"Homely, almost ugly. That's what I like about him best of all."

"That he's ugly?"

"And that he's so wonderful." Sophie gestured out the window toward the deep black of space and the waning cradle of the moon. "The fact is, you fell in love with a handsome man, Kala, and Ruth fell in love with Ephraim Savich, another handsome man, and Ekaterina, oh Ekaterina won't so much as blink at anyone who isn't splendid-looking, while I," she drew an exultant breath and then sang out, "have fallen in love with an ordinary-looking man with an ordinary-looking mustache . . . I'll draw you his picture." She struck a match, lit an extra candle, took up paper and pencil from a small drawer in the table by her bed, and, bending over, studiously formed circles, lines, dots, angles, and filled in a head of hair. When she had finished she affixed a skeptical eye to the results. "It isn't quite right; it doesn't do him justice. He doesn't even look like an ugly man."

"He looks more like a chicken."

"Then forget about the drawing." Sophie crossed it out and underneath she lettered the name, "Withold Swislocz." She turned the paper around.

"Withold Swislocz?" very cautiously Kala demanded.

"It's a Polish name, of course. He isn't Jewish. He's a Pole in the German army."

"A Pole?"

Sophie laughed. "Kala, don't look so alarmed! We don't plan to marry. Everyone needs a romance. Every girl needs a life of her own. And you would like him," Sophie crossed her arms, "because he comes from your kind of people—the kind you most approve of—from very poor and simple people. Yet he so impressed the Germans with his courage that they decorated him in the middle of battle. They made him a captain.

Captain Withold Swislocz. You can imagine how incredibly brave he had to be!"

"Brave," Kala repeated, still absorbed by her sister's cavalier manner and confession. "Courage," she muttered and recalled Mikhail's earlier obsession with proving himself. "If you ask me, these days courage is greatly overrated."

"No, you're wrong. I love courage." Sophie raised one of her crutches, waving it about her head. "And to have been chosen by a brave man, a brave captain! And with all of that, he's modest and unassuming and particularly kind to everyone in the bakery. He's not even like Major Kleist—he doesn't take any of the spoils. He's wonderful working with his hands and he's wonderful with animals. When he's on a horse they're like one animal—which is what you'll see when he rides in the cavalry exhibition on Sunday. Most stirring of all, he longs for the day when Poland will be free. He says only then will the Jews and all the other minorities be free too. But listen, Kala," Sophie cast a measuring eye on her sister, "if Withold and I should ever consider marrying, I know of course that Mama and Papa would rather see me dead and I respect that. But you, who disapprove of Palestine as a country only for the Jews—who claim there ought not be any separation between Jews and Christians—you, Kala, who believe in every sort of people, all races, all classes, mixing freely, how would you feel if I married Withold Swislocz, a Pole in the German army?"

A Pole in the German army, thought Kala, hardly a promising combination. It was a more extreme act than joining the Revolution.

"Would you support us—would you be glad?"

Kala lowered her head and tried to be glad. She imagined Sophie's expulsion from their family, the bakery, her race. She pictured Sophie's isolation and her parents' unhappiness. "Well, of course I'd support you since you'd be acting as I believe. You . . ." she faltered, realizing that all these years she had simply assumed that the role of rebellion belonged to her alone—that, indeed, she had counted shamelessly on the

[257]

acquiescence of her sisters, even of Ekaterina, to maintain the integrity and harmony of the Chodorovs' life. "Of course I would help you, Sophie, in every way I could. But in fact," she admitted, gazing with humiliation at the post at the foot of the bed, "I'd rather you married Hershel."

"Well, I'm not going to marry either of them," Sophie came back. She reopened the jar of cold cream and cheerfully dabbed bits of it all over her face. She then offered the jar to Kala. "But just wait and see how you change your mind when you see Withold Swislocz riding his cavalry horse at the fair."

All Sunday morning while the Chodorovs prepared for the fair, Kala waited impatiently for her first look at Sophie's captain. As usual Sophie opened the bakery early, but went home before ten and an hour later Malkeh closed up and returned to the house. Soon peasants, townspeople, retainers of neighboring estates, and citizens of surrounding villages began trailing through Lyesk in the direction of the aerodrome. Toward one o'clock, the Chodorov family set off with the others—Sophie in her wheelchair, Mordecai pushing the pram, and each person carrying something for the stall except for Naftali who, splendidly dressed, held nothing but his cane. Before they had covered half the distance, Ruth's two eldest daughters tired and Kala, transferring her cakes into Sophie's lap, picked the little girls up into her arms. The afternoon was clear and balmy, with no more than a few clouds drifting high in the light blue sky. Presently the sound of sprightly waltzes and thumping mazurkas beat out. Grunting, Ruth's daughters bounced in Kala's arms and struggled toward the ground, their large solemn eyes widening in surprise at the sound of the music and then at the sight of the bandstand which had been raised near the hangar. Here a group of military musicians in smart uniforms tooted upon their shiny instruments—the conductor smiling and waving his baton. Ruth's daughters squirmed out of Kala's arms and skittered like small birds toward the music, losing themselves in the crowd. Mordecai dashed after them, pushing the pram over the bumpy field and calling their names.

"And here come the so-called Polish gentry." With an ironic flourish of his cane Naftali pointed to the carriage and the same sway-backed horse driven by the sour Polish coachman who had conveyed Kala, Mikhail, and him from the railroad station. In the carriage, sitting upright, as suited their new stature, rode the owner of the hotel and next to him the watch repairman and his wife, the dressmaker, and the coachman's wife. "They think of themselves as important," Naftali added.

"There's the District Commander." Malkeh pointed to a group of officers standing behind the bandstand. "And you'll also notice other newcomers."

Naftali gazed around the airfield carefully. An entire complement of unfamiliar troops stood spaced out evenly around the field, their stance alert, their dress uniforms gleaming in the full sunlight. "A whole new troop of soldiers," Naftali said. "I've never seen one of them before."

"Why are there so many?" Malkeh said.

"To enjoy the fair," Naftali replied, dismissing Malkeh's question in his eagerness to join the festivities. "Just look!" Happily he swept his hand in an arc—for all about them the different booths with their limited treats had begun to thrive. Excited civilians, dressed in their brightest clothes as if asserting their right to an afternoon of pleasure, played a ring-toss game and a shell game; there was also a weight-lifting contest. In the middle of the airfield a live merry-go-round had been set up by Ekaterina, with horses pulling carriages, wagons, and carts in a great circle. Children clung to every possible projection, vying for the privileged positions on the horses' backs. A group of young women, both peasants and townspeople, danced to the band music. Another group cheered them on. On the sidelines Mordecai, bent over double and with his arms outstretched, danced with his daughters while Naomi Pearl Benjamin tried to coax her son, Pinchas, into hopping around with her and Leah tried to coerce her husband, Mendel Feldshpan, into a two-step. Meanwhile Rabbi Benjamin strolled among the different clusters of citizens clad in his severely tailored double-breasted suit, cut like a German uniform.

From the Chodorov booth, Malkeh said, "I've caught sight of men and boys who have been in hiding from the military for the past three or four years. I've seen widows I thought were still deep in mourning. I even saw an old friend I thought was lost in Russia."

"Kala," Sophie whispered into her sister's ear, "come with me. I'll introduce you to Captain Swislocz. Over there by the horses." Sophie began vigorously to wheel her chair in the direction of the corral that had been erected next to the hangar. Through the boards of the corral they could see the arched necks and heads of cavalry horses. Grooms busily prepared the animals—tying up their tails and manes and adjusting their saddles and bridles—a handful of officers directing the activity.

"He's one of the officers," Sophie said. "The short one."

"Which short one?"

"The shortest, with the stiff sandy-colored comical mustache."

"That one? Are you sure? But when do you get a chance to be with him?"

"Why almost every evening when I deliver our bread to the barracks. We've become great friends."

"Does Mama know?"

"I thought so at first. But now I think it's never entered her mind."

"Friends?" inquired Kala.

"More than friends."

"How much more?"

"I'm not sure that he loves me."

They were stopped just before the corral by a polite yet unyielding sergeant warning them that the area was off-limits to civilians. Turning back they ran into Ekaterina and demanded of her, "Why are the new troops here? What's happening?"

"The District Commander brought them," Ekaterina replied. "Where have the two of you been? I told you I was going to show you the airplane." She led them along the runway that had been freshly cut with scythes, the grass gathered in neat bundles at the edge of the grounds. As they came closer to the reconnaissance plane parked near the merry-go-round Kala recognized that it resembled the two-winged monster, complete with black crosses, that had bombed the refugees on the road to Baranovits.

"It's called an Albatross," Ekaterina instructed, "named after a bird in the South Seas. That's the propeller in front. It pulls you along while the wings lift you up. It can go over a hundred miles an hour. Kala," she accused, "you aren't listening."

"I am too," Kala said. "There was an airplane like this one on the road to Baranovits—when I left Lyesk during the evacuation. It threw bombs down at us."

"But this is a totally different plane!" Ekaterina growled, scratching her elbow. "And I'm learning how to fly it."

"This one," Sophie confirmed, "has nothing to do with bombs. It's a miraculous machine. Ekaterina promised to take me up in it one day. Can you imagine—to be flying high, high over Lyesk!"

Wearing smiles of varying widths, the three sisters headed back toward the fair. They arrived just as a roll of drums called the attention of the crowd to the upcoming cavalry exhibition. One by one the booths, stripped of their meager goods, closed. As quickly as she could, Ekaterina dashed about among the booths, checking that everything was in order, while Kala and Sophie hurriedly secured themselves a good spot from which to view the show. Turning about, Kala saw Mordecai toward the back of the crowd, but she caught no glimpse of Mikhail.

A second roll of drums thundered and hammered and then
—led by Captain Withold Swislocz—out rode the cavalry-
men. Wearing their full battle uniforms, capes, swords, and
polished boots, they proudly sat upon their magnificent bays,
roans, grays, and coal blacks—the horses single-stepping forward from the corral to the center of the field. In time to the
drums of the band, the horses danced: one, two, one, two.
Sophie leaned toward the spectacle, her cheeks scarlet, a faint
red touching her bare neck, her eyes luminous and filled with
anticipation. As the Captain went past the two girls, Kala
made out a broad tanned face, creased with lines of good
will—a homely yet appealing face that, above the graceful
arch of the horse's neck, altered for the briefest moment from
grim and impassive and took on, at the sight of Sophie, an
expression of eager tenderness. An astonishing, an electric
thrill sprang through Kala. "He loves you, Sophie, I can
tell," she blurted out, her outburst shocking them both so
that their eyes returned at once to the exhibition where, like
a well-trained ballet corps, the horses wheeled in unison.
Without apparent command the animals trotted to the right,
cantered, broke off in squads of four, wheeled backward and
forward, forming stars and crosses. The soft grass absorbed
the impact of the hoofs so that for all the straining of the
massive beasts only a muffled drumming upon the earth, the
wheezing of the horses, and the quiet sighs of satisfaction of
the riders could be heard. The crowd cheered.

As the last horse disappeared into the hangar and the doors
closed, the band struck up the most martial music of the
afternoon. Presently a single trumpet sang its song over
the aerodrome. The hangar doors swung open and out onto
the field again marched the familiar troops and officers of the
Lyesk command, led by Major Kleist and Captain Swislocz,
and now wearing marching packs and carrying rifles. The
District Commander rose from his chair on the bandstand.
Next to him a tall, rigid-looking officer stood up, gray of face
and hair, with a thin mouth primly closed.

Ekaterina suddenly appeared at Kala and Sophie's side.

"Something terrible has happened. That's the new major!" she pointed to the tall officer. "Major Kleist and his troops are being sent away!"

Kala quickly glanced at Sophie, who remained silent, her face expressionless and pale as she searched the field, where the unfamiliar troops trotted from their positions to form in front of the bandstand. The new major stepped down, approaching Major Kleist with a slight limp. The two majors saluted. Pennants were transferred from Major Kleist's troop to the new troop—after which Major Kleist, Captain Swislocz, and their men marched from the grounds, past the hangar and out onto the roadway where horses and supply wagons waited. Members of the new troops surrounded the entire field, so that none of the civilians attending the event could leave. Now squads of the new troops moved quickly through the crowd. Here and there cries of protest rose. Naftali came up to Kala. "Where's your husband?" he questioned. "Where's Mordecai?"

"They've got Lazar Dovitsky," someone yelled.

Bewildered, Kala scanned the airfield. "Mordecai was over there a second ago. I'm sure I saw him."

"And now he's somewhere else," Ruth said. She pointed toward the corral where, instead of the elegantly arched necks and heads of the bays, roans, grays, and coal black horses of the cavalry, the heads of Mordecai, Mikhail, Lazar Dovitsky, and some twenty-five other men peered out over the boards.

"Mordecai!" groaned Naftali, signaling to his son-in-law. "You're all penned in."

"They rounded us up like cattle," Mikhail shouted hoarsely.

"It's a labor draft. The Germans need laborers," Lazar Dovitsky called out over the boards. "They've captured whoever looked able to walk and Major Kleist and his soldiers are being sent with us to clear the forest at Bialowieza."

Naftali turned to Malkeh. "You must do something. It's a bad joke, using an entertainment in this way. You can't allow this to happen."

[263]

Malkeh surveyed the field, the bandstand, and the corral. "They've arranged it too cleverly, assigning the new troops to do the dirty work. There will be no bribes today under the eye of that District Commander. As for tomorrow, you see the new major's face—we won't manage so easily from now on."

"But it's all wrong. It's all wrong. This is no way for a civilized nation like Germany to act," Naftali protested as the Chodorovs moved slowly to the far side of the corral where Mikhail and Mordecai stood together. On their way they passed Naomi Pearl Benjamin, who was angrily commanding her husband, "Do something! Don't just stand there. And if you can't do anything, then go with them!" Then they skirted a row of indignant women who pressed their faces against the boards and wires surrounding the conscripts.

Kala and Mikhail embraced through the fence. "How ridiculous to be caught like this," Mikhail said.

"I wish we hadn't come to Lyesk."

"Well, at least they're not sending me to the front. I'll try not to chop down too many trees." He gave her a half smile. "If I find a way to escape, I'll send for you."

"But can't anything be done?"

"Nothing. Nothing but poetry. And somehow a poem doesn't pop into my mind." He laughed.

Next to them Naftali addressed Mordecai in a grieving tone, "My dear son-in-law, I had nothing against the Germans until a few months ago. Until a few months ago when their armies began to fare badly in the west, they treated us like gentlemen, they made you a foreman, Mordecai, and they left us all we needed to stay alive. We had animals and food—wood for fires—but now they're determined to take everything from us—even our forests, Mordecai. Even you."

Ruth folded her arms across her chest lightly. "So you won't be coming home?" she mused in a tone of wonder and speculation. "Poor Mordecai, they should have taken me away instead of you."

But to everyone's surprise Mordecai appeared jubilant. He

knelt at the fence to kiss his daughters, whom Ruth pushed forward. "They found me fit!" he repeated, his eyes, even his peach-colored ears glistening with pride, "they found your father fit! Ruth, they found your husband fit!"

Now a squad of troops entered the corral and lined up the conscripts, marching them one by one past an officer seated near the gate at a table. The officer examined each man's papers and took down his name. Kala and the family moved with the crowd toward the road where the former members of the local garrison waited in formation for their prisoners.

"So we've lost our men," said Sophie.

Ekaterina stamped her foot. "And what kind of entertainment was it anyway—nothing more than one small cake for every tenth family and a few puny games of skill. Germany's a dreadful disappointment—I'm through with Berlin." But as she spoke Ekaterina reached out her hand and groped toward Sophie's fingers, her head squeamishly turned the other way.

Now the conscripts marched down the road to join the convoy and the crowd moved forward to say farewell. Momentarily all order was lost. The conscripts and their families surged together. Commands were shouted, horses snorted and danced about, pounding their hoofs. Kala and Mikhail found one another in the hubbub. "I've thought of a poem," Mikhail said, hugging his wife. "It's to the point." Lifting his head he intoned:

> *This has all happened before:*
> *sad sighs on the road's edge.*
> *Learn to stand alone, my dear;*
> *life sings goodby, goodby.*

In the middle of Mikhail's recitation Captain Swislocz broke away from his troops across the road and strode toward the Chodorovs. He waited politely until the poem was finished and then he addressed the assembled family. "I am grateful to you for all your kindnesses," he said, "I hope to return one day soon. The truth is, I've never been in a place I've liked as well as Lyesk."

"In line! All conscripts in line!" The German soldiers rushed about, dragging the men of Lyesk from their relatives.

"I'll be back!" Mikhail shouted.

"Mikhail! Mikhail!" Kala cried after him.

Mordecai gathered his daughters to him one more time and at the last hugged Naftali convulsively. As he went off he called over his shoulder, almost gaily, "I'll be back too, just as soon as I finish clearing the forest at Bialowieza."

After a few minutes Naftali said, "They've all left us— Mordecai, Mikhail, the officers, the troops. It's a different town now."

Ekaterina added, "How dreary!"

CHAPTER TWENTY-THREE

IN THE AUTUMN OF 1918, WITH THE GERMAN CAUSE DETERIO-
rating in the war against the western allies, the new
major in command of Lyesk stripped the town and its surroundings ruthlessly of food, lumber, animals, and useful
machinery for shipment to the homeland. Hoping to protect
Sir Leslie, Emmanuelle, and Mishka, Kala helped her father
build camouflaged sheds in the wilderness behind the cottage.
Here they also stored and concealed apples and flour. But
there was no way to hide the birch woods from the Germans;
and as each tree was axed down and the large forest shrank
into fields of raw stumps, Kala—already estranged since her
return by the changes in Lyesk—experienced the odd sense
that she too was being severed bit by bit from her home.
Turning restless, feeling herself grow awkward and un-
defined—no longer a child in her own family or, for the
moment, an independent woman—she resolved that as soon as
possible she and her husband would go back into Russia, that

they would concentrate on what was decent and humane within the Revolution and, ignoring party politics, would again take up their unfinished work. Yet by October none of the labor conscripts had come back and presently word reached the town that the gangs employed in clearing the forest at Bialowieza had been shipped further and further toward Germany, working wherever they were needed.

When the supply of food in Lyesk had dwindled, Kala took to harnessing Sir Leslie to the cart and foraging through the countryside in the night, collecting wild grass for feed and trading apples and bread for whatever food the peasants were willing to barter. Gradually these sojourns evolved into a battle against the immense lethargy of the surviving peasant women and old men—those who had remained at home during the evacuation and who now barely cultivated the land on which they lived. Weeds and brambles invaded the once well-kept homesteads and the younger children, round-bellied with hunger, fled Kala's advances. Succeeding partially in breaking through the peasants' sullen movements, the young woman managed to warn them of impending German raids; she showed them how best to conceal their goods and their few remaining animals; she initiated a route of hidden trade between the peasants and the townspeople; and now and then she tried out on these sorry remnants of Little Lyesk and its surrounding countryside the favorite message of her heart: that the land the peasants tilled was theirs by right of their labor—that the landowners and bankers must never be allowed to take it from them. Invariably they then regarded her with a surprise mixed with skepticism and pity as if, in spite of her efforts to help them or perhaps because of her efforts, they judged her a bit demented. Frustrated by their response, conscious of how little of the land they'd tilled, she became aware that, unlike the peasants in Great Russia who had joined the Revolution, these people were far from ready to change their lives. It therefore relieved, even gladdened her, to wave goodby and ride away from them to join Sophie in the bakery where, at dawn, her sister was about to begin a day's meager baking.

One frosty morning in November, shivering from the cold as she returned from an expedition that had carried her all the way to the northern shore of Lake Lyesk, Kala found herself wishing that Sophie might suggest, as she'd occasionally suggested before, "Let's have some strong tea—even though Mama will be furious." Kala imagined her sister and herself seated at one of the tables, smiling at the warmth of the tea and its fragrance—their blunt noses in their tea glasses. The varnished wood of their father's furniture shone in the lamplight while the bright red and white curtains masked the dark windows rattling in the winter wind, and she had the impression that the war had never happened and nothing in Lyesk had changed.

Kala dozed. Her mind lit on Father Boris and Matryona. She seemed to make out their gaunt and wide figures with some burden in their arms—perhaps the twins—still roaming, wandering over the cold wastes. She beckoned them toward her to help save the ruins of Little Lyesk. "I have told the children," she informed Father Boris, "that if they have a piece of turnip they must eat it with bread. That makes a meal. Otherwise, they'll just be wastrels—no chance of growing up strong or tall."

Suddenly Sir Leslie stopped, snorted, and reared in his harness. Wakened, Kala recovered her balance and leaped down to the ground. She retrieved the reins that had been pulled from her lax grip, stroked the animal's forehead and muzzle to calm him, and peered around, fearful that a German patrol lay in the clammy emptiness ahead. Hearing odd sounds, she nevertheless murmured, "There's nothing wrong, Sir Leslie," led him to a field bordering the high road, and tied him to a low tree. Slowly she crept toward the road. Dense fog rose from the cold earth, passing over the bushes and the stunted trees to form threatening shapes. She parted the bushes along the verge, surveyed the high road, and, startled, made out a large throng of gray ghostlike figures moving westward through the cold damp morning, their bodies misshapen by bundles they carried on their shoulders. As the sky lightened into tones of a pale dusk-gray, gradually she recognized the proud peasants of Lomzha and Grodno provinces—without wagons or animals—trudging along silently like sleepwalkers shrunk in dreams, moving toward their villages. Was it possible, she wondered, that the war was over and her friends from the evacuation were coming home? She wanted to step into the procession and inquire if anyone had seen Father Boris, Matryona, Rivkah, or others from Lyesk, but there was something so spectral, so miragelike in the hushed steadiness of the peasants' advance that, intimidated, she stood motionless. Minutes later she turned and fled toward Sir Leslie, for the dawn was growing brighter. She led him into the orchard track and hid him again in the crude shed behind the cottage where Mishka and Emmanuelle impatiently awaited their morning feed. After hurling it into their troughs, Kala locked the door and set off on foot back to the high road.

By now a pale sun had cast a watery, pearly glow on the bushes and the gravel. When she reached the old post station, the road had emptied. In the distance she glimpsed the back of a column of refugees just disappearing over Raven's Hill and stood watching the halo of their dust. She was about to turn down Orchard Lane when to her right a different crowd of persons came milling into view—a mass of German soldiers hiking westward from the Russian border in scattered, random groups. Some appeared disheveled and very drunk, but most remained buckled and buttoned up, rifles on their shoulders and their heads held at a disciplined angle, as though they wanted to retain some pride despite the apparent lack of any superior authority to direct them. Twice, as Kala watched, automobiles full of officers bowled along, dispersing the infantrymen, and now and then an officer, riding proudly, trotted by on horseback, aloof from the disorder.

Kala walked in the direction of town, letting herself believe that the spectacle she had just witnessed signified the end of the war—that the borders had opened in the east and that in the west her husband and his fellow prisoners had been released from the German labor battalions. She decided that the Russian peasants, her friends, were coming home, and she hoped that even now Mikhail was making his way toward Lyesk. As she passed the barracks, she noted that a few townspeople had gathered across the road and were staring fearfully at the open gate, unoccupied by its usual guard. Without stopping to ask questions, she entered the gate and poked her head into the doorways of buildings. With the discovery that the buildings were empty, she headed for the entrance and called out to the townspeople across the road, caution mixed with her glee, "I think it's over—the war is over!" at which she and the group moved quickly toward the square, joining other citizens who were already hurrying to the station for news from the telegraph.

Kala made her way through the crowd and entered the station house. She glimpsed Ekaterina at the telegraph key, surrounded by Malkeh, Naftali, the Polish watch repairman, the Polish coachman, and Moishe Kantorovits. At the door, standing one behind the other, Naomi Pearl Benjamin and Leah Feldshpan relayed the messages Ekaterina received: "Armistice has been declared; a general strike has spread through Germany; the Kaiser has fled to Holland; Poland, under General Pilsudski, has become an independent nation . . ."

When the messages had ceased, a babble of voices shot up— everyone arguing and questioning what the new events would mean to Lyesk. Ekaterina rose from her seat and stretched. She said to her mother, "Well, it's a real mess! Who's in charge of Lyesk now? Are we German, are we Russian, are we Polish? What's the color of our flag?"

Malkeh's clear gray eyes widened. "For the moment Lyesk belongs to no one."

"To no one?" Ekaterina quavered crossly.

"It belongs to no one," Malkeh confirmed. "We'll have to

wait for the peace treaty before we know the color of our flag."

Yet as the weeks passed it became clear to Kala that the power of the town's Polish population was growing—a power controlled by the landlord, Pan Josef Potocki, through his Jewish manager, Moishe Kantorovits. Uneasily Kala kept wishing that more and more Russian faces would reappear but those who had joined the evacuation of 1915 slipped back only a few at a time. In their absence, Poles filled the town and for the first time, in addition to the Russian Orthodox Church, which, in Lyesk, remained without a spiritual leader, there was now a Catholic congregation and a Polish Catholic priest. Before the month of November was over, a new town committee had formed. Composed of Poles, Jews, and a few Russians, the committee fell under the control of the Polish party—the Jews only too happy to take their direction from Moishe Kantorovits, Pan Josef's manager, because he was Jewish. Malkeh was among the most important members of the committee and the most outspoken. Yet even Malkeh—Kala was appalled to note—consulted frequently with Kantorovits in order to retain a measure of power in the changing political scene.

In December Withold Swislocz sent the Chodorovs a note offering his warm regards and the information that he had been made a colonel in the Polish army. He reiterated his desire to visit Lyesk and claimed that this soon might be possible since he expected a large area of formerly western Russia would be turned over to Poland under the peace treaty. If this were the case, he hoped to arrange for a post near Lyesk.

"Just a friend," Sophie murmured to Kala that night in the bedroom the two again shared.

"I thought you said he's more than a friend." Kala threw her pillow at Sophie who picked it up and added it to her own.

"I can't know until he comes back."

"He loves you, Sophie, I saw that."

Sophie grew solemn. She touched her cheeks with her fingers. "I care for him. I love him."

In an instant Kala had walked across the room and was sitting on her sister's bed. "And Mama and Papa?"

Sophie nodded. "Since Withold's been gone, I've thought less about the disgrace."

"Don't think about disgrace at all. That can't be the point."

Sophie sat up. "Perhaps it wouldn't be the end of everything—even for Mama and Papa." She leaned toward her sister. "And when you think about it, Kala—this might be my chance to choose a life of my own."

Uncomfortable, Kala recalled that day, early in the war, when she had watched Sophie signal her fellowship to the wounded soldiers on the train. She murmured, "Your own life."

"But who knows if he'll come back or not. Don't fret, Kala." Sophie laughed. "You've got enough to occupy your mind. And I'll bet you'll see your husband long before Colonel Swislocz comes visiting on his horse."

But instead of Mikhail or Colonel Swislocz, it was Mordecai who showed up toward the beginning of January, having made his way across Poland in the company of a few of the other conscripts. When he stepped unannounced into the Chodorov kitchen, Ruth said, "Mordecai! How thin you've become!" And she herded their children together and stood them in between Mordecai and herself. Meanwhile Naftali enfolded Mordecai in his arms, released and held him a bit away, then clasped him in his arms again with shouts of pleasure.

"Ruth." Malkeh took her daughter aside and frowned. "Ruth," she reproved in a whisper. "He's your husband. Whatever are you thinking?"

Distractedly, Mordecai's gaze searched about the room. His eye lit on Kala who was waiting her turn to kiss him. "Is . . . has your . . . has Mikhail returned?"

Kala, too, then looked about the room, as though it were

possible Mikhail might pop out of a corner. Questioningly she stared at her brother-in-law's shaved, emaciated head.

"Where is Mikhail?" asked Malkeh.

"Wasn't he with you?" Naftali inquired.

"We got separated the first week," Mordecai stuttered. "I kept looking for him." He glanced hurriedly at Kala. "I'm sure Mikhail will come back. Give him a few more days."

Kala bit her lower lip. "Well, you're here, Mordecai—that's what's most important. You're here," she repeated, not realizing that she'd begun to shout. "That's what's most important —welcome Mordecai—won't somebody feed him!" And she set about pulling dishes out of the cupboards, pausing to bark at Ruth, "Hurry up, Mordecai's here! Can't you see that your husband's hungry?"

But if Ruth's motions were slow and almost dreamlike as she brought her husband a bowl of thin potato soup, Mordecai—clearly immersed in a life separate from the Chodorovs—seemed scarcely to notice. Appearing haunted and weighed down, his spirits failed to lift even when the baby, at present eleven months old, reached out for his ears— ears no longer peach-hued and winged, but thickened, dun-colored, and drooping.

"She remembers you, Mordecai!" offered Sophie. "What a clever baby!"

Mordecai's hand shot out and for an instant he waggled the baby's fingers. Then he abruptly withdrew his hand. "What I've seen!" he said, in a low voice. "What Lazar Dovitsky and I have seen."

"In the labor battalion?" Naftali inquired sympathetically while he, along with Malkeh, Kala, and Sophie crowded in a group behind Mordecai—each of them peering anxiously over Mordecai's shoulder at his untouched bowl of soup.

"Oh, the labor battalion—that was bad enough. But it was nothing compared to later on. Later on, when the Germans left, that's when the troubles got their worst. The Poles . . . as soon as they became a nation again there was nothing to hold them back, nothing to stop them, and they took out their anger on the Jews. The cruelty, the slaughter, the pogroms I saw among the Poles. There was no town we passed through in Poland where the Jews were not in mourning."

Blanching, Sophie objected, "Mordecai, you can't let yourself make villains of an entire nation. That makes no sense. Our Captain Swislocz has become a colonel in the Polish army."

"I saw a man . . ." Mordecai began, but Malkeh intervened, her eyes hooded and masked.

"Mordecai, the Poles in Lyesk are our friends. At least we hope . . . and we have every reason to believe they will be. While you were away," she lowered herself onto the bench by his side, "and after the Germans had left, the town got together and formed a governing committee." With a contemplative air Malkeh smoothed away a fold in the hand-stitched cloth that Ruth had laid for Mordecai. "I sit on the committee along with the most prominent Poles and a few members of the Jewish Council—with Moishe Kantorovits and Rabbi Benjamin. We've even found a distant relative of Luka Fomich's, an elder from the White Russian peasantry, to speak for the peasants, Pole and Russian alike. But when all is said and done, it's the Poles who wield the power."

"And mainly because of Moishe Kantorovits," Kala summed up, striding to the window and striding right back. "He may be a Jew and Leah Feldshpan's father but he's a Jew who puts his foot and his mouth in the Polish camp. He gives the Poles a majority in the management of the town—everyone's afraid to go against a representative of the Pan."

"And who's to say he's wrong?" Naftali pointed a finger in the air. "Poland's a new country. It's changing. At any moment it might outgrow its pogroms. Sophie, look how important Moishe Kantorovits has become to Pan Josef!"

"But not to us!" Kala shouted. "Can't you see—the Russian peasants are coming back now. They need land, and here is Moishe Kantorovits already grabbing it away for his Polish master—he's using his position on the town committee to make Lyesk a gift to Poland."

"Moishe Kantorovits," Naftali stuck his nose up with belli-
cose pride, "is my friend."

"Then give him up!" roared Kala. "Yes, give him up!"

Naftali shook his head. "A Jew like Moishe Kantorovits is
made in heaven. We should thank God he's got so much
influence."

Seated next to her son-in-law, Malkeh went on, "I suppose
you've heard—try your soup, Mordecai—the Red Army has
begun to move this way." She went on to explain that the
Russian army was being pushed on three sides by the soldiers
of the dead Tsar joined by American, French, English, and
Japanese troops. "They're marching toward us on their way
to Poland."

"And they have nowhere else to go," Naftali took up. "The
Bolsheviks—those hoodlums, those barbarians—they're oozing in our direction. Volozhin and Sluck have already fallen
into their hands."

"The Bolsheviks are marching in our direction?" Mordecai
appeared utterly amazed. Yet his interest faded in the next
second and he said, "What Lazar Dovitsky and I have seen."

Naftali looked at his son-in-law and sighed unhappily.
"You must eat, Mordecai, you're so thin."

"Eat, Mordecai," Malkeh urged.

"Please eat, Mordecai," Ruth pleaded.

"Do eat, Mordecai," echoed Sophie, and Ekaterina burst
out, "I'm hungry . . . I'm starving!"

At this—as though they'd become one creature the entire
family turned to look at Ekaterina, exclaiming in kind voices,
"Look at the table, Ekaterina. We've laid out a feast for
Mordecai. Look, there's everything. Ekaterina, help yourself."

"To what? To what? I don't want watery potato soup and
a frozen cucumber," Ekaterina hissed through tight lips. "I
don't want a slice of sawdust bread or that old piece of turnip." As she spoke, Mordecai reached out and handled the
items on his plate, examining and replacing them one by one.
"What I want," Ekaterina went on, "is a cake as tall as a
building, made even taller by piles of whipped cream and

butter icing and pink roses and chocolate slivers and sweet cherries and pistachio nuts. I want a loaf of soft white bread the size of this table," she said while the eyes of Ruth's daughters sprang wide open. "I want each slice of the white bread spread with a different kind of jam—apricot jam, strawberry jam, raspberry jam, peach jam . . ."

"Enough jams!" ordered Naftali, for around him the faces of his family were succumbing, one by one, to a constrained pinched look of longing.

"Listen, Ekaterina," Kala spoke out irritably, trying to free herself from a vision of raspberry preserves and a spoon. "If you had a bit more to do all day . . . if you came home and tried to help out instead of just sitting around at the telegraph office when there aren't any messages coming in . . . if you stopped lazing around like a parasite . . ."

Ekaterina gave a bitter laugh. "Like a parasite! Just listen to you! It's the language of the Revolution . . . the stupid language of the Revolution in your mouth. Even after everything, you're in love with that dismal dream of no one any different from anyone else—everyone humdrum and the same. Yes, you would leave us again for its sake in a second— just like you left us when the town was burning . . . you left us and you didn't care."

Dumbfounded that her departure had mattered to Ekaterina, Kala gaped at her sister. "Ekaterina," she said, regretting she had fretted so often over abandoning Sophie without once thinking to extend her anxiety so it included Ekaterina. Apologetically she looked into her sister's face, sorry she had always perceived her sister as needing no one's help—as swathed in layers and cloaks and clouds of crankiness, her psyche well-protected and nicely out of reach.

"And why do we stay here in Lyesk," Ekaterina scolded, "just so we can starve when there's all the food we want in Paris or London, even in Warsaw? It's not as if large cities don't need good bakers. Just think, we could wake up in the morning and not be hungry. We could go to bed at night and still not be hungry."

Infected by Ekaterina's dissatisfaction—undone by her talk about cakes and jam, Naftali suddenly demanded, "Then what about Detroit? What about Iosif and Detroit? Why not go to Detroit?"

At the rearing up of their father's old obsession, Ruth, Kala, and Sophie took to contemplating with varying degrees of embarrassment the table in front of them. Then Malkeh said, "Lyesk is our home. It's our own place. We'll try our best to stay here no matter who rules."

"But if Poland owns it next," Kala objected, "we'll all be in trouble."

"If Poland owns it next, we ought to run away," Mordecai said.

"Not the new Poland," Sophie interjected.

"We'll stay here, of course," Ruth stated firmly. With her smooth red-gold hair stretched starkly away from her cheeks, every one of her features—her eyes, her brows, her fine nose, her small mouth—seemed to draw together in intense concentration as though she were trying to reason her way out of suffering. "Where else would we go but here in the Pale where the learned have built God's house? Where else would God look for us when He turns back and wants to find us again? Certainly not in America. Certainly," she glanced at Ekaterina, "not in Paris or London. As for Palestine, the Messiah will lead us there in his own time. We'll stay here till then. Lyesk is our home."

Two days later, as Kala entered the bakery to help clean up for closing, Ruth informed her that a peasant, recently returned from Russia, awaited her outside the back door.

"From Russia?" Kala puzzled and hurried out the back where she found a ragged man munching slowly, thoughtfully on a piece of bread. His eyes were red-rimmed, his nose bloated and purple, and even through the cold she could smell the stench of whiskey.

When the peasant saw her he touched his cap and said, "In 1915 I went east with you and Father Boris and the rest. I found a pocket watch on the road. You fixed it for me, and now I'm back. But the watch is gone."

Kala peered at him and after a moment recognized him as one of the Rozumov peasants. "And your wife?" she inquired. "Your children?"

"Dead. Each one dead," he stated without hesitation. "We made it all the way to Siberia—to Omsk—and there, during our second winter—yes, even when I'd found work on an estate—they died of typhus. The journey and the newness of the place had weakened them. But God in His way was good. Except for the baby, Katya, they kept alive the first winter." The man's swollen nose quivered. "And so here I am . . . by myself. I came looking for your husband. But your sister said he isn't here."

Kala placed her gloved hand on the peasant's arm. "Come inside and warm yourself."

"No, no. If your husband isn't here . . . I saw him last in Omsk."

"You must be mistaken. My husband's in the west, working with the Germans."

"Kossoff, isn't it? Your husband, the fellow who used to wear the red kerchief around his neck. We were in prison together in Omsk."

"In Omsk?" Kala fell back against the door.

"He escaped from the German labor battalion—that's what he told me. He said something made him go back into Russia —that's exactly what he said."

"He promised to send for me."

"Why? Well, you see he was right not to. He ended up in prison. He and I and his friends," the man went on proudly, "were all in jail together—I for drunkenness and he because the authorities locked up all the politicals."

"Then I'll go to Omsk," she said. "The borders are open. I'll leave tomorrow."

"But he's not in Omsk any longer," the peasant said matter-of-factly. "He and I and all his friends escaped. Every single person—robbers, murderers, drunkards, politicals—simply walked away one morning. And if he hasn't arrived in Lyesk by now, either he's in some other jail, or else . . ." The man stopped and shrugged. "Your husband said that if I got here and he wasn't already with you I must give you a message. He said it's an important message: that he loves you and loves justice above all else. No . . ." He stopped and then began again. "He loves you the most, but to deserve you he has to prove he cares for justice first . . ." He scratched his head and squinted at Kala as if to determine whether these words meant anything.

Kala groaned, thinking that the drunken peasant possessed more common sense than Mikhail. She felt the need to be off by herself. "He went into Russia! How foolish," she said, leading the peasant into the bakery where she asked Ruth to give him tea and more bread. Then she said to Malkeh and Sophie, "I have news of Mikhail. He escaped from the German labor battalion and has gone into Russia."

"Gone back? Without you?" Sophie exclaimed in shock.

"I don't understand," said Malkeh.

"He had his reasons," Kala retorted heatedly. "You can't judge him."

"But not returning to Lyesk . . ." puzzled Malkeh.

"He wasn't abandoning me. It's not that simple. He understood I would try to persuade him to stay here. He may not have made a wise decision but I know Mikhail—his heart is good. It's more than that—he's noble." And with this, she quit the bakery and headed for the orchard though it was not yet time to feed the animals.

As she walked, she wanted nothing so much as to kick her husband. She addressed him aloud, "You fool! Why are you in Russia? Your party's leaders are all in prison or in hiding and no one's in power but the Bolsheviks. Did you go because of your old stupid courage?" All the same, she wanted to understand and forgive him—to believe that his motives were serious and worthy.

A light snow began to drift down above Kala's head. Minute by minute it increased until, by the time she turned off the high road, every inch of the air was filled with whiteness. Within this bright mist she tried to conjure up Mikhail's image. She recalled that he had shown himself inept at grand and individual gestures. She remembered that when the Volhynsky Regiment had fired upon the crowd at the Nikolaevsky Station in February 1917, he had reached the station square three minutes too late to be harmed. And in July of the same year he had leaped into the wrong entrance of the Tauride Palace, to his chagrin missing the bloody confrontation between the Bolshevik Kronstadt sailors and the Socialist Revolutionary leader, Chernov. Was it possible, she wondered, that after growing more sensible, Mikhail had succumbed again to a yearning for heroism? That seemed to her unlikely. Then could something have happened to make him want to escape their marriage? Doggedly she proceeded through the orchards toward the sheds where the animals were hidden.

In the sheds, Kala recoiled from the moist muzzles of the animals. "I don't have any treats for you," she told them. The three pairs of big dark eyes scarcely blinked at her abruptness. The three heads pulled forward and tried to prod at her hands and jacket. She jumped away from them, slammed the shed door, latched it, and climbed up the familiar shortcut through the banks of snow nestled against the bare tree trunks of the orchard. She decided to walk back across the river rather than take the high road. Sinking thigh-deep into the snow drifts, she clambered down the bank and out onto the frozen water. In the twilight of the day, the ice, swept clear by the wind, gleamed like burnished metal. She felt herself grow cold like the winter landscape around her.

CHAPTER TWENTY-FOUR

Two weeks later a Red Cross package of dried food-stuffs reached the Chodorovs, accompanied by a photo-graph of Iosif, his wife and three children, and a half-page of writing in which Iosif declared that through recent transactions he had become a wealthy man, in a position to bring his parents and sisters to America should they so decide.

"Iosif is wealthy! He has sent for us," gloated Naftali.

"But Lyesk is our home," Malkeh reminded them. And the family soon forgot Iosif's offer—even Naftali—for it came at a time when their minds were focused elsewhere: the negotiators at Versailles had not yet established definite boundaries for Poland and the Russian army was successfully continuing its westward advance. One by one the towns of Luninyets, Pinsk, and Baranovits had fallen into Russian hands. Anxiously Moishe Kantorovits, as head of the town committee, sent off three telegrams to Warsaw pleading for assistance from the newly constituted Polish Republic.

At first the replies from Warsaw counseled patience and promised nothing. Then on January 18, 1919, Paderewski, musician and politician, was proclaimed premier of Poland and almost immediately a reconnaissance unit—one lieutenant, two sergeants, and five enlisted men—arrived in Lyesk. Wearing uniforms decked out with assorted ribbons and bows, they rode all about town on horseback. Dismounting at the town hall, they declared martial law. Moishe Kantorovits then recommended that the town council hire, as Lyesk police chief and Lyesk police aides, the Polish coachman's three cousins from Brest, veterans of the German army.

Taller and larger than any other men in town—a good deal too wide, Kala thought, for the streets of Lyesk—the burly cousins filled passageways and lanes. They walked singly; they marched two or three abreast; they followed close behind the reconnaissance unit. Early one morning, coming into town from the orchard where her family still kept the animals, Kala saw, looming ahead across the lane, the massive figures of the Police Chief and one of the two sergeants of the reconnaissance unit. Both men, their legs outspread, stood in front of Rabbi Benjamin's house where the rabbi's father-in-law, the old teacher, Reb Chaim Pearl, his arms raised toward the rising sun, his shoulders shrouded in a voluminous *tallis*, his head and left arm bound by the black bands of the *tefillin*, chanted his morning prayers to God.

"What are you up to, up there?" the Police Chief shouted in German, his question repeated by the Sergeant when Reb Pearl gave no answer.

Kala stopped before them, clearing her throat to gain their attention. "Reb Pearl," Kala explained, "is simply reciting his morning prayers."

"Come down, come down," the Sergeant bellowed toward the roof, ignoring Kala's explanation. "If you keep on signaling the Bolsheviks we'll arrest you and put you in jail."

At this last, out of the house in their hats and coats came Reb Pearl's daughter Naomi, her husband Rabbi Benjamin, and their son Pinchas.

"Tell him to answer us," the Police Chief pleaded with Naomi.

"The truth is, he can't answer you," Naomi pointed out, confident and happy to be conferring information. Her face under its crown of thick tan curls gleamed bright pink and healthy. "My father can't speak—that is, he won't speak until he's done praying."

"He's signaling the enemy," the Police Chief said suspiciously.

"He isn't signaling anyone," Kala assured him.

"Of course he isn't," Naomi said. "Haven't I told you exactly what he's doing? Don't I know after all these years of living with him! My father doesn't like the enemy any more than you do—he's saying his morning prayers."

"Gentlemen," said Rabbi Benjamin, pushing his wife aside, "I know that you don't see a man praying on the roof every single day but my father-in-law climbs up there whenever he has the strength. He says he feels nearer to God. Let him finish praying, gentlemen. His wits aren't what they used to be."

"Papa, Papa," Naomi called up through cupped hands, "you'd better come down. Hurry and finish. You're making a spectacle of yourself. They want you to come down."

When nothing happened, the boy, Pinchas, gave a faint smile, puffed out his round full cheeks and declared in a child's smug bell-like voice, "There's no way in the whole world to make Grandpa hurry up."

"No way?" the Sergeant disputed. "Where there's a will there's a way." He was a puffy-faced man with a bulging stomach. He grasped hold of the rungs of a ladder that leaned against the house and mounted to the roof, his face and neck reddening as he climbed. On the roof he circled Reb Pearl. Keeping some distance between them, he hollered, "You're signaling our enemies, you ridiculous stubborn Jew!"

Reb Pearl went on mumbling out the words of his prayer—gazing up at the sky, his arms still reaching out toward God. At last the Sergeant approached him, lifted him onto his shoulder, and carried him down the ladder as if he were a recalcitrant sheep.

"What are you doing?" cried Kala.

"Take your hands off my father this instant!"

"He's a sick old man," objected Rabbi Benjamin. "What's your authority?"

"Our authority is martial law," replied the Sergeant, setting Reb Pearl down. "The town committee has put us in charge of defending Lyesk. This man is threatening public safety. He's under arrest." And he and the Police Chief each took one of Reb Pearl's arms and marched him up Merchant Lane toward the square—the two men taking great strides with the tiny frail figure in between, half running, half dragged along, the *tallis* fluttering from side to side. Behind them, protesting and complaining, hurried Naomi, Rabbi Benjamin, and their son Pinchas.

Kala headed for the bakery to inform her mother. On the way, outside Avrom Lavin's tailor shop, she met Mordecai and Naftali, who accompanied her. When they told Malkeh the news, Malkeh sent the men to the Potocki estate to bring back Kantorovits. "Thank heavens for Kantorovits—that he allied himself with the Poles," Malkeh said while she wrapped herself in her coat and pulled on her galoshes. "Your father was right, we're lucky he's one of us. Still we'd better do something ourselves. You and Ruth come with me. We'll alert the other members of the town committee and take up a collection wherever we can."

"But why must we always resort to bribery?" Kala objected, following her mother and sister. As she split off from them, she glanced with irritation at their stiff backs, their matching obstinate tread, their long black coats and babushkas. Today, she thought, could be one hundred years ago. The Poles could just as easily be Russians or Germans, they could be Mongols; it would make no difference: the system demanded that her mother and sister still try to bribe the powers. She wanted nothing to do with this; she felt above giving bribes. Yet the next instant she stepped into

Avrom Lavin's tailor shop and held out her hand for money.

"We'll give it back if we don't use it," she promised Lavin who stood before her pursing his lips. "Papa went to fetch Kantorovits. Kantorovits is supposed to save us. God knows whether Kantorovits or bribery is worse."

Twenty minutes later, Naftali and Mordecai joined Malkeh. "Kantorovits has fled." Excitedly Naftali waved his arms. "He packed up his family and ran to Warsaw in the middle of the night."

"He ran away," Mordecai said. "He heard the Bolsheviks are around the corner. He took his wife Leah and Mendel with him, and the children."

"Hurry," Malkeh said. "We have to hurry."

Naftali, Malkeh, Mordecai, Ruth, and Kala rushed to the square. "If only they had bothered to say goodby," Naftali complained.

Reaching the square, they found most of the Jews had gathered; yet not a single Christian, not one Polish member of the town committee had shown up. In front of the town hall a machine gun had been mounted and two soldiers carrying rifles guarded the door to the building. Kala let her mother go on ahead. Uneasily she put her arm around Ruth. Below the town hall the hunched figures of the dark-clad citizens resembled natural growths out of the cold ground, barely distinguishable from the dirty heaps of snow gathered here and there. An empty gray-white sky arched grandly over the scene. On all sides the question echoed, "Reb Chaim Pearl—why that good man?"

Very quickly the news of Kantorovits's unannounced departure made its way to Naomi, Rabbi Benjamin, and Pinchas, who had stationed themselves at the foot of the town-hall steps. Naomi's face lost its color. Lines cracked her skin from her nostrils down to the edges of her mouth. "Kantorovits gone, exactly when we needed him! And Leah, my best friend, my everyday closest friend, Leah went with him!"

Slowly, steadily Malkeh mounted the steps toward the soldiers. Ignoring the rifles cradled in their arms, she stopped just in front of them, and in a strong, reasonable, and pleasant voice asked in Polish to speak with the Lieutenant. One of the soldiers then rapped upon the door, stuck his head inside, and said a few words. Instead of the Lieutenant, the puffy-faced Sergeant stepped out. Just as amiably, yet with greater firmness than before, Malkeh inquired of the Sergeant, "Upon what charges do you hold Reb Pearl? Certainly he is no threat to anyone. Whatever the reasons—the town committee urges you to release him."

"I don't see any town committee here," the Sergeant replied, staring into the crowd, his hands on his hips. "The man has been charged with treason. The trial is going on right now."

"Treason?" Malkeh's shocked gasp was repeated by those nearest the steps. It spread through the crowd. When the word "treason" reached Kala, she said in a loud voice, "We have to stop them!"

"Don't be foolish," said Ruth, "they have guns."

"Save my father, save my father!" Naomi shrieked.

"We can storm the building," Kala said. "There are hundreds of us and only . . ."

Ruth's hand flew up to her sister's mouth. "Look around you and see who might be killed."

Naomi started up the stairs toward the door of the town hall. One of the soldiers thrust his rifle out to fend her off. Darting up the stairs, Rabbi Benjamin grabbed his wife by the waist and carried her back down where she struggled in his arms, cursing him and cursing Kantorovits.

Malkeh drew out a cloth bag from the folds of her coat. The Sergeant looked away. Then he looked inside the bag. A murmur started up within the crowd. "Malkeh will save Reb Pearl. You'll see, Malkeh will convince the Poles—better than Kantorovits." The Sergeant turned, went into the building, and promptly emerged with the Lieutenant, whose entrance at once brightened up the surroundings—dressed as he was in a grass-green tunic with gold braid twining up and down the breasts and the arms and with his red trousers tucked into soft leather boots. From the heavily ornamented scabbard at his side he unsheathed his sword and brought its tip to the fabric of the bag of money which Malkeh now offered him. "The new Poland," he declared in a high-pitched voice, his mouth wide open with the effort to carry his words to the crowd, "the new Poland is not interested in blood money."

Malkeh waited until any echo had died away. "I know that is true," she took up, her manner utterly grave. "The new Poland is above taking money dishonorably. But this is altogether different—a gesture of good intentions. This is a bond. All we ask is that you take one more look, a second look at Reb Chaim Pearl and decide for yourselves if he is a threat to anyone's security."

But her suggestion seemed to bore the Lieutenant, who had recently arrived in town, knew nothing of Malkeh's reputation for peacemaking, and had come into the bakery only twice—both times when the bread had run out and all the shelves were empty. The Lieutenant gestured to the Sergeant with his head, murmuring, "Bring out the old traitor," and again the Sergeant disappeared into the building and came back, this time pushing Reb Chaim Pearl ahead of him. The good teacher still wore his *tallis* and *tefillin*. Barely glancing at the old man, the Lieutenant raised his sword majestically in the air and the sword tip came down and pointed at Reb Pearl's wizened neck. "This man," shouted the Lieutenant in a high-pitched voice, "has been convicted of treason to the state. Let his fate be a warning to you all. Embrace Poland and she will embrace you. Betray Poland and you will die."

The Jews of Lyesk looked at each other. Embrace Poland? They found it hard to know what the officer had in mind. Reb Chaim Pearl a traitor, a criminal—this sweet, small, kind, generous man?

Growing more and more urgent, Malkeh's deep voice boomed out, "At least wire Warsaw for further instructions. At least you must contact Warsaw. And if the gift we present you is insufficient we can . . ."

The Lieutenant put his finger to his lips and with his other

[288]

hand brought the tip of his sword to Malkeh's chest. The crowd, angry and distressed, murmured its objection. The Lieutenant pointed to the steps and the Sergeant took Malkeh's arm to escort her. At this Ruth clasped Kala to her closely. But in fact there was no need to restrain her, for as Kala gazed at her mother she read in her face the determination that no additional blood be spilled. She understood that in this conflict, victory or failure belonged only to Malkeh— that she, Kala, had earned no right to interrupt or deflect it. It was, after all, her mother who, before Ruth's birth, had traveled to Minsk and changed the status of Lyesk so that Jews needed no permit to live there; it was her mother who had pursued peace for the Jews in Lyesk for almost twenty-five years, despite pogroms to the east, the north, and the south.

"Sergeant!" The Lieutenant ordered. A look of discomfort settled on his face, as though the present situation had brought on a stomach ache. The Sergeant and three soldiers turned and directed the old man into the passageway next to the town hall. As Reb Chaim Pearl walked along between the troopers he sang, *"Sh'ma Yisroel, Adonoy Elohenu, Adonoy Echod . . ."*

In low voices the Jews of Lyesk echoed his words: "Hear O Israel, the Lord our God, the Lord is one."

The execution of Reb Chaim Pearl stunned the Jews of Lyesk. Those who had assembled at the square blamed themselves for allowing it. Anger rose to screen their guilt, while for the rest of the town the execution seemed to encourage an old strain of racial scorn. In Lyesk, for the first time Kala saw Jews deliberately shouldered off the wooden sidewalks; she heard remarks behind her back about her father, mother, and fellow Jews; she noted that many Jews began to open their shops late and close them early. Still others obsessively spat over their shoulders at the idea that Moishe Kantorovits and the Polish representatives of the town committee had betrayed them.

"You would have thought," Naftali remarked glumly, "that under Paderewski, who was an artist, who was a pianist—Paderewski who could easily come to Lyesk and try out our piano—you would have thought that under such a leader, Reb Pearl would have been spared."

"Perhaps it has nothing to do with Poland," Sophie said. "Maybe it's just these men. If other men—if a different unit—if Colonel Swislocz's division had been in charge of this town." She broke off. ". . . How terrible that they murdered our Reb Chaim Pearl."

One day, soon afterward, Kala accosted Ruth on her way to the House of Study. "If you don't mind my asking, Ruth—does your belief in God help you?"

Ruth hesitated. "Sometimes."

"Only sometimes?"

Frowning, Ruth brushed a strand of red-gold hair from her face. "To be truthful, Kala, sometimes I think that God turns away, that He withdraws and leaves us to do as we will. Sometimes I think He isn't here all the time, that He wasn't in Lyesk when Reb Pearl was killed."

"But if you always go to the House of Study . . ."

"I go because if I study and pray, if I persevere in observing, that may bring back my faith. But I'm filled with doubts, Kala, I've had them since the war began."

Kala stared at her sister. She saw that the fierce anger that had marked her sister's face—clenched brows over fixed, accusing eyes—had given way to a wan despair. Horrified, Kala said, "But you can't give up, Ruth. I know that I've never put a great deal of store in God, but it would be terrible if everybody gave up on Him. And you have to remember, at least Reb Pearl went to his death praying to God."

"At least he went praying to God," Ruth echoed.

And because her sister sounded slightly heartened, Kala later repeated the same words to Malkeh.

But they did no good. The death of Reb Chaim Pearl

affected Malkeh the most of anyone. She had never intended to hand over Reb Chaim Pearl's life. Over the next month, when customers entered the bakery in pursuit of her advice, she no longer led them to a table and stood above them to listen and gaze at the wall like a queen. Rather she forced them to search her out and to sit down at one of the back tables where she roosted. Here she remained just as committed to listening as before. Yet no matter the question that was asked her—whether it was safe to buy lumber in the Ukraine, whether it was more advantageous to arrange for a daughter's marriage in Baranovits or Vilna—she answered: "There's no way to know. It's a different world. We can't settle anything. What we have to do is wait and see."

CHAPTER TWENTY-FIVE

N OT KNOWING WHERE TO TURN FOR NEWS OF MIKHAIL, Kala woke in the middle of the night in fits of terror, fearing he had been captured again by the Monarchists or murdered somewhere in great Russia by the Bolsheviks, or had fallen ill and died of hunger or the cold. Her ankles, her breasts, her arms ached from missing him—ached so keenly and insidiously that her hunger for her husband turned into an immense hot fury. Her family continued to question Mikhail's desertion, and though at first she had welcomed the support their anger gave her, it quickly saddened and depressed her.

Then one cold February afternoon Mordecai announced, "Thank God, the Poles are leaving us. But unluckily, the Bolsheviks are coming in." And indeed, three hours after the Polish reconnaissance unit had cantered out of Lyesk, the Red Army came rumbling in, trailing their wagons and cannons, the commands of the soldiers resounding through the streets. As the first Russian troop turned off the high road, all the shutters in town clapped closed, iron bars fell into place, the populace hid in cellars and back rooms, and Naftali said to Kala, "Now your husband's army has come to town."

"Will he be with them?" Mordecai inquired.

"My husband's army?" Kala asked in surprise. "You know Mikhail isn't a Bolshevik."

"They're all Bolsheviks now," Naftali declared. "Anyway, it's time Mikhail came back. And if he's here, even if he's a Bolshevik, we'll be glad to see him."

"Papa, he's not a Bolshevik. You know that as well as I. The truth is, he'd be safer entering Lyesk under the Germans or the Poles, considering the way the government feels about our party."

"Then why did he go off into Russia?" Ekaterina demanded.

Kala looked away from Ekaterina. "Why? Because he's a loyal man."

"A loyal man—and he left you behind?" said Ekaterina.

"Ekaterina," Ruth reprimanded, "Mikhail's concern has been with protecting Kala—keeping her free from danger. That's why he hasn't sent for her."

"And that's exactly how a husband ought to act," Mordecai stated firmly.

"Yes, that's how a husband ought to act," Naftali echoed. "If he thinks of it."

"Mikhail may well be capable of courage," said Malkeh cautiously.

Kala peered at her mother. Encouraged, she had the sense that Mikhail was gaining ground in the Chodorovs' estimation. But then her father said, "It's too bad he's a Bolshevik."

"He isn't," Kala murmured.

"And now, of course," Naftali went on, "the Red Army's arrived on our doorstep—who knows how they'll act? If there happen to be Cossacks or Ukrainians among them, then the Jews are out of luck. The whole town will be out of luck anyway—it isn't as though a real army will be taking over.

[293]

No, no," Naftali shook his head, "these are nothing but a bunch of marauders trying to feed themselves. And after all, what kind of army is it that elects its own officers?"

"The best kind," retorted Kala, measuring the Chodorovs with a truculent eye. "Why are you all looking at me like that? Just because I defend the way the Red Army chooses its officers doesn't make me responsible for the way they act. I never invented the Red Army and I certainly didn't bring them to Lyesk."

But despite these disclaimers Kala could not stop herself from watching and worrying over the Red Army's every move as it settled into town. To her relief, its take-over began peacefully. Within a few days normal business resumed. On market day the Division Commissar, a tow-headed young man with an open countenance, wide-set blue eyes, rosy cheeks, and a cleft chin, called a meeting of the townspeople, chiding them for their fearful behavior.

"Step forward, please." He urged the crowd to fill the large space they had left between them and him. "I won't bite. We're not monsters. Here we come bearing the gift of freedom and you bar your doors and windows."

With a slightly nervous grin Kala put her arm around Malkeh's shoulder. "You see, Mama, they're not monsters— just ordinary Russians—some of them even Jews."

"Your suspicious natures," the Commissar went on, "have hurt the feelings of our kindly Division Commander, Comrade Yushikov." The Commissar pointed across the square at the hotel where the division pennant hung over the door post. Standing on the porch, a young man in a plain jacket— broad-shouldered, slim-waisted, and balanced on thick bow legs encased in shiny boots—waved his riding crop joyfully at the crowd, a wide smile revealing a mouthful of broken teeth. Kala estimated his age as no older than twenty-five. She studied the faces of the townspeople and thought that the citizens seemed to look with favor on this genial and modest young man—that, in fact, they appeared more comfortable before this new ruler of Lyesk than they had with the mere lieutenant of the Polish reconnaissance unit who had presented himself a hundred times as grandly.

Cautiously she glanced at her mother. She had felt protective of her since shortly after Reb Chaim Pearl's execution. She pulled Malkeh to her more closely. "Mama," she coaxed, "do you notice how much the Commander resembles Luka's oldest son? Gregori had the same straw hair, the same broad nose, even the same loose teeth. You can't honestly say these men are monsters."

But all that happened was that Malkeh, her eyes judging, glanced first at the Commissar and then at the Division Commander. A chill passed over Kala.

"Nearer," pleaded the Commissar, "nearer so I don't have to shout." Russian soldiers, their coats patched with rags, their boots, full of holes and held together with emergency bindings, urged the townspeople forward. "Look about you!" commanded the Commissar. "Look at the buildings, the fields and the stores. Look at the cobblestones under your feet." The Commissar paused and waited.

Obediently the townspeople cast their gazes about, their eyes returning to the speaker when they discerned nothing different in the cobblestones or in the buildings than they had observed yesterday or the day before.

"Look! Look!" The Commissar squinted in all directions. "Everything you see today—not just one thing but every single thing—belongs not to some nobleman in Warsaw or in Moscow, not to a factory owner or a shopkeeper living in a high house—but to you, the people!"

Goose bumps rose on Kala's arms to hear such language again. She realized how sorely she had missed it. She remembered the February Days two years before when it had seemed such words had already come true. Fires had burned on the street corners of Petrograd, warming without distinction of birth, wealth, education, party, or profession all those men and women, those children of Russia who had risen up to depose the Tsar.

"You are masters of your own fate now," shouted the

Commissar. "You must elect your own Revolutionary Committee who will help bring about your evolution into freedom while we soldiers go on to liberate your countrymen to the west, and the laboring people of Poland too. Just remember that you are not alone. Everywhere in the world—in Germany, in France, in England and the United States, the people are rising to take back what belongs to them. The people are free."

Kala grasped her mother's arm, squeezing the flesh as if to stop Malkeh's judgment. "They want the people to be free. Mama, you have to admit—that's the right idea."

Skeptically Malkeh cast her eyes to one side. She murmured, "I've never questioned whether they have the right idea. What I want to know is—are we the people? Or are we the enemy?"

The young woman released her mother, acknowledging the truth of Malkeh's suspicion. The Chodorovs, with their bakery and orchard, would be considered bourgeois enemies of the revolution by any revolutionary party—her own included. Yet in the backward economy of Lyesk, most often it made little sense to distinguish between bourgeois and worker. In her own family they all worked physically long hard hours, caring for themselves and, in genuine communal fashion under Malkeh's tutelage, trying to care for others. Yes, reflected Kala, in the just society toward which she wanted to work, she was certain the Chodorovs deserved a respected place. At the same time she also knew that if a revolutionary tribunal were set up this moment in Lyesk, her arguments in defense of her family would fall to nothing and the Chodorovs, and perhaps the entire region of Lyesk with its scant buildings, poor soil, and knee-high mud, might be discounted as a complete loss in the socialist battle for the salvation of man. She slipped her hand into Malkeh's and said wistfully, "Almost everyone in Lyesk is the people, Mama."

Back they started toward the bakery, on their way stopping

to read a notice that had just been posted near the hotel. A long sheet of tattered paper urged all comrades of revolutionary Russia to come forward with voluntary contributions of sugar, tea, bread, salt, kvass, musical instruments, shoes, razors, soap. Kala grew alarmed: the list took up more than five columns.

"Can they be so blinded by their doctrine," questioned Malkeh, "that they actually believe their speeches will convince hungry people to starve and freeze themselves still further?"

"They've just gotten here," Kala apologized, somehow still wanting these men who bore the red banner to show themselves better and more humane than other armies. "When they're here awhile they'll understand how bad things are in the region and they'll act differently." With this she fixed a hopeful if stern eye on the Division Commander and his men.

But instead of acting better, they soon started acting worse. Unsuccessful in their quest for voluntary contributions, squads of soldiers regularly walked up and down Merchant Lane, employing the rhetoric and language of the Revolution and threatening to burn down the shops unless they were given money and food. From here they spread out around the countryside to declare that the peasants now owned all the land, including the buildings of Rozumov and Potocki—that the land had been given to the people in the name of the Revolution. In return for this great boon, each person was required to pledge an impossible amount of food and free labor. Those peasants who refused were beaten.

The army had been in town for three weeks when Sophie reported to Kala one night, "Now even Mama's given in to their demands. And it's not like in the old days. You could trust the authorities you were bribing then and if you couldn't, at least you didn't have to put up with their self-righteousness."

Ashamed, Kala lowered her head. "They'll leave pretty soon, Sophie," she tried to reassure her sister, now wishing only that the Red Army would get on with its work—that it would march ahead to liberate Poland and free Lyesk from its burden. "They're on their way to Poland."

"And whatever will you do when Mikhail returns? Will you really go back into Russia and live under people like that?"

"I don't know. Yes, probably I would." Kala picked up the smooth blue vase that stood on the table between her and Sophie's bed. She held it in one hand and leaned her cheek against its cool surface, remembering that Mikhail had bought the vase for her, as a surprise, in the Kitay-Gorod market in Moscow. Naftali had brought it back with them to Lyesk. "Yes, probably I would go back. Lots of people in Russia disagree with the government. Mikhail and I would join them." Kala looked at her sister for her response.

"Oh, I still think," said Sophie, nodding her head, "that if you believe in something, you ought to do it. I myself would go into Poland even after Reb Pearl's murder, if Withold asked me. Because things can change. Withold says there will be a new kind of Poland soon, based on equality and rights for everyone."

"What kind of equality and rights?" Ekaterina interrupted, abruptly entering the room. She sat down on Sophie's bed. "Who has rights? None of us here. Kala, your Bolsheviks are terrible, they're ruining everything. They found the flour Mama sewed into pillow cases—they stole the rest of the apples that we stored. Next thing I know, they'll steal my airplane."

"Your airplane?"

"My friends, the German pilots, hid it in the woods. They're ingenious, those Germans are. There wasn't enough petrol to fly it back to Germany so they decided that after the war they might come back and get some use of it themselves. After they'd gone I got to thinking—they probably left it for me." Ekaterina laughed, baring her numerous small bright teeth. "They left it so that when things get too awful, I can escape out of Lyesk."

"Ekaterina, you can't be that silly."

"Of course it's silly. But I think I could fly it if I wanted to. I could round up some fuel and fly off somewhere."

"Ekaterina, go away," said Kala, "you're bothering us."

"You go away. Go find your husband."

When Kala's face flushed, Sophie said, "Ekaterina, we don't know where Mikhail is."

But Ekaterina ignored her warning. "This is a peculair family, with both Ruth's and Kala's boyfriends running away from them. At least, Sophie, you and I are spared that tragedy."

"You and I? But I haven't been spared," said Sophie. "No, I haven't been spared." Then as though she just now registered these words she had uttered, her voice quickened and rose with pride. "I too am in love with someone who isn't here."

Ekaterina stared at Sophie. "I can't understand why you say that. I don't believe you, Sophie. You just say it to leave me out."

"No, not to leave you out. To include you by letting you know my secret."

Ekaterina retreated, backing into the corridor. "It doesn't include me at all. Not for a minute—such a lie. And it doesn't change the fact that Kala's Bolsheviks are terrible. This morning one of them stole a shirt of Mordecai's off the clothes line. I just wish they'd hurry up and go away."

"So do I," said Kala.

"I wish they'd go away," said Sophie.

But another month went by and still the division lingered on in Lyesk, stalled by new reports of civil war in Great Russia. With the winter of 1918–19 drawing to its close, counter-revolutionary forces backed by English, French, and American allies had claimed vast areas of the Russian nation. Battalions from within the Ukraine, Estonia, and from along the Volga threatened Russia's heartland from all sides, and contrary to the predictions of Lenin and Trotsky, the people of Poland failed to rise up against their oppressors and to embrace the units of the Red Army that did approach their border. Instead, the armies of independent Poland appeared ready to strike against western Russia. By the end of March a rumor circulated through Lyesk that General Pilsudski had crossed the Bug River and, with a large force, was pressing eastward against token Russian resistance. Trains filled with retreating Russian troops passed through Lyesk toward Moscow day and night, and the local garrison talked unhappily of an imminent retreat. On the first Friday in April, the Division Commissar called a meeting of the Lyesk population. When at ten o'clock, the appointed hour of the meeting, the town square remained almost empty, the Commissar sent out troops to invite the citizens to attend.

The weather was blustery—the morning unable to decide whether it was winter or spring. Numbing winds from the north alternated with warm breezes from the west and south. Clouds towered up here and there about the countryside. As the Commissar started his address, thunder sounded in the distance, from time to time accompanying the officer while he expressed his disappointment in the attitude of the populace toward their liberators. Here in Lyesk, mourned the tow-headed soldier, the Russian armies were starving and freezing; enemies threatened them from all sides; and yet they were forced to act like an occupying force over their own people. The Commissar declared that he found the lack of revolutionary fervor in Lyesk mystifying. The rosiness of his cheeks had now spread to his nose and eyes and Kala, thinking this speech a good deal less inspiring than the first, suspected he had recently been drinking spirits to ease his unhappiness. She perceived a furtive look of disillusionment in his boyish open face.

"Where is the proletariat which should rise up and take over the reins of government?" he inquired. "Why haven't you elected a Revolutionary Committee? Why do I walk through this town and still see capitalists shamelessly performing their bloodsucking trade?" The Commissar's voice blurred. He paused and lost his thought. Yet the soldiers would not allow the audience to depart. Shaking his head, the Commissar looked around and then focused his gaze on the hotel. "Look what you've done to our poor Commander!" He pointed across the square to the hotel steps where stood the Divisional Commander, that broad-shouldered, slim-waisted young man—the retinue around him looking thinner and even more ragged than the month before. Not only had the Commander's boots lost their shine, but his mouth had lost its winning smile and he scowled down fiercely at the residents of Lyesk, his broken teeth still showing, his riding crop held high in the air as if he were about to bring it down across their backs.

"Isn't it enough," continued the Commissar sorrowfully, "that the army fights your battles? Must we teach you your revolutionary responsibilities? In the name of Lenin, all capitalists will be made to pay for hoarding their goods away from the people's army. Before we leave you, I promise we will not be denied our roubles, we will not be denied our bread."

Uneasily Kala returned home to find her family celebrating the departure of the division. So relieved were the Chodorovs to be getting rid of this badly supplied army with its frayed clothes and nerves and explosive tempers that they appeared unwilling to take the Commissar's threats seriously. Their gaiety was tempered only by the possibility of another Polish occupation—a prospect, however, which did not bother Sophie, who speculated in a whisper to Kala that it might be Colonel Withold Swislocz who would lead his Polish division into Lyesk.

At the end of the afternoon—just before the early Friday closing—Mordecai entered the bakery and uttered into the ears of the Jewish housewives who had brought their casseroles to keep warm in the ovens over the Sabbath, "Thank God, the Bolsheviks are leaving. But the bad news is, next we'll be Polish."

The following morning the Red Army began to load its equipment onto railroad cars at the station. Two engines waited in readiness to haul the heavy load. From her family's house Kala could see the train's smoke rising into the sky, swept at a steep angle to the south by a frosty wind that had attacked the town during the night, ending the brief thaw. The hardened mud crackled underfoot as Malkeh and Naftali, Ruth and Mordecai set off for morning services at the synagogue. Kala, Sophie, and Ekaterina remained home with Ruth's children. Kala helped her sisters straighten the house and set the table for the Sabbath meal, after which she strolled over to the bakery to check on the casseroles left the evening before. As she was about to open the front door of the bakery, she heard a racket coming from the other side of town. She turned her head and listened. Through the cold air came the faint sound of shattering glass, splintering wood, shouts, and laughter. Recalling the Commissar's threats, she swiftly slipped up Merchant Lane to the square, where she viewed a procession of wagons filled with weapons, ammunition, and supplies proceeding steadily toward the station. She skirted the square, keeping close to the buildings, trying to remain as inconspicuous as possible. A bulletin flapped from the side of the hotel. She stopped to examine it: by order of the Division Commander, the bulletin read, prior to departure, squads of troops were required to visit the houses and shops of all "capitalists" in order to collect food and gold hoarded from the Soviet government.

Kala crept along the streets, approaching the origin of the shouts and the noise of crashing timbers. In a moment she caught sight of a mob of soldiers and a troop of Cossacks going in and out of the houses and stores, selecting only those buildings that belonged to Jews. She turned and ran back through the streets. Luckily, she thought, most of the Jews were at the synagogue; but as she raced in that direction, she grew terrified at the thought that her sisters and nieces had been left unprotected at home and she veered off down Merchant Lane. Without stopping at the house she entered the barn. Sir Leslie was openly stabled here as part of the bargain Malkeh had struck when agreeing to bake free for the army.

Harnessing Sir Leslie to the cart, Kala led him around to the front door. "Sophie, Ekaterina," she burst in, "the soldiers— who knows what they're up to! Leave the house! Take the children to the synagogue and tell the congregation! I'll close up the house, I'll warn the people who aren't at services." In a rush she helped dress her nieces in their coats. "Everyone had best stay inside the synagogue. It might be the safest place in town."

Inside the cart, Sophie took up Sir Leslie's reins and whipped them across the horse's rump. "I'll drop the children and come back for you."

"No! I'll meet you in the synagogue."

"I'll come back for you. If I don't, you'll just go chasing all over town."

"Aunt Kala," said Ruth's middle daughter, looking down at her coat, "you've buttoned my coat all wrong."

"Sophie, stay in the synagogue and be sensible."

"Aunt Kala," Ruth's daughter reminded more insistently, "you buttoned up all the wrong buttons."

Kala ran back to the house, fastened the doors and the shutters, and started up Merchant Lane. Ahead of her near the square she saw the squads of troops already hammering on the doors, breaking through the shutters. She noticed one or two neighbors fleeing out their back doors and she shouted for them to take refuge at the synagogue. Then without thinking, she continued ahead toward the troops who were approaching the large twin gates of Lazar Dovitsky's stable-yard. A half-dozen soldiers had ripped up the hitching rack in front and were preparing to batter in the gates. She approached two soldiers who directed the others. In her desperation she pleaded, "Comrades, please stop. Please tell the others to stop."

"She has a Moscow accent," giggled one of the soldiers, a tall, thin, black-haired man, more than a little drunk.

"She must be from Moscow," giggled the other.

Frustrated, Kala continued without letting herself pause, "You'd do much better to get on the trains before you're left behind. Comrades, listen—you're not helping the Revolution."

"We're not helping the Revolution? Ha! Ha! Tell that to the Commissar," the tall thin soldier roared, then giggled again and pointed as, down the lane from the square, the Commissar rode toward them on horseback, accompanied by several Cossacks in scarlet tunics and breeches. One Cossack wore a flowered woman's hat upon his head, a long feather boa streaming out behind. On the head of another's mount, a derby hat had been jammed with holes crudely cut out for the ears. The faces of all the riders were flushed.

"Comrade Commissar!" Kala called out. "Your men here are going to miss their train." She looked around sharply, trying to decide where she could run if they came after her.

The Commissar stared at Kala, unable to believe what he heard. He turned to his companions on horseback. "What's she saying? Who is she?"

"From the bakery," came a voice.

"I'm an aide to the Central Committee," Kala declared.

"One of the daughters at the bakery," said a soldier.

A great smile appeared across the face of the Commissar. "Where is your sister? The one I like best. The crippled one with the black hair."

"I don't know, she's not in the bakery," Kala answered in a loud voice, preparing to run now through the narrow passageway to the left of the stable. If she could get to the fields beyond, she would be able to hide from them.

"Look! There's her sister!"

Kala turned and, stupefied, saw Sophie driving down Merchant Lane in the cart pulled by Sir Leslie. Instead of diving into the passageway, Kala headed toward Sophie. Angrily she yelled, "Why are you here?" and Sophie answered, "Come Kala, quick, get in the cart."

"That's her!" exulted the Commissar. "And just in time!" he chortled. "Let's have her. Stop the nag!" he ordered the Cossack wearing the woman's hat.

The Cossack spurred his horse forward until it was abreast

of Sir Leslie. He reached down and seized the reins, pulling Sir Leslie to a halt.

Kala snatched the reins away from the Cossack's grasp, slapping the muzzle of the Cossack's mount smartly with the flat of her hand so that the horse danced backward nervously and reared. She leaped into the cart and whipped at Sir Leslie's back. He lumbered forward toward the bakery.

Shouts rose all about the girls. On either side of the cart, Cossacks galloped, reaching down to seize the rains.

"Jump, Kala, jump!" called Sophie. "You can get away."

"I want the one with the black hair! You can have the other one," came the drunken cry of the Commissar behind them.

"They're ours now!" shouted the Cossack wearing the woman's hat. He stood in his stirrups and looked back at the girls and then over their heads at the Commissar, laughing. Kala stared at him as at a dream. He was a tall swarthy man on a large bay stallion. He wore a heavy cloak over his tunic and a shining sword curved down along his scarlet trousers and boots.

Kala yanked the reins back and forth, trying to free them from the grasp of their captors, but the two Cossacks kept control of Sir Leslie, leading him and the cart down the lane. From the square another two riders galloped toward them, leaning in at the girls as if to snatch them off the cart and carry them away. Kala and Sophie linked their arms around each other's waist and kept close to the center of the cart to avoid the grasping hands of the riders.

Kala's mind, her body, all of her senses concentrated upon one object: to rescue her sister from this cart. Time slowed almost to a stop as she sought the small opening that would free them. The hind quarters of Sir Leslie and the two horses flanking him seemed to swell before her eyes. She could see each drop of sweat drying upon the hides, each coarse hair of the three tails flickering in the breeze, the steady nervous lifting of hind leg and hind leg, pulling her and Sophie forward. From one side, into her vision came the pink nostrils and starred forehead of another horse bearing down upon them. A scarlet arm and black glove cut through the air, brushing over their clasped bodies. The shop fronts of Merchant Lane moved slowly by, a great distance on either side of them. Kala felt as if the name of each merchant burned its way into her mind—Avrom Lavin, Tailor; Lazar Dovitsky, Stables—as yet another horse and arm swept by. And then, when the lane ahead looked clear for a moment and the two girls allowed themselves a brief sigh, hoofbeats and a shout from behind startled them and Kala felt intense pain across her scalp as a rider grasped her hair from behind and attempted to lift her bodily from the cart. She loosed her hold on Sophie's waist and braced both hands upon the cart, her head jerking forward until she was looking straight down at the muddy lane and the hoofs of the horses. Surprised by the unexpected resistance, the rider was pulled half off his horse. At the same moment, Sophie launched herself across Kala's back and bit the hand holding her hair.

With a shout of pain, the rider loosened his hold and, barely keeping his seat, rode off, calling out, "Bitches!"

Tears of pain streamed down Kala's face. Blindly she reached out to grab Sophie again, but a rider bore down upon the cart from the other side and managed to get his arm around Sophie's waist. As he lifted her clear of the cart, Sophie swung the whip she held in her right hand, snapping it across the eye and cheek of her assailant. It was the Commissar, who shouted in pain and dropped his burden.

"Sophie!" wailed Kala in horror as she saw her sister falling helplessly in front of the moving cart. The cart canted in the air as it passed over Sophie's body. Kala heard a cracking sound as if something brittle had been crushed.

From that moment Kala lost all consciousness of what happened. Without an instant of hesitation she leaped over the back of the cart and ran two steps to her sister who lay face down in the trampled mud of the lane. Across the back of Sophie's head and shoulders the track of the cart made a clear raw mark, from which blood oozed slowly. Kala rolled Sophie over. She gasped when she saw the mud and snow caked over her sister's features, filling her open mouth. "It's all right, it's all right," Kala muttered again and again as she attempted to brush the muck from her sister's face, to dig it out of her mouth. The eyes stared up at her without recognition. The galloping horses of the Cossacks pounded past, riders leaning down from their saddles in trick positions as if the crouching girl were part of a circus act. Filled with anguish and rage, Kala clasped one arm under Sophie's neck and the other under her legs and heaved her up. She staggered down Merchant Lane, veering right and swerving left to confuse the riders pursuing her—her sole object to get Sophie back to the bakery where she could wash her off and make her whole again.

Now it appeared the riders were merely playing with Kala, passing on one side or the other, forcing her this way and that without making any serious attempt at grasping her. One of the Cossacks came cantering by with his sword flourishing and caught the end of her skirt. Sliding to her knees in the mud, Kala could feel her dress and pettitcoat tear as if a dressmaker slit the seam with a razor. The brisk cold air blew in upon her thighs and backside. Crouching there in the mud, she thought for a moment that she heard Sophie breathing. "Alive! She's alive." Her heart leaped. But then she realized that she heard only her own panting, her lungs heaving with the effort of carrying her sister.

"A moment, Sophie! We'll be home in a moment! Please wait."

Behind her the Cossacks and the mob of troops deserted the street. Silence fell upon Merchant Lane. In a second's time Kala was left alone, dazed, holding Sophie to her, kissing her face, murmuring to her. Slowly she rose with her burden and stumbled toward the bakery, thinking to enter through the back. As she emerged behind the building a voice called out in a hushed whisper, "Kala! Kala! Over here." Kala looked around and caught sight of Ekaterina in the loft of the barn, signaling to her.

Barely able to support Sophie, Kala moved toward the barn. In a moment Malkeh, Naftali, and Ekaterina were at her side, helping her carry Sophie into the barn. Ekaterina swung the door closed. She said, "We just came looking for you and Sophie."

"Wash her face, wash her face," said Kala. "Where's the water? Clean the dirt and breathe into her mouth."

Malkeh crouched on the floor of the barn, Sophie's head cradled in her lap. From Malkeh's mouth came a strange low wrenching sound as if rusty iron bars were rubbing against one another.

"She's alive, she's alive!" protested Kala.

Ekaterina brought a bucket of water and sponged off Sophie's face. Blood leaked out of both sides of Sophie's mouth. Naftali knelt, his head to Sophie's heart. Kala clawed him away, pushed Ekaterina aside, and cried out, "Sophie, Sophie!"

Sophie's eyes stared up into the air, seeing nothing. Malkeh swayed, keening. Naftali stood, his eyes closed, beating his breast.

Kala rose. She tried to stop her father's fist from striking upon his breast. "She won't die, she won't die."

"The Tsar crippled our Sophie," Naftali wept, "and the Revolution has murdered her."

Kala stumbled back. She fell against one of the wooden pilings supporting the roof. The barn door creaked open and Sophie's family looked up in terror. Then light flooded in as Sir Leslie, still harnessed to the empty cart, stubbornly pushed his way into the barn.

CHAPTER TWENTY-SIX

"COME WITH ME," EKATERINA WHISPERED INTO KALA'S ear. "Come with me right now."

Kala neither blinked nor made any other sign that she'd understood. She was watching her mother loosen Sophie's hair and brush it down on either side of her shoulders. She was looking at her mother smooth Sophie's brow, close her eyes and lips.

"Come with me," pleaded Ekaterina. "It's for Sophie."

At the word "Sophie," Kala let Ekaterina pull her along by the hand.

"We'll need an ax, lamp oil, twine, matches, and kindling to start a fire."

Automatically—as though she were sleepwalking—Kala helped her sister load the cart and then climbed in after Ekaterina. They drove out onto the deserted Merchant Lane and turned away from the square, making their way cautiously through deserted side streets and glimpsing, through the gaps of houses, the scarlet uniforms of the band of Cossacks who continued to plunder the town.

"The Jews have barricaded themselves in the synagogue," said Ekaterina. "We'll have to hurry before something happens." She urged Sir Leslie forward, out a country road. "Kala, make Sir Leslie hurry. We might not have much time."

Pressing closer to Ekaterina, Kala closed her eyes. She cried out, "No, no! The horse is too tired!" They were trotting smartly in the direction of the country and she remembered that the Sunday before, she and Sophie had gone out for an early morning ride and that at the last minute Ruth's two oldest children had jumped in with them. It was a blustery day, a morning when the wind had rushed over the land in squalls, gusting here and there, bringing to their nostrils an intermittent scent of warm earthy air.

"Spring is coming!" Sophie had shouted. "Just smell the air!" she instructed her nieces, hugging the little girls when they dutifully lifted their heads to breathe in deep, long draughts. The air blew warm one moment and icy the next. Above them huge thunder heads towered up in billows of white and black. Close by roared still another thundering sound and soon they had passed over the river, which boiled along so high they could feel the wisps of water on their cheeks. Below the wheels, the timbers of the bridge trembled. Chunks of ice careened along the current, followed by branches, trunks of trees, whole bushes uprooted by the swift water. The quiet little girls, at once thrilled and frightened, clutched at their aunts who laughed back at them boldly—laughed out of pleasure in the excitement of their excursion and at the wildness in the spring and the fact they were all together. From the river they entered the forest, where the wind bellowed through the high pines. They left the forest and rode back and forth along country lanes, the land presenting itself to them empty of people but filled with the movement of air, water, trees, and clouds. High overhead a flock of rooks wheeled in the gusting wind, beating slowly against the air and then swiftly sideslipping with the currents to cross one another's paths in daredevil swoops.

"See how free they are!" said Sophie.

And the little girls, who rarely said anything, echoed, "See how free!" and begged their aunts that they not turn back just yet but continue to the top of Raven's Hill so that they could all look down and see the view, see the forest of Nechaelvo, which had somehow escaped the German axes.

"You won't be able to see the woods," Kala had told them. "Look at all the clouds. It'll be raining down there. All you'll see is black mist." Nonetheless she had ascended the long rise and, topping it, reined in Sir Leslie, and there to the south— even though to the north Lake Lyesk was completely obscured—the great forest of Nechaelvo stood out clearly, the dark evergreen of the pines interwoven with the bare branches of the birches and the willows beyond.

Turning to Kala, Sophie had said, "How beautiful it is here!" her fiery-bright cheeks like apples in the wind, her blue eyes almost black.

"Sophie, my Sophie!" Kala now called out—blissful yet somehow desperate. She grabbed hold feverishly of her sister's hand.

"I'm not Sophie," Ekaterina said. Her eyes, rimmed with red, lacked all color, her small teeth bit sharply into her lips. "I'm not Sophie. I never have been." Ekaterina's white-gold hair hung down, exaggerating the pallor of her cheeks. "And she wasn't just yours. I loved her. She was mine too. I always wanted to show her how I loved her, and now there's something I can do."

They had reached the airfield. Before them the abandoned and damaged buildings of the aerodrome loomed up. Storms had collapsed the roof of the office and torn one of the hangar doors from its support. Ekaterina directed Sir Leslie up the field where patches of dirty snow lay in between the dark brown stubble of the cleared runway. Here and there touches of new grass sprouted, the green nurtured by the few warm days the week before. The weather cold again, a brisk chill wind blew in the girls' faces and the wheels of the cart made a grinding sloshing sound as they cut through the thin frozen layer of soil and snow to the thawing earth.

"Why have we come here?" asked Kala.

"To chase the soldiers out of Lyesk before they reach the synagogue."

"The Red soldiers?"

They were entering a copse of wood and brush that grew within a natural declivity of a small hillside well beyond the end of the airfield. Ekaterina jumped off the cart and ran toward a large oak that appeared to be growing out of the center of the hill. At the base of the oak she threw aside some limbs and rocks, uncovering the corner of a heavy tarpaulin. "Kala, come help me. I can't do any of this unless you help me."

Kala climbed down and helped Ekaterina shove a small boulder aside. Then the two sisters pulled the tarpaulin partially away to reveal an opening. Creeping inside, they beheld the form of a German plane. Around its structure the pilots had built a wooden frame, nailed in the front to the oak and to a smaller pine, the top of which had been lopped off. The back of the frame was supported by the rising hillside. Over the frame the Germans had nailed heavy canvas to camouflage and protect the vehicle, spreading branches and leaves above the top so that the entire edifice looked like an extension of the hill. At the back of the man-made cave were piled boxes, cannisters, and several large drums.

"This is my airplane," said Ekaterina, surveying the machine. "My escape." She laughed at the idea. "What do you think of it? It's a lovely creature, isn't it?"

"Yes," answered Kala vaguely, thinking that the airplane looked like some great insect still wrapped in its cocoon—the strange propeller canted across its nose, the double wings that projected out of each side bound together by delicate struts and stays, the tail with its own twin ears. She had the sense that her youngest sister was going to take it up into the air, "Are we going to fly?"

"Don't be foolish, Kala. The machine's been sitting out here the whole winter. We'd never get it started by ourselves —and certainly not when we're in such a hurry. I have a different plan." She mounted the wing of the plane and climbed into the back cockpit. "Everything's here," she called down, "just as they left it. Here's the machine gun." She swiveled the gun around above Kala's head. "Do you see those crates back there—I want you to carry one of them here and hand it up to me. But be careful, they're full of grenades and flares and every kind of ammunition."

Obediently, though without understanding, Kala ran to the back of the cave and picked up a case. It was so heavy that her knees buckled. She managed to get her arms around the case, and cradling it to her stomach, she stumbled toward the plane, where she rested her cargo against the fuselage. Kneeling down, she put her shoulder to the end of the case, boosting it up to Ekaterina, who then was able to tip the case into the cockpit.

After the second case had been dumped into the front cockpit, Ekaterina asked Kala to bring her one of the small cannisters, informing her it contained petrol. Ekaterina opened the cannister, balancing it carefully in her fingers, away from her body, and pouring its contents over the front and back cockpits, down over the wing and along the ground of the cave toward the back. "Now all we need is for you to get the ax. Only hurry!"

Still obedient, Kala ran to the cart and back and at Ekaterina's command split the top of a large drum that stood near the cases at the back of the cave. Then the girls tipped the drum over on its side.

"Be careful. Don't get any on you," Ekaterina warned.

Slowly the petrol seeped out of the drum, forming a pool that began to trickle along the ground toward the airplane. The fumes of petrol filled the cave now. Passively Kala stood, breathing in the fumes, waiting for what would happen, the vapors intoxicating her. "Kala!" Ekaterina scolded, pulling her older sister along, out of the entrance, and ordering her to build a small fire, well away from the cave. "Use the kindling and the lamp oil and whatever twigs you can find. I'll lead Sir Leslie and the cart over there across the field."

Shortly after Kala started the fire, Ekaterina returned. Warming her hands, she remarked, "How odd it is—everything I tell you to do, you do it." The idea seemed to please her. "Now we'll make torches out of kindling and twine."

"Torches?" Kala asked.

"Kala, I know what I'm doing. That's why you're listening to me. We'll soak the end with lamp oil. The torches are for the explosion so we can frighten away the Red soldiers. It's just a chance. I need to try it for Sophie." Ekaterina took a breath. "I'll throw mine first, you throw yours and then we have to run toward the cart as fast as we can. Do you understand? Run as fast as you can!"

Kala nodded. And when it came time, the sisters, carrying the flaming ends of their torches high in the air, proceeded to the open tarpaulin leading into the cave. For just a moment Ekaterina peered in, and then she hurled her torches, one after the other, as far as she could. Kala stepped up and hurled hers next, much farther, almost to the back of the cave. Without a pause, the two sisters tucked their skirts up and ran toward the hangar building where Sir Leslie was tethered. To Kala it seemed as if they ran for an hour and yet nothing happened. She was about to look back when she heard a whoosh, then a roar, and felt a warm draft of air pushing behind her. The first explosion deafened her and almost knocked her off her feet. Ahead, Sir Leslie reared up and whinnied. Kala raced to the horse, fearing he would injure himself. It took both young women to hold him down.

Now the flares and the grenades and ammunition began to go off in a series of lesser explosions, while up the field, brilliant orange and red flames shot from the hillside. At the center of the blaze, a magnificent plume of black smoke spiraled into the sky and was swept by the wind toward the town.

"I promised Sophie she would fly," said Ekaterina, her face stricken in the uneven light of the fire.

Kala stared at the fire and its black smoke—the remnant of Ekaterina's airplane—mounting the skies above Lyesk. Overhead the smoke billowed, dropping scorched fragments of the airplane, the tarpaulin, the trees, the dirt of the hillside over the two girls. "I promised Sophie she would fly," repeated Ekaterina, brushing the ashes from her clothing and face.

Kala shut her eyes and willed Ekaterina and Sophie into the airplane. She willed them to sit upright, comfortable in their cockpits, happy in the fragile contraption—layers of plywood held together by filaments of wire and columns of metal tubing. She concentrated on their jolting down the field, the wind whipping across their faces and the propeller biting into the air and pulling them off the ground at a steep angle. Then quite suddenly, while the plane was still climbing, she heard Sophie's extraordinary laughter and it became clear to Kala what she and Ekaterina had done. They had taken Sophie's soul and were sending it up to heaven. From above Lyesk, Sophie could see the river, the railroad station, the roofs of the town, the bare orchards near their father's cottage, and the trees along Orchard Lane. She could view the land where they'd spent almost all their lives. Indeed she could see all the way to the high road and the old Post Station, for her spirit was ascending with the plume of smoke and would soon spread out, as released and free as the wheeling rooks they had seen early Sunday morning near Raven's Hill. Kala wanted to call out to Ekaterina and tell her what was happening but she had the certain sense Ekaterina already knew—had even known long before her. "Ekaterina," she said, "let's not be the way we were before. Let's be good friends."

"Of course we'll be," Ekaterina replied. "We'll have to be, since I don't suppose we'll ever get out of Lyesk."

In the distance they heard a train whistling frantically and, faintly to their ears, the long hiss of steam being vented as the train began to move. They mounted the cart and drove Sir Leslie back toward town. It was close to noon when they reached Merchant Lane and the gray sky had brightened. A quick wind blew down the streets, billowing out the coats of men and women as they bent over to gather up debris from the looting. As the sisters approached the bakery, Mordecai ran out to them. "Where have you been? Did you hear the explosions? The Polish army's coming and the Cossacks have fled from them on the train. Go inside, your mother's out of her mind with worry. Kala and Ekaterina, why are you just sitting there?"

But Kala and Ekaterina made no move to leave the cart. They merely clasped one another stubbornly and tightly, each one unwilling to step down and enter the streets of Lyesk without Sophie.

CHAPTER TWENTY-SEVEN

Mᴇ Dᴇᴀʀᴇꜱᴛ Wɪꜰᴇ Kᴀʟᴀ,
      I write to you from San Francisco, California, in
the United States of America. No doubt you will be surprised
to learn that I am here—yet perhaps no more surprised than
I. My darling, please forgive me for breaking my word and
not sending for you when I escaped the German labor battalion. I decided—correctly I still believe—that it would be
wrong to bring you with me into Russia where there was so
much danger. You might well have died, as I almost did. As
it turned out, there was nothing either of us could have done
in Russia. The very sad news, Kala, is that our party is dead.
The Left Socialist Revolutionaries, the party of the peasant
and the land, the only party we could have belonged to, no
longer exists. The Bolsheviks have completely dismantled it.
This was what I discovered when I reached Omsk early last
October. In Omsk itself, the Right Socialist Revolutionaries

had united with the Monarchists—both parties fearing the Bolsheviks more than they did each other. You can imagine my disgust that matters had deteriorated to such a degree. It goes without saying, of course, that a few weeks later, the Monarchists performed a treacherous coup and threw everyone in jail, including me when I rallied a crowd against them. You will be pleased to know, I wasn't worrying about my courage at that moment—only about the outrageous behavior of the Monarchists. Fortunately, my jailers proved altogether untrustworthy and allowed everyone to escape, taking the opportunity to depart themselves.

From Omsk, dear Kala, I then started out attempting to move toward Lyesk, determined to return to you no matter what. But for every step I took in your direction I was forced two, five, ten steps away—in flight both from the Monarchists and from the Bolsheviks. Each band of fugitives I came across carried me further and further away from you until at last I gave myself up to my fate, seeking only to find some haven to which I could summon you. Finally, starving and sick with influenza, I reached Vladivostok, where I contacted a distant cousin, a furrier and a sportsman, who took care of me. He was even able to inform me that all my immediate family was safe—my parents and older brother with his family in Berlin and my other brother in Paris. You can imagine my relief at this news and my gratitude to my cousin (he is related to me both through my mother and my father, but I will explain that to you another time). As it turned out, my cousin, who is a widower, was about to emigrate to America and since he did not want to leave me in my weakened condition, he convinced me that rather than attempt to cross a hostile Russia, I might well have an easier time getting back to Lyesk via America—pointing out that a similar plan had recently been considered by the Czech Legions. I had just experienced what it was like to move about in Russia, and so this far-fetched suggestion made a sort of sense to me. I therefore traveled with my cousin to Shanghai and from Shanghai here—recovering from a general haziness and confusion and regaining my health on shipboard.

Kala, now I come to the remarkable, the extraordinary portion of my account. Through conversations with three or four of the ship's passengers and particularly with the ship's first mate who spoke French, I learned that in America, particularly in the West, there are vast farmlands where it is possible for free peasants—"farmers" they call them—to thrive and govern themselves and to lead their own lives. There are great cooperatives, there are socialist and progressive farmer parties in areas called Minnesota and North Dakota (Indian names). Dearest Kala, after learning of these cooperatives, I stood on deck, surrounded by the long powerful swells of the ocean, and imagined the two of us amidst a community of equal farmers—without a single army sweeping through to destroy orchards and fields and towns. Oh, admittedly there are many enemies of our dream in America. But you and I, we're used to such things.

Let me try to convince you. One night I recited some Russian poems to the ship's first mate. In turn he told me about an American poet named Walt Whitman who sings not only to the mountains, rivers, and plains of this continent, not only to its animals and plants, but also to the common people whom he calls the genius of the United States. This poet speaks of the Americans' attachment to freedom, of their curiosity, their welcoming of novelty. He ascribes to Americans an air of never knowing how it feels to stand in the presence of superiors. Evidently in this country the custom is for the President to take his hat off to the people, not they to him. So affecting did I find this that I immediately felt an overpowering urge to take off my hat to the President.

Kala, I didn't really choose to come to this New World, but being here, I see its possibilities. I would like to try to settle on the land as a farmer, and I ask you, humbly, to join me in pursuing our dream here. As soon as I send this letter, I will set out for Detroit to find your brother Isoif, in care of

[319]

whom you may address your reply. If you do not agree, please write out your reasons fully so that we can discuss the matter. I will keep on writing until I hear from you. I will live nowhere without you. If need be, I will find a way to return.

Your husband, Mikhail Kossoff

San Francisco, California

Kala read the letter twice and examined the envelope carefully. "My husband's alive!" she said, dazed. In a rush she made her way outside. She cut across the stableyard and back along the path toward the river. On either side the grasses of the hillside sprouted in brilliant green waves. Ahead, the few standing birch trees glowed pale white, while the stumps that stretched around them sprouted slim flexible branches tipped with green. Exulting at Mikhail's survival, she advanced toward one of the trees and embraced it. She imagined herself and Mikhail in one another's arms. By the river's bank she stopped and listened to the water, still swollen with the spring rain.

But where would their reunion take place? Kala contemplated Mikhail's proposal that they become American farmers. How odd, she reflected, to be choosing a loyalty and a nation. Wasn't that somehow assumed—part of one's birthright? Yet the fact was, she and Mikhail had been cast loose by war and revolution, and now he was asking her to choose America over Russia. She turned from the river and moved purposefully around the town toward the site of Sophie's grave just below Raven's Hill.

As she approached the cemetery she noted that the fields off in the distance had been touched with the light green shadow of new grass. Up close the graveyard had an untidy look, with stones leaning this way and that. Heartsick to be visiting her sister here—that these stones and this ground had become her sister's place—she wound her way through the paths and at Sophie's grave discovered her mother setting a lilac bush in the earth. She guessed that Malkeh had dug up Sophie's favorite plant from behind the barn and carried it here to Sophie. Kala stood back, watching her mother's lips open and close soundlessly—pained by the unfamiliar humility she witnessed in her mother's movements. Next to Malkeh, Ruth worked diligently on her hands and knees, planting a border of red and white flowers.

"You just missed Hershel," said Ruth, lifting her head.

"I'm sorry, I'll see him when he comes tomorrow."

"He told Mama and me he'll be leaving soon. He and his pioneer group are emigrating to Palestine, legally or illegally —whatever the obstacles."

Squatting, Kala helped her mother and sister dig in the soil. She waited until the planting had been finished before she handed Mikhail's letter to her mother. Then she waited while Malkeh read, reflecting she would now have to write Mikhail about Sophie's death and remembering with regret she had not yet been able to bring herself to write Withold Swislocz.

"San Francisco?" said Malkeh, returning the letter. "Everyone else goes the other way. Thank God he's safe."

"Yes, thank God he's all right," Kala breathed, offering the letter to Ruth. "And thank God he didn't try to come back to this terrible part of the world." She glanced uneasily at her mother. "You read that Mikhail wants me to come to America?"

Malkeh nodded.

"I want to go, except . . . I don't want to live so far away from the rest of you—across an ocean. Besides, I'm not certain I want to leave Russia."

Malkeh gazed with great sorrow at the mound of dirt and the lilac bush. She brushed something from her face. "We may very well come with you, Kala. Now, with Sophie dead . . ." Suddenly she cried out in a fierce and outraged voice, "God knows this land has been defiled. Nothing can flower here but our graves."

Stunned to hear so passionate an outburst from their mother, Ruth and Kala grouped themselves on either side of her as they headed back toward town. Indeed, they walked so close to Malkeh it was hard to tell whether they leaned on her or she on them. Presently Ruth hazarded quietly, "I wonder if Detroit looks very different from White Russia."

"We'll find out before long," Malkeh said. "Now that we've heard from Mikhail, it's possible to make a decision."

They walked on in silence, Kala moved by the fact that Mikhail had figured so prominently in her mother's thoughts. Entering the house they found Naftali working on the walls of the parlor and Ekaterina sitting on the piano bench, reading. Feigning a casual air, Ruth and Kala addressed their sister.

"Ekaterina, how would you feel about leaving Lyesk?"

"Delighted," said Ekaterina.

"But wouldn't you miss it here? Don't you remember our dressmaker Dunya—how many pins she could keep in her mouth?"

"And Luka. Our good friend Luka, with so many blond grandchildren?"

"And Matryona, how fat she was? She's probably still fat."

"There's no reason to finish the parlor, Naftali," Malkeh informed her husband. "We're moving to Detroit. We'll make arrangements to join Iosif as soon as possible."

"Why Detroit?" questioned Ekaterina. She put down her book.

"Detroit?" laughed Naftali, as though his wife had tried her hand at a foolish joke. "To Detroit?" he repeated, sounding alarmed.

"It's exactly what you've wanted since Iosif left. To be with your son," Malkeh said.

"So you've changed your mind, wife? You want to leave Lyesk? Ah yes. Yes, yes," Naftali went on. He seemed not to know where to place his hammer. As a last resort he left it in his hand. "Yes, yes, wife. But will Iosif remember us? Think of the years in between. Will he," Naftali amended since this was more to the point, "remember me?"

At this it occurred to Kala that if Iosif no longer remembered his father, Mikhail might no longer properly remember her—that by the time she met him in the new country they might have grown in such different ways as to have almost nothing in common and to care for each other even less. Nevertheless, she let herself continue, "I might not actually stay in Detroit. It could be the wrong place for Mikhail and me to pursue our beliefs."

"Your beliefs," grumbled Naftali, momentarily distracted by Kala's words. "Those same beliefs. I thought you got rid of them."

"I haven't tried," retorted Kala.

But Naftali's attention had already drifted elsewhere. "To Detroit . . . to Detroit—to Iosif," he resumed, and began pacing back and forth the length of the room until at last he burst out the door of the house into the yard, clearly beside himself with unexpected and conflicting emotions.

That summer the Chodorovs settled up their affairs. Naftali sold the orchard lease to Lazar Dovitsky. As part of the bargain, Dovitsky promised Sir Leslie, Mishka, and Emmanuelle a comfortable old age in his stable, and Dovitsky's children undertook to tend Sophie's grave. The bakery was sold to a cousin of Avrom Lavin's from Pinsk who, finding herself unable to move to Lyesk, hired Naomi Pearl Benjamin as manager. And Naomi, having long suspected that her son Pinchas possessed musical talent, convinced her husband, Rabbi Benjamin, to buy the Chodorov piano, along with the Chodorov house.

As the summer progressed, the Lyesk Jews took to following Malkeh about, complaining to her, "Malkeh, why are you leaving us?" to which she often framed the reply, "I no longer have the heart to understand what's coming in Russia and in Poland. A younger woman is needed. Naomi's grown strong since her father's death. Even if she can't bake, she can hire assistants to help her—I've given her every one of my recipes. And if anyone these days can find enough flour and sugar under Polish rule—if anyone can ferret out eggs—it's Naomi." And Malkeh indicated the tall figure of Naomi Benjamin already standing like a military commander inside the Dutch door of the bakery, her blue eyes flashing like stars in the midst of the halo of tan frizzy hair.

On the last day of August Ephraim Savich, Ruth's former fiancé and now a neighbor of Iosif's in Detroit, stopped in Lyesk to bring the Chodorovs their final immigration papers. Ephraim was traveling through Poland as a member of the Hoover Relief Commission. Since the Chodorovs had seen him last he had grown a sizable belly and pouches under his eyes that bulged big as purses. Aside from distributing supplies to the victims of the war, Ephraim was also looking for a wife. "Ekaterina," he began, bowing chivalrously and extending a plump yet manly hand, "you see before you a man so successful in the lumber business that he keeps two brand-new automobiles in his garage—one of them for whoever will be his wife."

"An automobile?" said Ekaterina, twirling her fingers with contempt. "I can fly airplanes."

"Look how fat he's become," Kala whispered to Ruth, pointing out that, by comparison, Mordecai had remained quite slim.

Finally, in the autumn of 1919, the Chodorovs visited Sophie's grave and said goodby with bowed heads—after which they gathered on the platform of the railroad station to embrace their friends and neighbors. From Lyesk they traveled by train to Warsaw and Gdansk, embarking on their sea journey by way of Antwerp and Southampton. The October crossing was rough, the ship crowded, and as they descended onto the dock at Montreal, Canada, where Iosif had arranged to meet them, it seemed to Kala that all her family, including Ruth's daughters, looked and smelled like packages of old fish wrapped in soiled newspaper. Beyond the barriers stood Iosif, his wife, and three small children—all five pressed, starched and shining, with Iosif himself still short and squat but now bearing fluffy side whiskers and a narrow mustache. "Iosif! Iosif!" called Naftali and Malkeh—at which an expression of horror settled onto the faces of Iosif and his wife as they understood that the dank and smelly creatures heading toward them were their family.

Off to one side Mikhail waved and shouted, "Kala, my darling, my love—Kala!" Kala and Mikhail ran into each other's arms.

Meanwhile Iosif remained rooted to one spot while his wife took charge, bravely plunging forth to deliver a dutiful kiss on each of the newcomer's cheeks, taking care to keep her jacket clear of their coats. With the gold of her bracelets clanging, she propelled her husband into the arms of his father and his mother and then herded her children forward to receive their kisses. As the children reluctantly offered their faces, Kala observed that her nephew, Iosif's smallest child, possessed Sophie's expressive mouth and blunt nose, that the next child, Kala's three-year-old niece, owned Sophie's high cheekbones and rosy cheeks, that the four-year-old was endowed with Sophie's blue, almost black, luminous eyes. Could she possibly hope, Kala asked herself, that one of them also possessed Sophie's laughter? Would they remind her of Sophie as they grew up? Would her American nephew and nieces understand their kinship to that corner of Russia where Kala's dreams and anger had been born? Or would they flinch and back away, uneasy and embarrassed by her strangeness?

She turned to Mikhail. Their arms fell naturally about one another's waists. They walked together from the dock. The entire family was about to follow when Malkeh put out her arm and barred their way, allowing the young couple to move on alone, Mikhail speaking to Kala about the possibility of justice in North Dakota and Minnesota, his auburn hair fluttering in the breeze.